JOHNNY PANIC
AND THE BIBLE OF DREAMS

*the text of this book is printed
on 100% recycled paper*

Sylvia Plath

JOHNNY PANIC AND THE BIBLE OF DREAMS

Short Stories, Prose and Diary Excerpts

HARPER COLOPHON BOOKS
Harper & Row, Publishers
New York, Cambridge, Hagerstown, Philadelphia, San Francisco
London, Mexico City, São Paulo, Sydney

Contents

Introduction

Sylvia Plath wrote a considerable amount of prose. About seventy stories, mostly unpublished, are extant. She started several novels, but only one sizeable fragment—"Stone Boy with a Dolphin"—survives from anything before *The Bell Jar*. After *The Bell Jar* she wrote some 130 pages of another novel, provisionally titled *Double Exposure*. That manuscript disappeared somewhere around 1970.

Besides fiction, she wrote pretty consistently at some form of journal —sometimes in large hardback notebooks, occasionally on loose typed sheets, occasionally in small notebooks from which she tore the pages she wanted to save. (The rest of the notebook would be filled with drafts of poems, etc.) Her motive for keeping the journal varied. The handwritten notebook entries were generally negative self-castigation, or a means of rallying her determination to get through something or other. The typewritten sheets share a good deal of this, but they expand more easily to general comment and description, and are always written in sharper and swifter style. She wrote noticeably better prose on a typewriter than with a pen. These typewritten sheets provided a warming-up exercise, before she went on to other things. At various times she set out to type three large pages a day, though unfortunately she never kept it up for very long. When she moved to Devon she set about making an archive of all the new people she met, and of all her dealings with them. She planned to case the whole region, with the idea of accumulating details for future stories. Some of this material is unpublishable. She regarded these sheets not only as an archive, but as an arena for exercising her observation in Flaubertian style. After visiting a neighbor's house, she would detail the décor and furnishings with laborious tenacity, and upbraid herself for failing to remember exactly what motif adorned that particular lamp, and exhort herself to get a mental photograph of it on her next visit. Similarly with what people wore. She had a special eye for this. At the same time she had a great suspicion that her real inclination might be to ignore such things altogether. What is especially interesting now about some of these descriptions is the way they fed into *Ariel*. They are good evidence to prove that poems which seem often to be constructed of arbitrary surreal symbols are really impassioned reorganizations of relevant fact. They show just how much of the poetry is constructed from the bits and pieces of the situation at the source of the poem's theme. A great many of these objects and appearances occur somewhere or other in the journals.

Finally, there is a certain amount of journalism. She had a special respect for this form of writing: it was an essential key to her life plan. She declared her ambition about two things. The first was to become a proficient story writer, of the high-power practical, popular American type, whose stories could appear in the big journals and earn huge sums of cash and give her the feeling of being a professional with a real job in the real world. The second was to become a proficient freelance journalist, who could wander about the world and finance her adventures by writing about them. One might imagine there can have been few writers so naturally endowed to become a readable travel writer. But all her efforts in that line, right up to her last year, were curiously numb. Part of the stiffness probably came from the fact that she was always trying to write a pastiche of the sort of writing she imagined was wanted by the journal she had in mind. But during her last year, the liberation that occurred in her poetry and in her fictional prose occurred also in her journalism. The three or four commissioned pieces she wrote then seem to me among her freest things. She had suddenly become a natural writer of the casual brief essay.

Her ambition to write stories was the most visible burden of her life. Successful story-writing, for her, had all the advantages of a top job. She wanted the cash, and the freedom that can go with it. She wanted the professional standing, as a big earner, as the master of a difficult trade, and as a serious investigator into the real world. And finally, not least, she wanted a practical motive for investigating the real world. The fear recurs constantly in her journals that these were all things not naturally hers, they would have to be fought for, as if they belonged naturally only to her opposite. She behaved as if she believed that. So her life became very early a struggle to apprentice herself to writing conventional stories, and to hammer her talents into acceptable shape. "For me," she wrote, "poetry is an evasion from the real job of writing prose."

Throughout the years between college and *The Bell Jar* the great tension of her character was inseparable from her inability to write these stories to her satisfaction. Either she couldn't find ideas, or she despised her ideas, or she couldn't get writing, or she was dismayed by what she wrote. She couldn't understand why it was so difficult for her, when other writers seemed to find it so easy, and when even she had found it fairly easy in the past, during her teens. How had it become such an impossibly stubborn language for her, and why was the whole effort loaded with such terrors?

She analyzed the stories by various popular writers, taking them apart and studying their machinery. Of Frank O'Connor's stories she wrote: "I will imitate until I can feel I'm using what he can teach." From one writer she wanted one thing, from another another. But mainly what she wanted in her stories was the presence of the objective world. "I must write about the things of the world with no glazing." She fought doggedly against the great suction into her own subjectivity: "I shall perish if I can write about no one but myself." Something like this went through nearly every entry in her journal over long periods.

In 1958. at the end of her year of teaching, when she left college for the last time (it was also the first time), and faced her decision to become a writer living on her writing, she wrote: "I ran through my experience for ready-made 'big' themes: there were none. . . . [she then cites a few calamities that had happened to her friends] . . . All paled, palled—a glassy coverlid getting in the way of my touching them, too undramatic. Or was my outlook too undramatic? Where was life? It dissipated, vanished into thin air, and my life stood weighed and found wanting because it had no ready-made novel plot, because I couldn't simply sit down at the typewriter and by sheer genius and willpower begin a novel dense and fascinating today and finish it next month. Where, how, with what and for what, to begin? No incident in my life seemed ready to stand up for even a twenty-page story. I sat paralyzed, feeling no person in the world to speak to, cut off totally from humanity, in a self-induced vacuum: I felt sicker and sicker. I couldn't happily be anything but a writer and I couldn't be a writer. I couldn't even set down one sentence. I was paralyzed with fear. . . ."

She escaped from this into a job in the records office for mental patients in the Massachusetts General Hospital in Boston, and a few months later, after writing the story "Johnny Panic and the Bible of Dreams," where she turned that experience into a private literary breakthrough which ran on underground through the rest of that year, she wrote: "It is the hate, the paralyzing fear, that gets in my way and stops me. Once that is worked clear of I will flow. My life may at last get into my writing: as it did in the Johnny Panic story." What that story had actually done was tap the molten source of her poetry as none of her poems up to then had. She found that source again, nine or ten months later, in the poem printed at the end of her collection *The Colossus,* and titled "Poem for a Birthday," where the voice of *Ariel* first makes itself heard. Yet just before writing that short sequence of poems, she set down in her journal: "Wakeful last night. Tossed and turned. *New Yorker* fear, as if I could by main force and study weld my sensibility into some kind of articulateness which would be publishable." At that time her greatest ambition was certainly to get a story into *The New Yorker* or the *Ladies Home Journal*—the two alternating according to her mood. At the same time she was noting: "Read over the stories written in Spain. They are so dull. Who would want to read them?" or again, "My Shadow story reads mighty thin, mighty pale," and "Still sick on waking and will be until the story is more interesting than my self-musings," while everywhere there are references to her "paralysis," her "desperation" and even her "despair," when she confronts the story in progress.

It is strange that she was so much more patient with her poems. She would sit down to compose poetry in a fever, like an addicted gambler, yet afterwards she would ponder over and correct the results that disappointed her—resigned, wistful, but loyal, even material. Her story-writing, on the other hand, always took place in an atmosphere of locked combat. Here, her intense ambition had clearly met something equal but opposite. If a story is inevitably a fantasy, and if every fantasy leads eventually to the heart of the labyrinth, her problem was that she could not linger among the outer twists and turns and complications, where the world is still solidly itself and comparatively safe, however thrilling. She had an instant special pass to the center, and no choice but to use it. She could no more make up an objective ingenious narrative than she could connect up all the letters in her handwriting, where nearly every symbol seems to sit perched over a gulf. This lightning pass through all the walls of the maze was her real genius. Instant confrontation with the most central, unacceptable things. So her dogged, year-in year-out effort to write conventional fiction, in the hope of preparing herself to make a livelihood, was like a persistent refusal of her genius. In September of '59 she wrote in her journal: "Disgust with the seventeen-page story I just finished: a stiff, artificial piece about a man killed by a bear, ostensibly because his wife willed it to happen, but none of the deep emotional undercurrents gone into or developed. As if little hygienic trap-doors shut out the seethe and deep-grounded swell of my experience. Putting up pretty artificial statues. I just can't get outside myself. Even in the tattoo story I did better. . . ." It was only when she gave up that effort to "get outside" herself, and finally accepted the fact that her painful subjectivity was her real theme, and that the plunge into herself was her only real direction, and that poetic strategies were her only real means, that she suddenly found herself in full possession of her genius—with all the special skills that had developed as if by biological necessity, to deal with those unique inner conditions.

Nevertheless, her stories are much more interesting than she thought. They seem livelier now, in some ways, than they did when she wrote them. And their vitality comes from the very thing she was always striving to escape: the themes she found engaging enough to excite her concentration all turn out to be episodes from her own life; they are all autobiography. They have the vitality of her personal participation, her subjectivity. And all are circling the flames which the poetry, encouraged by "Johnny Panic" and *The Bell Jar*, eventually jumped into.

Typically, they begin like some objectively detailed event described in her later journals, and they tend to go on in the same way. Among the stories she scrapped were quite a few that never managed to make that artful turn off the rails of observed fact into the adventure of imagined fiction. A story which almost went the same way is "The

Fifteen-Dollar Eagle." That story recounts an ordinary encounter from beginning to end in the most faithful way, and perhaps finally it isn't a story. But it is a real image, something uniquely Plathian, an authentic lump of her dream life. Yet she deplored its "imagey, static prose," and wondered why she couldn't make it read like an O'Connor story.

What she really coveted was a natural colloquial style. It was the arithmetical, sophisticated syntax of her earlier poetry, "imagey and static," that laid the dead hand on her narratives, and her vain efforts to throw it off were a big part of her labor. Interestingly enough, the stories that use her experience of working in the Massachusetts General Hospital are the ones where her own natural voice begins to come through. The voice that speaks in "The Daughters of Blossom Street," and even more confidently in "Johnny Panic and the Bible of Dreams," is moving straight towards *The Bell Jar* and the more direct poems of *Ariel*. The material of these stories, just as in the others, is basically description of first-hand experience, but the urgent expressiveness is a new thing for her. The change in her fluency and narrative skill is noticeable. After finishing "Johnny Panic," in December 1958, she wrote: "It's so queer and quite slangy that I think it may have a chance somewhere. Will send it out 10 x before I get sorry: by then I should have two or three more stories."

She wasn't able to hang on to her new freedom. She relapsed to a series of attempts in her old manner—"The Fifteen-Dollar Eagle," "The Fifty-ninth Bear" and several total failures—before she launched herself into *The Bell Jar* in 1960.

Among her papers at the time of her death were the manuscripts of about seventeen stories. These included those of her stories she wanted to keep, plus others written during her last two years in England.

A collection of her prose, published in England in 1977, was made up of a selection from these seventeen stories, together with some pieces of her journalism and extracts from her journal. At that time, as editor, I had to assume that she had either lost or destroyed as failures all the other stories I remembered her having written. Just as that collection was being published, however, a large quantity of Sylvia Plath's papers emerged in the Lilly Library, at Indiana University, acquired by the library from Mrs. Aurelia Plath, the writer's mother, and among these were the typescripts of over fifty stories—

dating from her first attempts at writing up to roughly 1960, though most of them very early work. Apart from duplicates of a few of those she had kept by her, these were all stories she had failed to publish and eventually rejected.

This present collection contains the thirteen stories published in that 1977 English edition, with a further seven selected from the Indiana archive.*

Interspersed among the stories are five of her more interesting pieces of journalism, and a few fragments from her journal. All items have approximate dates of composition and are roughly in reverse chronological order, insofar as that is possible.

Sylvia Plath herself had certainly rejected several of the stories here, so they are printed against her better judgment. That must be taken into account. But in spite of the obvious weaknesses, they seem interesting enough to keep, if only as notes toward her inner autobiography. Some of them demonstrate, even more baldly than the stronger stories, just how much the sheer objective presence of things and happenings immobilized her fantasy and invention. The still-life graphic artist in her was loyal to objects. Nothing refreshed her more than sitting for hours in front of some intricate pile of things laboriously delineating each one. But that was also a helplessness. The blunt fact killed any power or inclination to rearrange it or see it differently. This limitation to actual circumstances, which is the prison of so much of her prose, became part of the solidity and truth of her later poems.

In 1960 she tried her hand at stories for the more sentimental English women's magazines, and with these she managed a slightly freer range of invention. One of them, "Day of Success," is included here as an example of her efforts at pastiche. But even here one can feel the rigidity of the objective situation elbowing the life out of the narrative.

No doubt one of the weaknesses of these weaker stories is that she did not let herself be objective enough. When she wanted merely to record, with no thought of artful shaping or publication, she could produce some of her most effective writing—and that appears in her journal.

Much of this journal either describes people still alive or is very private to her. How much of it ought to be published is not easy to

*The seven stories are "Sweetie Pie and the Gutter Men," "That Widow Mangada," "Stone Boy with Dolphin," "Above the Oxbow," "The Shadow," "Tongues of Stone," and "Among the Bumblebees."

decide. Her description of neighbors and friends and daily happenings is mostly too personal, her criticisms frequently unjust. A few of the more harmless pieces—by no means the best—from the later entries have been selected to illustrate, among other things, the close correspondence between the details she took possession of in those pages and the details she was able to use subsequently in her poems. The piece about Charlie Pollard is a loose prose draft of "The Bee Meeting." The coolness and economy of her observation is something to note. But nearly all the poem's essential details are there, the beginnings of her interpretation and the mood, even the eerie movement of some of the phrases. And "Rose and Percy B" is in effect a draft for the death and funeral in "Berck Plage," while "Among the Narcissi" takes a phrase or two from it.

The Cambridge passage, from diary pages typed early in 1956, might stand as some supplement to the style of self-revelation used in the letters. Though less naked than some of her poems, this piece gives an idea of the state of mind behind what she was writing just before the first of the poems of her first collection, *The Colossus*.

The logical thing, no doubt, would be to publish this more private side of her journal complete. It seems probable that her real creation was her own image, so that all her writings appear like notes and jottings directing attention towards that central problem—herself. Whether this is right or wrong, with some personalities it simply happens. As an editor of Sylvia Plath's unpublished writings, watching this happen to her, I am more and more inclined to think that any bit of evidence which corrects and clarifies our idea of what she really was is important, insofar as her writings persuade us of her importance. But living people figure everywhere, even in her most private discussions with herself, and—an editor has to face it—some things are more important than revelations about writers. The vivid, cruel words she could use to pin down her acquaintances and even her close friends were nothing she would want published and would be no joke to the recipients, still less so now that she is internationally famous and admired for her gift of phrase. This shouldn't need to be said.

Except for four small deletions of a few words, these journal passages are complete in themselves. In her journals, as a form of typed shorthand, Sylvia Plath occasionally referred to people by their initials. This practice has been extended here on occasion for obvious reasons.

Reading this collection, it should be remembered that her reputation rests on the poems of her last six months. Nearly all the prose brought together here was written before her first collection of poems, *The Colossus*, was completed, three years before her death.

The only bits of prose written during the time of the *Ariel* poems are the three brief journalistic pieces, "America! America!" "Snow Blitz," and "Ocean 1212-W." In other words, this collection does not represent the prose of the poet of *Ariel*, any more than the poems of *The Colossus* represent the poetry of the poet of *Ariel*. But it does give glimpses into early phases of the strange conflict between what was expected of her and what finally was exacted.

Our thanks are due to the Lilly Library, Indiana University, for their generous help in our examination of the Sylvia Plath archive for the purpose of this collection.

Ted Hughes
May 1978

Mothers

Story, 1962

Esther was still upstairs when Rose called in at the back door. "Yoo-hoo, Esther, you ready?" Rose lived with her retired husband Cecil in the topmost of the two cottages in the lane leading up to Esther's house —a large, thatched manor farm with its own cobbled court. The cobbles were not ordinary street cobbles, but pitch cobbles, their narrow, oblong sides forming a mosaic melted to gentleness by centuries of boots and hooves. The cobbles extended under the stout, nail-studded oak door into the dark hall between the kitchen and scullery, and in old Lady Bromehead's day had formed the floor of the kitchen and scullery as well. But after old Lady Bromehead fell and broke her hip at the age of ninety and was removed to a home, a series of servantless tenants had persuaded her son to lay linoleum in those rooms.

The oak door was the back door; everybody but the random stranger used it. The front door, yellow-painted and flanked by two pungent bushes of box, faced across an acre of stinging nettles to where the church indicated a gray heaven above its scallop of surrounding head-stones. The front gate opened just under the corner of the graveyard.

Esther tugged her red turban down around her ears, then adjusted the folds of her cashmere coat loosely so that she might, to the casual eye, seem simply tall, stately and fat, rather than eight months pregnant. Rose had not rung the bell before calling in. Esther imagined Rose, curious, avid Rose, eyeing the bare floorboards of the front hall and the untidy strewing of the baby's toys from front room to kitchen. Esther couldn't get used to people opening the door and calling in without ringing first. The postman did it, and the baker, and the grocer's boy, and now Rose, who was a Londoner and should have known better.

Once when Esther was arguing loudly and freely with Tom over breakfast, the back door had popped open and a handful of letters and magazines clapped onto the hall cobbles. The postman's cry of "Morning!" faded. Esther felt spied on. For some time after that, she bolted the back door from the inside, but the sound of tradesmen trying the door and finding it bolted in broad day, and then ringing the bell and waiting until she came and noisily undid the bolt, embarrassed her even more than their former calling in. So she left the bolt alone again, and took care not to argue so much, or at least not so loudly.

When Esther came down, Rose was waiting just outside the door, smartly dressed in a satiny lavender hat and checked tweed coat. At her side stood a blond, bony-faced woman with bright blue eyelids and no eyebrows. This was Mrs. Nolan, the wife of the pub-keeper at the White Hart. Mrs. Nolan, Rose said, never came to the Mothers' Union meetings because she had no one to go with, so Rose was bringing her to this month's meeting, together with Esther.

"Do you mind waiting just another minute, Rose, while I tell Tom I'm off?" Esther could feel Rose's shrewd eyes checking over her hat, her gloves, her patent leather heels, as she turned and picked her gingerly way up the cobbles to the back garden. Tom was planting roller berries in the newly spaded square behind the empty stables. The baby sat in the path on a pile of red earth, ladling dirt into her lap with a battered spoon.

Esther felt her little grievances about Tom's not shaving and his letting the baby play in the dirt fade at the sight of the two of them, quiet and in perfect accord. "Tom!" She rested her white glove, without thinking, on the earth-crusted wooden gate. "I'm off now. If I'm late getting back, will you boil the baby an egg?"

Tom straightened and shouted some word of encouragement that foundered between them in the dense November air, and the baby turned in the direction of Esther's voice, her mouth black, as if she had been eating dirt. But Esther slipped away, before the baby could heave up and toddle after her, to where Rose and Mrs. Nolan were waiting at the bottom of the court.

Esther let them through the seven-foot-high, stockade-like gate and latched it behind them. Then Rose crooked out her two elbows, and Mrs. Nolan took one, and Esther took the other, and the three women teetered in their best shoes down the stony lane past Rose's cottage, and the cottage of the old blind man and his spinster sister at the bottom, and into the road.

"We're meeting in the church today." Rose tongued a peppermint drop into her cheek and passed the twist of tinfoil round. Both Esther and Mrs. Nolan refused politely. "We don't always meet in church, though. Only when there's new members joining up."

Mrs. Nolan rolled her pale eyes skyward, whether in general consternation or simply at the prospect of church, Esther couldn't tell. "Are you new in town, too?" she asked Mrs. Nolan across Rose's front, leaning forward a little.

Mrs. Nolan gave a short, joyless laugh. "I've been here *six years.*"

"Why, you must know everybody by now!"

"Hardly a *soul,*" Mrs. Nolan intoned, causing misgivings, like a flock of chilly-toed birds, to clutter at Esther's heart. If Mrs. Nolan, an Englishwoman by her looks and accent, and a pub-keeper's wife as well, felt herself a stranger in Devon after six years, what hope had Esther, an American, of infiltrating that rooted society ever at all?

The three women proceeded, arm in arm, along the road under the high, holly-hedged boundary of Esther's acre, past her front gate and on under the red cob wall of the churchyard. Flat, lichen-bitten tombstones tilted at the level of their heads. Worn deep into the earth long before pavements were thought of, the road curved like some ancient riverbed under its slanted banks.

Along past the butcher's window, with its midweek display of pork hocks and cartons of drippings, and up the alley by the constabulary and the public conveniences, Esther could see other women converging, singly and in groups, to the lych-gate. Burdened by their cumbersome woolens and drab hats, they seemed, without exception, gnarled and old.

As Esther and Mrs. Nolan hung back at the gate, nudging Rose ahead, Esther recognized the uncommonly ugly person who had come up behind her, smiling and nodding, as the woman who had sold her an immense rutabaga for one-and-six at the Harvest Festival. The swede had bulged like a miraculous storybook vegetable above the rim of Esther's shopping basket, filling it entirely; but when she got round to slicing it up, it turned out to be spongy and tough as cork. Two minutes in the pressure cooker, and it shrank to a wan, orange mash that blackened the bottom and sides of the pot with a slick, evil-smelling liquor. I should simply have boiled it straight off, Esther thought now, following Rose and Mrs. Nolan under the stumpy, pollarded limes to the church door.

The interior of the church seemed curiously light. Then Esther realized she had never been inside before except at night, for Evensong. Already the back pews were filling with women, rustling, ducking, kneeling and beaming benevolently in every direction. Rose led Esther and Mrs. Nolan to an empty pew halfway up the aisle. She pushed Mrs. Nolan in first, then stepped in herself, drawing Esther after her. Rose was the only one of the three who knelt. Esther bowed her head and shut her eyes, but her mind remained blank; she just felt hypocritical. So she opened her eyes and looked about.

Mrs. Nolan was the one woman in the congregation without a hat. Esther caught her eye, and Mrs. Nolan raised her eyebrows, or rather, the skin of her forehead where the brows had been. Then she leaned forward. "I never," she confided, "come here much."

Esther shook her head and mouthed "Neither do I." That was not quite true. A month after her arrival in town, Esther started attending Evensong without a miss. The month's gap had been an uneasy one. Twice on Sundays, morning and evening, the town bell-ringers sent their carillons pounding out over the surrounding countryside. There was no escape from the probing notes. They bit into the air and shook it with a doggy zeal. The bells made Esther feel left out, as if from some fine local feast.

A few days after they had moved into the house, Tom called her downstairs for a visitor. The rector was sitting in the front parlor among the boxes of unpacked books. A small, gray man, with protruding ears, an Irish accent and a professionally benign, all-tolerating smile, he spoke of his years in Kenya, where he had known Jomo Kenyatta, of his children in Australia, and of his English wife.

Any minute, now, Esther thought, he's going to ask if we go to church. But the rector did not mention church. He dandled the baby on one knee and left shortly, his compact, black figure dwindling down the path to the front gate.

A month later, still perturbed by the evangelical bells, Esther dashed off, half in spite of herself, a note to the rector. She would like to attend Evensong. Would he mind explaining the ritual to her?

She waited nervously one day, two days, each afternoon readying tea and cake, which she and Tom ate only when the tea hour was safely past. Then, on the third afternoon, she was basting a nightdress of yellow flannel for the baby when she happened to glance out of the window toward the front gate. A stout, black shape paced slowly up through the stinging nettles.

Esther welcomed the rector with some misgiving. She told him right away that she had been brought up a Unitarian. But the rector smilingly replied that as a Christian, of whatever persuasion, she would be welcome in his church. Esther swallowed an impulse to blurt out that she was an atheist and end it there. Opening the Book of Common Prayer the rector had brought for her use, she felt a sickly, deceitful glaze overtake her features; she followed him through the order of service. The apparition of the Holy Ghost and the words "resurrection of the flesh" gave her an itchy sense of her duplicity. Yet when she confessed that she really could not believe in the resurrection of the flesh (she did not quite dare to say "nor of the spirit"), the rector seemed unperturbed. He merely asked if she believed in the efficacy of prayer.

"Oh yes, yes, I do!" Esther heard herself exclaim, amazed at the tears that so opportunely jumped to her eyes, and meaning only: How I would like to. Later, she wondered if the tears weren't caused by her vision of the vast, irrevocable gap between her faithless state and the beatitude of belief. She hadn't the heart to tell the rector she had been through all this pious trying ten years before, in Comparative Religion classes at college, and only ended up sorry she was not a Jew.

The rector suggested that his wife meet her at the next Evensong service and sit with her, so she should not feel strange. Then he seemed to think better of it. She might prefer, after all, to come with her neighbors, Rose and Cecil. They were "churchgoers." It was only as the rector picked up his two prayer books and his black hat that Esther remembered the plate of sugared cakes and the waiting tea tray in the

kitchen. But by then it was too late. Something more than forgetfulness, she thought, watching the rector's measured retreat through the
green nettles, had kept back those cakes.

The church filled rapidly now. The rector's wife, long-faced, angular,
kind, tiptoed back from her front pew to pass out copies of the Mothers' Union Service Book. Esther felt the baby throb and kick, and
placidly thought: I am a mother; I belong here.

The primeval cold of the church floor was just beginning its deadly
entry into her footsoles when, rustling and hushing, the women rose
in a body, and the rector, with his slow, holy gait, came down the aisle.

The organ drew breath; they started on the opening hymn. The
organist must have been a novice. Every few bars a discord prolonged
itself, and the voices of the women skidded up and down after the
elusive melody with a scatty, catlike desperation. There were kneel-
ings, responses, more hymns.

The rector stepped forward and repeated at length an anecdote
which had formed the substance of his last Evensong sermon. Then
he brought out an awkward, even embarrassing metaphor Esther had
heard him use at a baptism ceremony a week earlier, about physical
and spiritual abortions. Surely the rector was indulging himself. Rose
slipped another peppermint between her lips, and Mrs. Nolan wore
the glazed, far look of an unhappy seeress.

At last three women, two quite young and attractive, one very old,
came forward and knelt at the altar to be received into the Mothers'
Union. The rector forgot the name of the eldest (Esther could feel him
forgetting it) and had to wait until his wife had the presence to glide
forward and whisper it in his ear. The ceremony proceeded.

Four o'clock had struck before the rector allowed the women to
depart. Esther quitted the church in the company of Mrs. Nolan, Rose
having caught up with two of her other friends, Brenda, the wife of
the greengrocer, and stylish Mrs. Hotchkiss, who lived on Widdop
Hill and bred Alsatians.

"You staying for tea?" Mrs. Nolan asked, as the current of women
ferried them across the street and down the alley toward the yellow
brick constabulary.

"That's what I came for," Esther said. "I think we deserve it."

"When's your next baby?"

Esther laughed. "Any minute."

The women were diverting themselves from the alley into a court-yard at the left. Esther and Mrs. Nolan followed them into a dark, barnlike room which reminded Esther depressingly of church camp-outs and group-sings. Her eyes searched the dusk for a tea urn or some other sign of conviviality, but fell on nothing but a shuttered upright piano. The rest of the women did not stop; they filed ahead up an ill-lit flight of steps.

Beyond a pair of swinging doors, a brightly lit room opened out revealing two very long tables, set parallel to each other and swaddled with clean white linen. Down the center of the tables, plates of cake and pastries alternated with bowls of brass-colored chrysanthemums. There was a startling number of cakes, all painstakingly decorated, some with cherries and nuts and some with sugar lace. Already the rector had taken a stand at the head of one table, and his wife at the head of the other, and the townswomen were crowding into the closely spaced chairs below. The women in Rose's group fitted themselves in at the far end of the rector's table. Mrs. Nolan was jockeyed unwillingly into a position facing the rector, at the very foot, Esther at her right and an empty chair that had been overlooked at her left.

The women sat, settled.

Mrs. Nolan turned to Esther. "What do you *do* here?" It was the question of a desperate woman.

"Oh, I have the baby." Then Esther was ashamed of her evasion. "I type some of my husband's work."

Rose leaned over to them. "Her husband writes for the *ra*dio."

"I paint," said Mrs. Nolan.

"What in?" Esther wondered, a little startled.

"Oils, mainly. But I'm no good."

"Ever tried watercolor?"

"Oh yes, but you have to be good. You have to get it right the first time."

"What do you paint, then? Portraits?"

Mrs. Nolan wrinkled her nose and took out a pack of cigarettes. "Do you suppose we can smoke? No. I'm no good at portraits. But sometimes I paint Ricky."

The tiny, extinguished-looking woman making the rounds with tea arrived at Rose.

"We can smoke, can't we?" Mrs. Nolan asked Rose.

"Oh, I don't think so. I wanted to the worst way when I first came, but nobody else did."

Mrs. Nolan looked up at the woman with the tea. "Can we smoke?"

"Ooh, I shouldn't think so," the woman said. "Not in the church rooms."

"Is it a fire law?" Esther wanted to know. "Or something religious?" But nobody could say. Mrs. Nolan began to tell Esther about her little boy of seven, named Benedict. Ricky was, it turned out, a hamster.

Suddenly the swinging doors flew open to admit a flushed young woman with a steaming tray. "The sausages, the sausages!" pleased voices cried from various parts of the room.

Esther felt very hungry, almost faint. Even the ribbons of clear, hot grease oozing from her sausage in its pastry wrapper didn't stop her —she took a large bite, and so did Mrs. Nolan. At that moment everybody bowed their heads. The rector said grace.

Cheeks bulging, Esther and Mrs. Nolan peered at each other, making eyes and stifling their giggles, like schoolgirls with a secret. Then, grace over, everybody began sending plates up and down and helping themselves with energy. Mrs. Nolan told Esther about Little Benedict's father, Big Benedict (her second husband), who had been a rubber planter in Malaya until he had the misfortune to fall sick and be sent home.

"Have some dough bread." Rose passed a plate of moist, fruity slices, and Mrs. Hotchkiss followed this up with a three-layer chocolate cake.

Esther took a helping of everything. "Who made all the cakes?"

"The rector's wife," Rose said. "She bakes a lot."

'The rector," Mrs. Hotchkiss inclined her partridge-wing hat, "helps with the beating.'

Mrs. Nolan, deprived of cigarettes, drummed her fingers on the tabletop. "I think I'll be going soon."

"I'll go with you." Esther spoke through a doughy mouthful. "I've to be back for the baby."

But the woman was there again, with refills of tea, and the two tables seemed more and more to resemble a large family gathering from which it would be rude to rise without offering thanks, or at least seeking permission.

Somehow the rector's wife had slipped from the head of her table and was bending maternally over them, one hand on Mrs. Nolan's shoulder, one on Esther's. "This dough bread is delicious," said Esther, thinking to compliment her. "Did you make it?"

"Oh, no, Mr. Ockenden makes that." Mr. Ockenden was the town baker. "There's a loaf over, though. If you like, you could buy it afterwards."

Taken aback by this sudden financial pounce, Esther almost immediately recollected how church people of all orders were forever after pennies, offertories and donations of one sort or another. She had found herself walking out from Evensong recently with a Blessings Box—an austere wooden container with a slot into which one was apparently intended to drop money until the next year's Harvest Festival, when the boxes would be emptied and handed round again.

"I'd love a loaf," Esther said, a bit too brightly.

After the rector's wife returned to her chair, there was a muttering and nudging among the middle-aged women in best blouses, cardigans and round felt hats at the table's foot. Finally, on a spatter of local applause, one woman rose and made a little speech calling for a vote of thanks to the rector's wife for the fine tea. There was a humorous footnote about thanking the rector, too, for his help—evidently notorious—in stirring the batter for the cakes. More applause; much laughter, after which the rector's wife made a return speech welcoming Esther and Mrs. Nolan by name. Carried away, she revealed her hopes of their becoming members of the Mothers' Union.

In the general flurry of clapping and smiles and curious stares and a renewal of plate-passing, the rector himself left his place and came to sit in the empty chair next to Mrs. Nolan. Nodding at Esther, as if they had already had a great deal to say to each other, he began speaking in a low voice to Mrs. Nolan. Esther listened in unashamedly as she ate through her plate of buttered dough bread and assorted cakes.

The rector made some odd, jocular reference to never finding Mrs. Nolan in—at which her clear, blonde's skin turned a bright shade of pink, then said, "I'm sorry, but the reason I've not called is because I thought you were a divorcee. I usually make it a point not to bother them."

"Oh, it doesn't matter. It doesn't matter now, does it," muttered the blushing Mrs. Nolan, tugging furiously at the collar of her open coat. The rector finished with some little welcoming homily which escaped Esther, so confused and outraged was she by Mrs. Nolan's predicament.

"I shouldn't have come," Mrs. Nolan whispered to Esther. "Divorced women aren't supposed to come."

"That's ridiculous," Esther said. "I'm going. Let's go now."

Rose glanced up as her two charges started to button their coats. "I'll go with you. Cecil will want his tea."

Esther glanced towards the rector's wife at the far end of the room, surrounded now by a group of chattering women. The extra loaf of dough bread was nowhere in sight, and she felt no desire to pursue it. She could ask Mr. Ockenden for a loaf on Saturday, when he came round. Besides, she vaguely suspected the rector's wife might have charged her a bit over for it—to profit the church, the way they did at jumble sales.

Mrs. Nolan said goodbye to Rose and Esther at the Town Hall and started off down the hill to her husband's pub. The river road faded, at its first dip, in a bank of wet blue fog; she was lost to view in a few minutes.

Rose and Esther walked home together.

"I didn't know they didn't allow divorcees," Esther said.

"Oh, no, they don't like 'em." Rose fumbled in her pocket and produced a packet of Maltesers. "Have one? Mrs. Hotchkiss said that even if Mrs. Nolan wanted to join the Mothers' Union, she couldn't. Do you want a dog?"

"A what?"

"A dog. Mrs. Hotchkiss has this Alsatian left over from the last lot. She's sold all the black ones, everybody loves those, and now there's just this gray one."

"Tom *hates* dogs." Esther surprised herself by her own passion. "Especially Alsatians."

Rose seemed pleased. "I told her I didn't think you'd want it. Dreadful things, dogs."

The gravestones, greenly luminous in the thick dusk, looked as if their ancient lichens might possess some magical power of phosphorescence. The two women passed under the churchyard, with its flat, black yew, and as the chill of evening wore through their coats and the afterglow of tea, Rose crooked out one arm, and Esther, without hesitation, took it.

Ocean 1212-W

Essay, 1962

My childhood landscape was not land but the end of the land—the cold, salt, running hills of the Atlantic. I sometimes think my vision of the sea is the clearest thing I own. I pick it up, exile that I am, like the purple "lucky stones" I used to collect with a white ring all the way round, or the shell of a blue mussel with its rainbowy angel's fingernail interior; and in one wash of memory the colors deepen and gleam, the early world draws breath.

Breath, that is the first thing. Something is breathing. My own breath? The breath of my mother? No, something else, something larger, farther, more serious, more weary. So behind shut lids I float awhile; I'm a small sea captain, tasting the day's weather—battering rams at the seawall, a spray of grapeshot on my mother's brave geraniums, or the lulling shoosh-shoosh of a full, mirrory pool; the pool turns the quartz grits at its rim idly and kindly, a lady brooding at jewelry. There might be a hiss of rain on the pane, there might be wind sighing and trying the creaks of the house like keys. I was not deceived by these. The motherly pulse of the sea made a mock of such counterfeits.

Like a deep woman, it hid a good deal; it had many faces, many delicate, terrible veils. It spoke of miracles and distances; if it could court, it could also kill. When I was learning to creep, my mother set me down on the beach to see what I thought of it. I crawled straight for the coming wave and was just through the wall of green when she caught my heels.

I often wonder what would have happened if I had managed to pierce that looking-glass. Would my infant gills have taken over, the salt in my blood? For a time I believed not in God nor Santa Claus, but in mermaids. They seemed as logical and possible to me as the brittle twig of a seahorse in the Zoo aquarium or the skates lugged up on the lines of cursing Sunday fishermen—skates the shape of old pillowslips with the full, coy lips of women.

And I recall my mother, a sea-girl herself, reading to me and my brother—who came later—from Matthew Arnold's "Forsaken Merman":

> Sand-strewn caverns, cool and deep,
> Where the winds are all asleep;
> Where the spent lights quiver and gleam;
> Where the salt weed sways in the stream;
> Where the sea-beasts rang'd all round
> Feed in the ooze of their pasture-ground;
> Where the sea-snakes coil and twine
> Dry their mail and bask in the brine;
> Where great whales come sailing by,
> Sail and sail with unshut eye,
> Round the world for ever and aye.

I saw the gooseflesh on my skin. I did not know what made it. I was not cold. Had a ghost passed over? No, it was the poetry. A spark flew off Arnold and shook me, like a chill. I wanted to cry; I felt very odd. I had fallen into a new way of being happy.

Now and then, when I grow nostalgic about my ocean childhood—the wauling of gulls and the smell of salt, somebody solicitous will bundle me into a car and drive me to the nearest briny horizon. After all, in England, no place is what? more than seventy miles from the sea. "There," I'll be told, "there it is." As if the sea were a great oyster on a plate that could be served up, tasting just the same, at any restaurant the world over. I get out of the car, I stretch my legs, I sniff. The sea. But that is not it, that is not it at all.

The geography is all wrong in the first place. Where is the gray thumb of the water tower to the left and the sickle-shaped sandbar (really a stone bar) under it, and the Deer Island prison at the tip of the point to the far right? The road I knew curved into the waves with the ocean on one side, the bay on the other; and my grandmother's house, halfway out, faced east, full of red sun and sea lights.

To this day I remember her phone number: OCEAN 1212-W. I would repeat it to the operator, from my home on the quieter bayside, an incantation, a fine rhyme, half expecting the black earpiece to give me back, like a conch, the susurrous murmur of the sea out there as well as my grandmother's Hello.

The breath of the sea, then. And then its lights. Was it some huge, radiant animal? Even with my eyes shut I could feel the glimmers off its bright mirrors spider over my lids. I lay in a watery cradle, and sea gleams found the chinks in the dark green window blind, playing and dancing, or resting and trembling a little. At naptime I clinked my fingernail on the hollow brass bedstead for the music of it and once, in a fit of discovery and surprise, found the join in the new rose paper and with the same curious nail bared a great bald space of wall. I got scolded for this, spanked, too, and then my grandfather extracted me from the domestic furies for a long beachcombing stroll over mountains of rattling and cranking purple stones.

My mother was born and brought up in the same sea-bitten house; she remembered days of wrecks where the townspeople poked among the waves' leavings as at an open market—tea kettles, bolts of soaked cloth, the lone, lugubrious shoe. But never, that she could remember, a drowned sailor. They went straight to Davy Jones. Still, what mightn't the sea bequeath? I kept hoping. Brown and green glass nuggets were common, blue and red ones rare: the lanterns of shattered ships? Or the sea-beaten hearts of beer and whisky bottles. There was no telling.

I think the sea swallowed dozens of tea sets—tossed in abandon off liners, or consigned to the tide by jilted brides. I collected a shiver of china bits, with borders of larkspur and birds or braids of daisies. No two patterns ever matched.

Then one day the textures of the beach burned themselves on the lens of my eye forever. Hot April. I warmed my bottom on the mica-bright stone of my grandmother's steps, staring at the stucco wall, with its magpie design of egg stones, fan shells, colored glass. My mother was in the hospital. She had been gone three weeks. I sulked. I would do nothing. Her desertion punched a smoldering hole in my sky. How could she, so loving and faithful, so easily leave me? My grandmother hummed and thumped out her bread dough with suppressed excitement. Viennese, Victorian, she pursed her lips, she would tell me nothing. Finally she melted a little. I would have a surprise when mother came back. It would be something nice. It would be—a baby.

A baby.

I hated babies. I who for two and a half years had been the center of a tender universe felt the axis wrench and a polar chill immobilize my bones. I would be a bystander, a museum mammoth. Babies!

Even my grandfather, on the glassed-in verandah, couldn't woo me from my huge gloom. I refused to hide his pipe in the rubber plant and make it a pipe tree. He stalked off in his sneakers, wounded too, but whistling. I waited till his shape rounded Water Tower Hill and dwindled in the direction of the sea promenade; its ice-cream and hotdog stalls were boarded up still, in spite of the mild pre-season weather. His lyrical whistle beckoned me to adventure and forgetting. But I didn't want to forget. Hugging my grudge, ugly and prickly, a sad sea urchin, I trudged off on my own, in the opposite direction toward the forbidding prison. As from a star I saw, coldly and soberly, the *separateness* of everything. I felt the wall of my skin: I am I. That stone is a stone. My beautiful fusion with the things of this world was over.

The tide ebbed, sucked back into itself. There I was, a reject, with the dried black seaweed whose hard beads I liked to pop, hollowed orange and grapefruit halves and a garbage of shells. All at once, old and lonely, I eyed these—razor clams, fairy boats, weedy mussels, the oyster's pocked gray lace (there was never a pearl) and tiny white "ice-cream cones." You could always tell where the best shells were— at the rim of the last wave, marked by a mascara of tar. I picked up, frigidly, a stiff pink starfish. It lay at the heart of my palm, a joke dummy of my own hand. Sometimes I nursed starfish alive in jam jars of seawater and watched them grow back lost arms. On this day, this awful birthday of otherness, my rival, somebody else, I flung the starfish against a stone. Let it perish. It had no wit.

I stubbed my toe on the round, blind stones. They paid no notice. They didn't care. I supposed they were happy. The sea waltzed off into nothing, into the sky—the dividing line on this calm day almost invisible. I knew, from school, the sea cupped the bulge of the world like a blue coat, but my knowledge somehow never connected with what I *saw*—water drawn halfway up the air, a flat, glassy blind; the snail trails of steamers along the rim. For all I could tell, they circled that line forever. What lay behind it? "Spain," said owl-eyed Harry Bean, my friend. But the parochial map of my mind couldn't take it in. Spain. Mantillas and gold castles and bulls. Mermaids on rocks, chests of jewels, the fantastical. A piece of which the sea, ceaselessly eating and churning, might any minute beach at my feet. As a sign.

A sign of what?

A sign of election and specialness. A sign I was not forever to be cast out. And I *did* see a sign. Out of a pulp of kelp, still shining, with a wet, fresh smell, reached a small, brown hand. What would it be? What did I *want* it to be? A mermaid, a Spanish infanta?

What it was, was a monkey.

Not a real monkey, but a monkey of wood. Heavy with the water it had swallowed and scarred with tar, it crouched on its pedestal, remote and holy, long-muzzled and oddly foreign. I brushed it and dried it and admired its delicately carved hair. It looked like no monkey I had ever seen eating peanuts and moony-foolish. It had the noble pose of a simian Thinker. I realize now that the totem I so lovingly undid from its caul of kelp (and have since, alas, mislaid with the other baggage of childhood) was a Sacred Baboon.

So the sea, perceiving my need, had conferred a blessing. My baby brother took his place in the house that day, but so did my marvelous and (who knew?) even priceless baboon.

Did my childhood seascape, then, lend me my love of change and wildness? Mountains terrify me—they just sit about, they are so *proud*. The stillness of hills stifles me like fat pillows. When I was not walking alongside the sea I was on it, or in it. My young uncle, athletic and handy, rigged us a beach swing. When the tide was right you could kick to the peak of the arc, let go, and drop into the water.

Nobody taught me to swim. It simply happened. I stood in a ring of playmates in the quiet bay, up to my armpits, rocked by ripples. One spoiled little boy had a rubber tire in which he sat and kicked, although he could not swim. My mother would never let my brother or me borrow water wings or tires or swimming pillows for fear they would float us over our depth and rubbish us to an early death. "Learn to swim first," was her stern motto. The little boy climbed off his tire, bobbed and clung, and wouldn't share it. "It's mine," he reasonably said. Suddenly a cat's paw scuffed the water dark, he let go, and the pink, lifesaver-shaped tire skimmed out of his grip. Loss widened his eyes; he began to cry. "I'll get it," I said, my bravado masking a fiery desire for a ride. I jumped with a side flap of hands; my feet ceased to touch. I was in that forbidden country—"over my head." I should, according to Mother, have sunk like a stone, but I didn't. My chin was up, hands and feet milling the cold green. I caught the scudding tire and swam in. I was swimming. I could swim.

The airport across the bay unloosed a blimp. It went up like a silver bubble, a salute.

That summer my uncle and his petite fiancée built a boat. My brother and I carried shiny nails. We woke to the tamp-tamp of the hammer. The honey color of the new wood, the white shavings (turned into finger rings) and the sweet dust of the saw were creating an idol, something beautiful—a real sailboat. From the sea my uncle brought back mackerel. Greeny-blue-black brocades unfaded, they came to the table. And we did live off the sea. With a cod's head and tail my grandmother could produce a chowder that set, when chilled, in its own triumphal jelly. We made suppers of buttery steamed clams and laid lines of lobster pots. But I never could watch my grandmother drop the dark green lobsters with their waving, wood-jammed claws into the boiling pot from which they would be, in a minute, drawn—red, dead and edible. I felt the awful scald of the water too keenly on my skin.

The sea was our main entertainment. When company came, we set them before it on rugs, with thermoses and sandwiches and colored umbrellas, as if the water—blue, green, gray, navy or silver as it might be—were enough to watch. The grown-ups in those days still wore the puritanical black bathing suits that make our family snapshot albums so archaic.

My final memory of the sea is of violence—a still, unhealthily yellow day in 1939, the sea molten, steely-slick, heaving at its leash like a broody animal, evil violets in its eye. Anxious telephone calls crossed from my grandmother, on the exposed oceanside, to my mother, on the bay. My brother and I, knee-high still, imbibed the talk of tidal waves, high ground, boarded windows and floating boats like a miracle elixir. The hurricane was due at nightfall. In those days, hurricanes did not bud in Florida and bloom over Cape Cod each autumn as they now do

—bang, bang, bang, frequent as firecrackers on the Fourth and whimsically named after women. This was a monstrous specialty, a leviathan. Our world might be eaten, blown to bits. We wanted to be in on it.

The sulfurous afternoon went black unnaturally early, as if what was to come could not be star-lit, torch-lit, looked at. The rain set in, one huge Noah douche. Then the wind. The world had become a drum. Beaten, it shrieked and shook. Pale and elated in our beds, my brother and I sipped our nightly hot drink. We would, of course, not sleep. We crept to a blind and hefted it a notch. On a mirror of rivery black our faces wavered like moths, trying to pry their way in. Nothing could be seen. The only sound was a howl, jazzed up by the bangs, slams, groans and splinterings of objects tossed like crockery in a giants' quarrel. The house rocked on its root. It rocked and rocked and rocked its two small watchers to sleep.

The wreckage the next day was all one could wish—overthrown trees and telephone poles, shoddy summer cottages bobbing out by the lighthouse and a litter of the ribs of little ships. My grandmother's house had lasted, valiant—though the waves broke right over the road and into the bay. My grandfather's seawall had saved it, neighbors said. Sand buried her furnace in golden whorls; salt stained the upholstered sofa and a dead shark filled what had been the geranium bed, but my grandmother had her broom out, it would soon be right.

And this is how it stiffens, my vision of that seaside childhood. My father died, we moved inland. Whereon those nine first years of my life sealed themselves off like a ship in a bottle—beautiful, inaccessible, obsolete, a fine, white flying myth.

Snow Blitz

Essay, 1963

In London, the day after Christmas (Boxing Day), it began to snow: my first snow in England. For five years I had been tactfully asking "Do you ever have snow at all?" as I steeled myself to the six months of wet, tepid gray that make up an English winter. "Ooo, I do remember snow," was the usual reply, "when I were a lad." Whereupon I would enthusiastically recall the huge falls of crisp and spectacular white I snowballed, tunneled in and sledded on in the States when *I* was young. Now I felt the same sweet chill of anticipation at my London window, watching the pieces of darkness incandesce as they drove through the glow of the streetlight. Since my flat (once the home of W. B. Yeats and so marked on a round, blue plaque) has no central heating, my chill was not metaphorical but very real.

The next day the snow lay about—white, picturesque, untouched— and it went on snowing. The next day the snow still lay about— untouched. There seemed to be a lot more of it. Bits plopped in over my boot tops as I crossed the unplowed street. The main road had not been plowed either. Random buses and cabs crawled along in deep white tracks. Here and there men with newspapers, brooms and rags attempted to discover their cars.

Most of the local shops still foundered in a foot or two of fluff, the customers' footsteps like bird tracks looping from door to door. A small space in front of the chemist's had been cleared. Into this I gratefully stepped.

"I suppose you don't *have* snowplows in England, heh, heh!" I joked, loading up with Kleenex paddipads, black-currant juice, rose-hip syrup and bottles of nose drops and cough medicine (labeled The Linctus in Gothic script)—those sops and aids to babies with winter colds.

"No," the chemist beamed back, "no snowplows, I'm afraid. We in England are simply not prepared for snow. After all, it falls so seldom."

This seemed to me a reasonable, if ominous, reply. If England was due for a new ice age, what then?

"Shall I," the chemist leaned forward with a confidential smile, "show you what *I* have found helpful?"

"Oh, yes, do," I desperately said, thinking of tranquilizers.

The chemist lifted, shyly and proudly, a rough six-foot plank from behind a counter of Trufoods and cough pastilles.

"A board!"

"A board?"

The chemist closed his eyes and gripped the plank, blissful as a housewife with a rolling pin.

"With this board I simply *push* the snow aside."

I stumbled out with my bundles. I smiled. Everybody smiled. The snow was a huge joke, and our predicament that of Alpine climbers marooned in a cartoon.

Then the snow hardened and froze. Sidewalks and streets became a rugged terrain of ice over whose treacherous crevices old people teetered, clutching dog leads or steered by strangers.

One morning my doorbell rang.

"Shovel your steps, lydy?" asked a small cockney with a vast canvas pram.

"How much?" I cynically wondered, not knowing the going rate and expecting extortion.

"Oh, thruppence. A penny."

I melted and said all right.

Then, foreseeing slackness: "Mind you chip off the ice!"

Two hours later the boy was still working. Four hours later he rang to borrow a broom. I glanced out of the window and saw a pram full of tiny icebergs. Finally he had finished. I inspected the job. He seemed to have cleaned between the railing struts with a chisel. "Looks like it might snow again." Hopefully he surveyed the low gray sky. I gave him a sixpence and he vanished in an avalanche of thanks with the snow-mountained pram.

It did snow again. Then came the cold.

The morning of the Big Freeze I discovered the bathtub half full of filthy water. I could not understand it. I do not understand plumbing. I waited a day; maybe it would go away. But the water did not go away, it increased, both in depth and dirtiness. The next day I woke to find myself staring at a stain in my beautiful new white ceiling. As I looked, the ceiling discharged, at various spots, drops of viscous liquid that plopped onto the rug. The ceiling paper sagged at the seams.

"Help!" I cried to the house agent from a puddle of black water in the telephone kiosk. I had no home phone because getting one took at least three months. "My ceiling is leaking and the bathtub is full of dirty water."

Silence.

"Not *my* dirty water," I hastened to add. "Water that floods up into the tub of its own accord. I think there is snow in it. Maybe it's roof water."

This last information was a bit apocalyptic. *Had* I seen snow in the tub water? It certainly sounded more dangerous.

"The water may well be from the roof," the agent faintly said. Then, more sternly, "You realize there is not a plumber to be had in London. Everyone has the same trouble. Why, I have had three burst pipes in my flat."

"Yes, but you know how to fix them," I resolutely cooed. "There is no cold water in the cold water taps either. What does *that* mean?"

"We," muttered the agent, "shall soon see."

The builders and the agent's assistant arrived within the hour, booted and puffing and tracking up black muck. With shovels and picks they crawled through the attic trapdoor and soon great masses of snow were thunking from the roof into the yard.

"Why does the roof leak?" I asked the agent's assistant.

"These are old roofs. It's all right when it rains, but when it snows, the snow piles up and up behind the gutters. It's all right as long as it stays cold." He smiled. "But when it melts!"

"But where I come from there is snow every winter and the roofs *never* leak."

The agent's assistant blushed. "Well, there *is* a faulty gutter just over your bed."

"Over my bed! Hadn't you better repair it? If it snows and melts any more I'll wake up in a mess of wet plaster. Or maybe I won't even wake up."

The agent's assistant didn't look as if he had seriously considered repairing the gutter. After all, I could see him hoping, there might not be any more snow.

"You better repair it. I don't want to have to bother you *again!*"

The men descended and began to swab the discolored and still dripping ceiling with a general air of having things fixed. I ran into the babies' room in answer to a crash and a scream. My son, in an access of energy, had just shaken his cot apart, snapping all the screws. When I returned, coddling his sobs, I heard the men saying "Whoops" to one another. They were holding a yellow plastic bucket to a geyser of ceiling water with the embarrassed air of covering some obscenity.

"How long," I demanded, "is this leakage going to go on? You know it's like Chinese water torture, don't you, drip drip drip all night. Can't you put a bucket up in the attic?"

"Ooo, mum, there's not room to stand a candle in that attic. The gutter lays straight atop your ceiling."

They left the bucket on the floor, just in case, and with promises to repair the gutter before the weekend, stumped off.

I have not seen them since.

Then the agent himself arrived, with bowler and moisture detector, to see about my leakage, the failure of cold water and the tubful of Alpine fluid.

With the moisture detector he pricked the bedroom ceiling and assured me that it would not, in the immediate future, fall.

"You realize, though, that you are in danger of having no drinking water."

I said no, I had not realized it. Why?

"The builders haven't properly layered the pipes to the house and they are frozen. I would turn off your immersion heater in case it burns out the empty tank. When the water in the upstairs cistern is finished, that's the end."

I tried to recall some of the things one cannot do without water besides washing one's face and making tea. There were many.

"I'll try to get the pipes fixed by tonight," the agent promised. "The drinking water situation is more important than your tub."

He stepped onto the snowy balcony to survey the maze of ancient pipes against the wall, then went in to fiddle with the water taps in the kitchen. "Aha!" he finally said. "At first I thought the plumbers might have connected a pipe wrong and that the tub water could indeed be coming from the roof. But look!" He instructed me to stand and watch the tubful of water while he went into the kitchen and ran the hot tap.

Bubbles and rings plopped up from the open drain hole.

"You see," the agent accused, "it is *your own water* filling the tub. You have a frozen waste pipe, so it can't escape."

Then he invited me out on the balcony.

With dazzling glibness he rattled off the sources and origins of the twining pipes. "That is your sink pipe, that is your bath pipe, those going up into the air are air pipes." I stared in despair. The bath waste pipe alone ran some twenty feet down the wall and along the balcony before it bent to drop its load into an open drain below.

"Somewhere the bath waste pipe is frozen."

"What happens," I asked, "if you run hot water in the tub?"

"Oh, it just melts the top bit of ice and freezes again."

"Then what can I do?"

"Hold candles to the pipe. Or pour hot water on it. Of course I *could* have the builders put a blowtorch to it, but you'd have to have it done at your own expense."

"But *you* are responsible for the outside repairs, and the pipes are outside the house."

"Ah, but," the agent evilly gleamed, "the *bath* is inside. Have you been plugging your drains every night to prevent water escaping and freezing?"

"No-o. Nobody told me to. But I always turn off the taps very tightly."

I felt cornered. "Granted," said the agent loftily, "the Water Board should have sent round leaflets telling what to do in such an emergency."

"What do *you* do at *your* flat?"

"Oh, I run great douches of boiling water through several times a day and bung up the drains at night. Terrible waste of electricity, of course, but it seems to work."

After the agent had folded himself into muffler, gloves and bowler and left with his moisture detector, I pondered his advice. Douches of boiling water would do nothing if the pipes weren't already cleared, and I had a limited, perhaps even now extinct, supply of water. The candle cure seemed miserably Dickensian. Still, to be doing something, I filled a bucket with hot water and shivered out onto the balcony. At random I emptied the almost immediately lukewarm water onto a spot of black, recalcitrant pipe. Then went in to look at the tub, hoping for a miracle. There wasn't any.

The dirty stuff didn't stir.

All that materialized was the downstairs tenant.

"Did you happen to empty some water on your balcony just now?"

"The agent told me to," I confessed.

"The agent's a fool. There is a puddle leaking through onto my kitchen floor. And my front walls are dripping. *That*, of course, is not your fault. But how can I lay carpets over a whole lot of water?"

I said I had no idea.

In the street that evening I passed great frozen fields of water. From, I presumed, burst pipes. At a tap newly raised from the sidewalk at one corner, an old-age pensioner stopped to fill a fat flowered china pitcher.

"Is that *drinking* water?" I called above the mean east wind.

"I suppose," he croaked, "they put it there for that purpose."

"Shocking!" we both cried at the same moment, and passed in the darkness like sad ships.

Later that night I heard the noise of a Niagara overhead and feet thudding up my hall stairs and a frenzied knocking. The taps gurgled and choked. I flung open the door and a ruddy young plumber rushed in. "Is the water coming?"

I covered my eyes and pointed up to the roaring. "You look. I can't. Will it flood everything?"

"Oh, it's just filling the cistern. It's all right."

And it was. We had water to drink, we were lucky.

As for the tub, I decided to wait until the thaw—that mystical, unpredictable date when affairs would better. Every day I emptied its dirty contents by bucket into the toilet and flushed them away.

Oddly enough, no one really beefed.

I asked a man holding a small blue gas flame to a button of pipe at the side of the house if the flame helped. "Hasn't yet," he cheerfully said.

The cheer seemed universal. We were all mucking in together, as in the Blitz. An Indian girl in the Chalk Farm tube told me her house had been without any water for three weeks, when the pipes burst and flooded the lot. They had to go out to eat, and the landlady rationed out buckets of water each day.

"Sorry to get you out of the warm," the milkman apologized, calling for his weekly ten-and-six. "What we got now is nine months of winter and three of bad weather."

Then came the power cuts.

One soot-colored and frigid dawn I snapped on the two buttons of the electric heater the builders had stuck, like a Martian surgical mask, in the middle of my otherwise beautiful Georgian wall. A red, consoling glow—two bars of it. Then nothing. I snapped on a light. Nothing. Had I blown a fuse with my piecemeal heating—the little mushroom-shaped childproof electric fan heaters I lugged round from room to room (there were never enough)? *They* had been going defunct lately, one by one, fanning out icy air. I peered into the gray street. No light showed anywhere. My personal concern must be universal. Still, I felt dismal. What had happened? How long would it last?

I knocked at the flat downstairs. A warm oil stench flooded the hall, from one of those paraffin heaters I would never buy because of my fear of fire.

"Oh, didn't you know, there's a power cut," said the tenant, who read newspapers.

"Why?"

"Strikes. A baby died in hospital because of it."

"But what about *my* babies? They've got flu. They can't do this to us, it isn't right!"

The tenant shrugged with a resigned and helpless smile. Then he loaned me a green rubber hot-water bottle. I wrapped my daughter in a blanket with the hot-water bottle and set her over a bowl of warm milk and her favorite puzzle. The baby I dressed in a snowsuit. Luckily I cooked by gas.

Hours later my little girl crowed, "Fire on." And there it was—dull, red, ugly, but utterly wonderful.

The next power cut came unannounced a few days later, at tea. By this time I had flu too—that British alternation of fever and chills for which my doctor offered no relief or cure. You either die or you don't.

A neighbor popped in with prize booty—night lights. To see by. The shops were sold out of tapers, candles, everything. She had stood in a queue to get these. In the street old people were being helped down the perilous steps of cellar flats by candlelight. Candles filled the windows, mellow and yellow; the city flickered.

Even after the power cut, the instinct to hoard remained. One iron-monger simply wrote CANDLES in his window and sold out the piles of red and white boxes from some secret source—no other ironmonger had refills yet—in a few minutes. I bought a pound of wax fingers and stuffed my pockets.

An electrician told me the generators simply weren't equipped to take care of the load of new electrical appliances. They were building new generators but not fast enough. The statisticians hadn't envisioned the demand.

Then, just a month after the first snowfall, the weather relaxed. Eaves began to drip. With a sordid gurgle my bathtub emptied of its own accord. In the street I saw official-looking men sprinkling shovelfuls of powder on the already half-melted ice.

"What's that?" I demanded.

"Salt and sawdust. To make it melt."

I also saw my first London snowplow—small, doughty, with a crew of men helping it along by chipping and chopping the truculent remnants and dumping them into an open van. "Where have you been all month?" I asked one of them.

"Oh, we've been coming."

"How many plows do you have in all?"

"Five."

I didn't ask whether the five served our zone only, or the whole of London. It didn't really seem to matter.

"What do you do with the snow?"

"We empty it down the sewers. Then there's floods."

"What will you do if this happens every year?" I asked my agent.

He blenched. "Oh, it's not been this bad since nineteen-forty-seven."

I could tell he didn't want to think about it—the possibility of an annual snow blitz. Dress up warm, lots of tea and bravery. That seemed the answer. After all, what but war or weather breeds such comradeliness in a big, cold city?

Meanwhile, the pipes stay outside. Where else?

And what if there *is* another snow blitz?

And another?

My children will grow up resolute, independent and tough, fighting through queues for candles for me in my aguey old age. While I brew waterless tea—*that* at least the future should bring—on a gas ring in the corner. If the gas, too, is not kaput.

The Smiths: George, Marjorie (50), Claire (16)

From Notebooks, Spring 1962

First George comes bustling out of the National Provincial Bank—he is the manager. "My wife has been meaning to come to see you." Oh, tell her to come any afternoon after three, I say. Much, much later after no wife: "My wife fell downstairs and hurt her leg, that's why she hasn't been up before this, I didn't want you to think she was being rude." Well, I hadn't thought of it before that; then I did think of it. Almost immediately after three o'clock one afternoon the front bell rang and a woman—narrow, sharp, all in browns, I thought, kerchief, coat, boots—came in. Ted joined me for tea in the red front room—only it wasn't red then, it still had the old green & orange rug and the bare wood window seat. Marjorie Smith talked. Her anecdotes. Finding rubber poncho or some odd bit of value on the roadside and bringing it to the police station. The mustached town constable saying she should bring it to her nearest police station. "This *is* my nearest." He peering, trying to guess, then she

revealing her identity, he sweeping a seat clean with a pocket handkerchief—"Oh, do come in." Her wry, sarcastic, critical talk. The
rector came to tea with his wife when he first came to town some six
years ago. Afterward George saying "Why didn't you tell me?" (he
having been dead silent all through tea). "Tell you what?" "That she
was much the *ugliest* woman?" George could hardly talk, he thought
the rector's wife so ugly. Marjorie hadn't mentioned her looks to
him, he always called her too critical. Marjorie Irish, born in Athlone (province? town?). George a Devonian, with four brothers and a
queer sister named Sylvia—his father a man of consequence. Marjorie's father a bank manager in Ireland.

New Year's party—Saturday night before Sunday New Year's.
Drinks. I still pregnant, within seventeen days of Nicholas, immense
in Chinese blue-satin maternity top. A sense of In. Rang at the side
door of the bank. Came up into dining room—a tree hung with
lights, plastic streamers, Christmas cards. Warmth, people standing
round about. I recognized Dr. Webb, his blond, side-look, weak Cor-
nish chin. His dark wife Joan my target. The Smiths' daughter, six-
teen-year-old Claire, home from Headington, the fashionable private
school in Oxford Marjorie liked because of the wonderful parquet
floor and curving entrance stair. The private school in Plymouth was
all wrong—the playing field was miles from the school, and think of
the girls catching cold on the drafty bus journey after playing out in
the rain! Claire pretty, with short auburn hair, clear skin, pale, fashionable, baby-faced. A striving to be with-it sort. Bad at math. Good
at what? Notion of her going to University giving Ted idea of "saving" or educating her. Inviting her round to sample our books. A
fine crowd of festivity and merriment. Marjorie's sister Ruth, a
housekeeper in London and humorous gray-haired lady, and Claire
passing miraculously replenished snacks—a hump of hollowed bread
filled with mustard and stuck with small hot sausages on picks. Pine-
apple, cheese, cream cheese and prunes, hot pasties. I drank an immense amount of sweet sherry. No lacunas in food or drink. A
white-haired Danish architect turned British farmer talked first to
Ted, then me. We were enchanted with him. I talked to Joan, short,
dark, intelligent-seeming, about help, babies, her sister who turned
from actress to nurse in London. Marjorie interrupted us, shifting us
round. A Welsh mathematician from Dulwich College telling me of

his navy days in California, Coos Bay, the girl he left off in a pine forest. When he went to refind her, found her living in unimaginable squalor in a huge tent with immense family. The friend—Dick Wakeford, oddly mechanical, pale fellow, who is scientific-farming his hundred acres in Bondleigh. His lively wife Betty (who never makes her beds before noon, Claire reported to Marjorie, & has washing machine, spin-dryer, dishwasher, but no fridge!). She's the blond one, I said later to Marjorie, trying to place people. Marjorie wrinkled her nose: Mouse, I'd say. A curious desperate sense of being locked in among these people, a cream, longing toward London, the big world. Why are we here? Ted & I very excited. Our first social event in North Tawton. Our last, so far. Also met short, dark, Jewy-looking Mrs. Young, whose husband is head of the Devon Water Board—the impression she wears green eye shadow. Came home almost three hours later to a pink, desperate Nancy, left alone with no radio or TV or work to do.

Later Claire came over, very dressed for the occasion with a dark ribbon binding back her short auburn hair, black stockings, dark dress and rich brown-black scarf knit by her grandmother. Her obvious bid for Ted's interest. He wanted to give her *Orlando*. I groaned and gave her *The Catcher in the Rye*. Ted's biblical need to preach. She dutifully read this: thought Salinger's style "went on too long." Her absolute uncritical sense—recommended *Angelique and the Sultan*. Ted later wrote her a letter at school analyzing *The Windhover*. Her cutely theatrical account of listening to Ted's play (part of it) on the wireless, the romantic little-girl part "a part I'd love to play myself." I felt awfully old, wise, entrenched. But very inclined to pull up my stockings. Breathless over *Winnie the Pooh*. I shall be, in the future, omnipresent. A young girl's complete flowerlike involvement in self, beautifying, opening to advantage. This is the need I have, in my thirtieth year—to unclutch the sticky loving fingers of babies & treat myself to myself and my husband alone for a bit. To purge myself of sour milk, urinous nappies, bits of lint and the loving slovenliness of motherhood.

My tea at the Smiths'. My stiffness with George vanishing. He came up from the bank for tea. I had wanted to talk and gossip with Marjorie & Claire. Claire in Bondleigh at the Wakefords'. While George was out, I talked with Marjorie about childbirth. She hadn't wanted children. Married George late. He wanted children. Went to war. Claire "unexpected." Marjorie had her in Ireland. Had a nurse. Never woke up at night. Fed her on bottle on return to England. During courtship George deluged her with cookbooks. "Have you read the one I gave you last week yet?" Her dislike of babies, cooking, housewifery. What, I wondered, did she like? She plays a lot of golf, loved living in London. They have accounts at Harrods, Fortnum's. Couldn't tell what their living room had in it. Vague impression of stuffed, comfortable sofa and wing chairs. A dun beige quality brooding over everything. I *still* don't know. Reproductions of an Oriental. Pot ducks flying up wall. Probably very expensive. Must catalog rugs, upholstery, next time. Talked of choosing private schools. Their tour for Claire. Didn't want to turn out a queer person like George's sister Sylvia—she, if she came into the room, wouldn't say a word to me, had no social graces. A sense of silence about her—repressed horrors. I fascinated. She had stood behind Marjorie in a bus queue during the war with a strange man. Marjorie myopic, wondered if it was Sylvia. "Is that you, Sylvia?" Why, yes, Marjorie, I was wondering when you'd notice me. The strange man her husband. One of George's brothers, Marjorie told me later, committed suicide. In bad health, though young. Marjorie afraid of George doing same—he has had two heart attacks, lives under the shadow. Won't drive far. Gets giddy, depressed, in bad weather.

Since—George has come over a great deal. His tender, nervous concern for Frieda, very sweet and genuine. "She'll fall." Waiting for her to climb down from window seat. My initial awe melting. He calls for Marjorie—got Ted onto good radio just in time for play-broadcast of *The Wound*. George is a hi-fi fan. His collection of records. Subscribes to *The Gramophone*. Our local electrician an expert. Everything, it turns out, thrives in North Tawton. We have a great clambering Ariel. George's bright red cheeks. Marjorie brought out Mrs. Von Hombeck's woven skirts and stoles—handsome, one rich red with pale silver-beige embroidery. Marjorie's stories of sharp retorts to the rector (her refusal to volunteer to mind a local old people's recreation room), to a Plymouth landlady who peered out the door every time someone came in ("I don't think a robber would be interested in anything of *yours*") and so on.

Both came over last week after days in London. Got seats at *Beyond the Fringe* by way of Ruth's employer, who is in ITV—raved over Jonathan Miller. Marjorie's story of getting the Right spring coat for nine guineas. A drama. Their pub in Mayfair (or Kensington?) that has the thinnest of rare roast beef. They stay at the Ivanhoe. Claire away at schools since very young. Her emergency appendectomy— Marjorie did not visit her (George had been ill). Took her oddly long-legged bear Algy, a white-gray creature dressed in period suit I saw at Marjorie's. Lost Algy in hospital. Eventually he returned, but missing one arm. Even at sixteen took Algy out of hotel during fire alarm. Have invited the lot of three to dinner this Sunday.

FEBRUARY 22

Knocked, or rather rang the Smiths' bell, after hearing George had a mild heart attack and the Smiths wouldn't be coming to dinner. Met by Marjorie, very brisk and handsome—nursing seems to bring a fine self out. Brown, pleasantly waved hair, stockings, brown, gracefully heeled but sensible shoes, a brown cashmere cardigan over a yellow blouse and brooch. I lingered in the pink-and-blue gleaming kitchen while she put tea things on a tray. George was in bed. He was to eat nothing but chicken and fish. We went into the parlor, with its big bay over the Square and the white and red of Blogg's garage. The sun poured in. I dragged myself to look round and put colors into words. Yes, it *was* all brown and cream.

Shiny cream-colored wallpaper with a minute white embossed pattern. Brown, medium brown, window curtains. Two chairs in window bay. A cream radiator under window, with newspaper on it. A great dull blue-eyed television set. The walls crammed with awful reproductions of Devon hills, a country gate, and a big reproduction of an Indonesian girl in muted tans, silver-grays and lilacs I thought looked familiar. George had bought it in London, & that was where I remembered it from. The trouble about my noticing had been that there was so *much*. The living-room suite in a brown tone, with a pattern of dull yellow and pink flowers, probably roses. A green— unpleasant verdigris green—rug with flowers patterned over it. And a bookcase from which the complete Rudyard Kipling leapt out, and all sorts of other dull old books in dated bindings, with the air of a secondhand shop. A table with curios laid out, from Marjorie's mother—a Duke of Wellington conserve bowl, a French bud vase of glass, embossed with silver filigree, a smashed and mended Oriental vase, all pink cherry blossom and green vines. And an incredible pottery alligator, upright, with green paws holding a purse, in a sunbonnet and long skirt, with brown glass eyes! Awful, but compelling. A primitive drollery. Then the mantel—tiny china children or angels on candlesticks, a minute Crown Derby teacup and saucer, lots of big Oriental pitchers. I had more biscuits and lots of tea. We talked of cooking (M was making G sweetbreads for supper; the family can't stand fat; M had a pork casserole dish she always serves for company), the butcher (M's complaints about his filet steak, her bringing back cuts not tender or thick enough), banking (M's description of it as a competitive business—she has no entertaining because there is no other bank in town; the abusiveness of some customers; a bank manager has to know all sorts of intimate details to give loans, etc.; she forgot to sign a check to the the butcher). My very pleasant sense of warmth, hot tea, and being neatly dressed for a change. George called out from the bedroom to give me some sherry. I asked the name of the sherry, it was so good: Harvey's Bristol Milk. And how to make tea, complaining my tea was so bad. Six o'clock struck twice, the church clock, and then the Square clock. I poked my head in at George—he very dear, tousled gray hair, red cheeks, propped up on pillows, like a young boy. Felt refreshed, enlivened, renewed. Very at home.

FEBRUARY 24

C came for tea. I managed a girdle & stockings & heels and felt a new person. Set up the table in the playroom, with the westering sun, instead of the cold, darkening back kitchen. She in a charcoal-gray cashmere twin set, dark skirt, stockings, flats with gold buckles, furry dark pea jacket, newly from hairdresser's. A hard, catty, snippety nature. I sat & talked with her for a while. She talked completely of herself—what she said to the headmistress, how she got her hair done, how she loved Brigitte Bardot, how she wanted to reduce to have a nice shape (What's wrong with your shape, says Ted). Called Ted down. She talked on & on. *The Seven Samurai* "bored her." It was Ted's favorite film, but it bored him too. She will of course take anything from him, & who doesn't love to have bright young youth listen to pontificatings. "Everybody is always saying I'm bumptious." The product of finishing school: finished. I took her up to see the baby—she couldn't care less, perfectly natural. Was dying to peer into other rooms with shut doors and upstairs—remembered house vaguely from Arundel's time. Talk of prefect's privileges to shop in Oxford, her white mac & blue head scarf, told again how she listened to Ted's radio program, how an English teacher was a fan of his. Terribly critical of Lady Arundel, the midwife's poor son who "blushes whenever he meets her." Small wonder.

SUNDAY, FEBRUARY 24

I should have known it. My instincts were right. At ten-thirty the doorbell rang. I should have answered it. I was in my slippers, without make-up, my hair down on all sides, when Claire came in. "I'm not too early?" Oh, no, said Ted. He made her a cup of tea and she stood in the kitchen while I finished my coffee and Frieda her bacon. I had made the mistake of saying I'd be interested in seeing her poetry anthology at school. Ted & I ridiculed it gently. I kept wanting to get to work. Furious that Ted had invited anyone in. The morning gone, eleven-thirty by the time I gave her her book back and said I didn't think I needed to keep it—which would have involved dropping it round before ten tomorrow. Now I have a respite till April 4 in which I may get started on my book. She is shrewd, pushing, absolutely shameless. I shall ask Marjorie when the moment arrives to confine visits to afternoons. I *must* have my mornings in peace. Her incredible angling last night to get driven to the movies in Exeter (I want to see *Fanny*, how should I get there?). It did not occur to Ted to offer to drive her; he suggested a taxi. I mentioned how we despised Maurice Chevalier, & how Ted in particular disliked musicals. On the assumption that I am as fascinating as T, I shall be omnipotent—chauffeur, entertainer, hostess, if the occasion arises. A charming ignorance as to any difference between us. Her models: Brigitte Bardot & Lolita. Telling.

Friday, March 2

Drawn in spite of myself to ring the Smiths' bell, having been to the
bank at five minutes to three with two American checks and imagined
the boys would be horror-struck at having extra work before closing
time. Then thought the S's might think it a snub if I went to town
without Frieda & didn't ask how George was. These dim things in
back of it. I rang the bell & Marjorie popped to the door in her brown
cashmere, very neat and fine. Went up, feeling ponderous & clumpy
in my suede jacket *and* big green cord coat. "I like your coat," Marjorie said, in a way that made me feel the opposite behind her words.
We sat in the sun-filled front room. I could see, suddenly, that the
wallpaper was a glossy embossed cream, and the ceiling a shiny embossed white, very newish. "I hope Claire didn't bother you." I saw
immediately that Claire had retailed the whole of her two visits in a
fashion which escapes me, because I consider our life so natural, but
which I can construct from her usual critical malices ("Lady Arundel
never looked smart when she came into North Tawton"). Talked of
the wallpaper—they had had the Bank House redecorated at the expense of the bank when they came: a new kitchen and bath, as the
former man had been a bachelor with an old mother who had someone do for her. The bank allowed 15s. for the parlor, 12/6 for the
bedroom and 7/6 for the spare room. "Well, if *that's* all they feel the
manager deserves." This is George's first managership. (Late?) Then
a story about a darling boy in the navy they knew who ended up
marrying a terribly drab American girl with stringy hair to her
shoulders. Why? She must have had money. *He* didn't have money.
Two terribly drab children. I read this as a sort of allegory—the
usual infuriating assumption American girls have lots and lots of
money. Felt terribly sorry for this poor girl. Then the bell, just as
Marjorie asked me, with no feeling, and perfunctorily, to stay for tea.
Betty Wakeford. She came bounding up in a suede jacket with
glasses, a long Jewy nose and open grin, and fresh-crimped high-
fronted hairdo (done in Winkleigh that morning). "So sorry I didn't
come to tea at your place yesterday." She had a pile of new books for
Marjorie. A sense of their close relation. They talked of the Hunt
Ball to be held in the Town Hall that night. Betty & Dick were
going; and Hugh and Joan Webb; and the chemist, Mr. Holcombe,

and his wife. "Bulgy." Why? When strapless gowns came in she wore one and bulged all over it; Marjorie's eyes glinted cattily. Later it occurred to me that "Bulgy," whom I imagined as a drab fat, was probably the voluptuous blonde I'd seen off & on in the chemist's: a good excuse for cattiness. Betty would "twist," she's seen how on the telly. I had the strong intuition Marjorie had peered into our life all she needed to make a judgment, had judged, and now our relation would be quite formal. Mine certainly will be. C shall visit if she visits, not live here as she might. I later sobbed—for the poor heard-of American girl, and for the flat malice of people I keep dreaming into friends.

Noticed, for the first time, a set of luster jugs on top of M's sideboard. A raw copper luster. With pink highlights, and a blue enameled band round the middle on which were badly painted fruits and flowers. What fruits, what flowers? Next time must see. Asked how George was, but M really said nothing. Turned out Betty had seen him in the morning ("I hope I didn't tire him out"). A sly sense of being just by that much shut out.

FRIDAY, MARCH 9

Met M in Boyd's. "Do come up just for two minutes." I had Frieda in her soiled pale blue snowsuit jacket. A completely different atmosphere. Me? She? Carried Frieda up the steep steps. The wallpaper in the lower half of the hall (or rather on the lower half of the hall wall up- and downstairs) a pleasant pattern of a few wheat stalks in red, brown, and black on white. Ruth, down from London, in a rust-colored shantung blouse, to the left of the fire, George, with his iron-gray hair down in front, looking handsome and raffish, with a red silk, handkerchief looped to counterfeit a bloom in his buttonhole. Very hot and snug. I had a glass of Bristol Milk. Frieda stared. They brought out a straight child's wood chair with a brown upholstered seat, and two fine antique teddy bears—one huge, with a naïve primitive expression, big glass eyes and fur that had been pale lavender, worn now to smoky gray, and a little purple-and-black bear. Frieda smiled. M said Mr. Fursman was an admirer of hers ("Have you seen her *smile?*"). Frieda pushed the little bear through the chair back and onto the floor. Threw down the big bear. Laughed charmingly. "Claire is trying to imitate Ted"—a letter from C with a "poem" brought out, about her trying to study and her brain being vacant.

Last time, how Marjorie's glasses kept reflecting the light, in glittering oblongs, into my eyes. She was facing the bright bay window, and I could not look at her mouth, or an ear, but forced myself to try to pierce the glancing shields of light to the eyes behind them. Got a headache, continually deflected. R had seen a huge white owl in a toy shop in Gloucester Road. Her gray tight hair. An Agatha Christie housefrau. We talked of the fine old toys. M told of going to a shop down a row of teddy bears with a friend. "Now *that's* the only one with the *right* expression." The saleslady, overhearing, was delighted: "That's just what *I* said when I was unpacking them—that's the only one with the *right* expression."

APRIL 18

There have been many visits, back & forth. Now there is the astounding & relieving fact of imminent departure. George had a heart attack. He is being retired from the bank. They are moving to Richmond, Surrey, bag, baggage. And Claire. Claire is home from school on a month's Easter holiday. She came yesterday afternoon. I was on the toilet on the landing in a tangle of my workman's overalls. Heard the professionally husky voice: Anybody home? Ted went down. I hauled myself together & flew down. She wore a dark pea jacket, green blouse & gold heart locket. Very pale pink lips & white complexion. Auburn hair. Can I take Frieda for a walk? I stared, smiled, in my pleasant, obtuse way which I so enjoy now that I am a scatty mother of almost thirty. Walk? Walk? Isn't it the right time, she asked. I thought: she has been put up to it. Oh, any day but today, I said. Frieda, as it happens, has been bitten by a crow. She is very upset. I have just been trying to get her to go to sleep. Claire admitted that the weather—suddenly cold, gray & overcast—was not very good. I blithered on about the crow bite—how Ted had introduced Frieda to this big black baby crow in spite of my motherly forebodings, & how the crow had, indeed, snapped at her & drawn blood. I knew Frieda was pottering around upstairs in her bare bottom. Ted, very harassed, went up to do his Baskin article & put her away. He said later she had shat on the floor in the interval. I held & arranged the baby, nosing him idly like a bunch of white flowers. Saw George at the gate. Claire was asking me what I was going to do that afternoon: could she help. I saw Marjorie more & more clearly behind this. O I am going to mow the lawn, I said vaguely. I don't quite see how *help*, there's only one mower. I welcomed George. He looked very ruddy & Tyrolean in a green felt hat, walking tweeds & a cane. We talked about the crow. I think he had come to see how Claire was doing. She was very catty about her eighty-year-old grandmother whom she was to visit with her father the next day, he having asked for a bunch of daffodils to take. The old woman always talked business (so boring), thought she was older than she was and should therefore be respected, couldn't cook anymore & insisted on serving terrible pastries. I felt very sorry for the old woman. George had never seen the property. So I led the two through the tennis court up onto the back hill of daffodils. Claire was holding Nicholas, pale & blinking in his white bonnet & knitted blanket. She had no "feeling" for him as a baby, a person. She was doing something, learning to do something, like making a salmon kedgeree. She grew misty-eyed, even wet-eyed. Now she was going to miss North Tawton. O Claire, I jokingly said, I thought you were very eager to leave this dull town. Oh, no, not now that it came to the point. George said, somehow deftly fitting it in, that maybe now we would "ask Claire down." I was dumbfounded, but only smiled obtusely. What in God's name, I thought, would she find of interest in staying with us. Then, of course, it came: a husband. Or at least an entry ticket into literary London society. Ted had mentioned John Wain was coming down, & they'd seen him on television. Then that Marvin Kane was down, doing a recording of me for the BBC. So Marjorie emerged behind Claire's sudden helpfulness (very clever, too) and advance nostalgia for the town she couldn't, till this moment, stand. Claire left with George, a little defeated. The weather closed in and became very mean and cold. I got Frieda out, and the lawnmower.

Thursday, April 19

Claire tripped in, in heels and a white silk scarf with large and fashionable black polka dots, to collect the large bunch of forty daffodils I had arranged to give George for the trip to the grandmother. I asked if Marjorie would be home that afternoon. Yes. I felt called upon to do something. Claire had remarked loudly and somehow meaningfully that she only had two more weeks in North Tawton. It occurred to me I was somehow intended to do something. Dinner, as I had once thought, seemed out of the question for six, with Ted's family coming. So I stopped, after my shopping, to ask the three ladies, Ruth, Marjorie and Claire, to tea on Saturday. I rang. Marjorie knocked from the upstairs bay window over the square. She was offish and a bit scatty. As if something had not come to pass. Her first remark was about trying to fit the furniture into the rooms of the new flat, hopelessly. I thought that if they had cut the price of their imitation old-fashioned Welsh dresser, refectory table & unsatisfactory wheelback chairs by two-thirds, from the preposterous £150, we might have relieved her of some of her baggage. I sat for a minute in the sunny room, noticing the huge, ugly floor lamps, one of a giant size, and both with frightful shades, frightful in pattern and color too. Almost immediately the bell rang. It was a Mr. Bateman from Sampford Courtenay with an aged terrier named Tim, whose muzzle was gray (he was twelve years old) and who shook upsettingly, as if with palsy. Mr. Bateman was very stiff & dapper. A skyey blue chiffon neckerchief, cinnamon-colored check tweeds. We spoke perfunctorily of animals, after my crow account: of myna birds, talking crows, & the like. I rose to leave just as Ruth melted into the room, stooped a bit effacingly, her gray hair tightly crimped from the hairdresser's in Exeter. Marjorie accompanied me downstairs. I made much of the coming arrival of Ted's relatives and the immense work they would involve.

Recollections: Ruth came to tea alone. Talk almost solely of her very fat girlhood in Athlone, and suspicious advances by monks and gay priests. Chucking her under the chin, asking to accompany her to horseraces, playing tennis, et cetera. My reply, almost continually: I didn't know priests would do that. My, my. The incredible fixed reminiscences of a spinster. Her looking out at German bombers, realizing she was in a nightgown, & retreating in blushes from the window, and the ring of young men leaning from neighboring windows. Then the scone & Devon cream tea for Frieda & me at the Smiths': Frieda glowing & beautiful & good at table, everybody, Ruth especially, playing with her. She seizing on a few fuzzy animals that were conspicuously put out. Of a koala bear, Claire said, it was bumpy & stiff. Marjorie chided: Oh, you mustn't say that of some-

thing you are trying to *sell*. The odd ambiguity—they have given us
large old bears, old baby pillow slips by the half dozen; then they
bring out books at a shilling each, a fusty urine-yellow doll's tea set.
Their noses sharpen: that's twenty-five bob.

Recollections: My visit to Marjorie, in bed, with bronchitis. She gray &
quenched. I brought back the christening gown of Limerick lace
from her grandmother's wedding dress she had loaned me, & showed
her a little picture of Nicholas in the gown. I left Frieda in the living
room with Ruth Pearson. Marjorie was drinking lemonade. She had
that queer camouflaged look, of blending into obsequious gray-
brown surroundings obsequiously and gray-brownly, so that I would
be at an utter loss to describe the furnishings of the room, except to
say my impression was of immense and depressed wardrobes, tower-
ing. George joined us. They looked at each other. Shall we tell Sylvia
our news? I surmised it. Good or bad? Both; George had been
"retired." They were leaving in six weeks for a flat that had miraculously and independently turned up in Richmond. I felt uncomfortably like bursting out laughing. I managed tears. My worries of C's
increasing limpetlike cling in the next three years disappeared. I
could be magnanimous.

Almost immediately, they gave me a price list of things they were
going to sell. I was astounded. They were letting us have the favor of
"first choice." The prices were very high. Trust a banker, I thought.
He must think my grant installments are a life legacy. My first
thought: what in God's name would I want of their stuff. There
turned out to be, startlingly, an antique oak drop-leaf table I coveted
for Ted. We bought it for £25, which I felt wiped out any obligations
to buy anything else. But bought also a handsome round, brass tray-
table & a coal scuttle in brass like a shining embossed helmet, and a
mirror. The brass & the table complete our living room. The table is
a heavenly find. Then they loaded Frieda with old toys Claire did not
want. Showed others that were for sale. I smiled, admired, but said
no more about them.

Ted went to tea after the scone & Devon cream tea. Came home at
seven. After the harrowing visit of the Roses, those ghastly two girls.
I very tired & faint, heard two voices. Flew down with the baby and

materialized in the front door. Claire & Ted standing at opposite sides of the path under the bare laburnum like kids back from the date, she posed & coy. I came out, sniffing the baby like a restorative. I just brought back some of Daddy's records, she said. May I come over Friday and listen to your German Linguaphone records? I have a better idea, I said, and rushed in and took out the records & booklet & thrust them into her hands. "This way you can study them to your heart's content all the rest of your vacation." She had asked Ted if the secretary in his "Secretary" poem was a real person. So hopes begin. For some time I seriously considered smashing our old & ridiculous box Victrola with an ax. Then this need passed, & I grew a little wiser.

APRIL 21

I had invited the three ladies to tea in George's absence over Easter, visiting his mother: Ruth, Marjorie, Claire. Only Marjorie & Claire came. Ruth had a heavy cold & was sorry. Hilda and Vicky had arrived earlier that morning, surprisingly, and in the heavy rain had helped me clean house. I had baked a big yellow sponge cake. We all sat in the living room for a bit, Claire on the window seat talking to me, and Marjorie almost, but not quite, ignoring Hilda & Vicky. Obviously it was a shock to the Smiths not to be our only & honored guests. Their self-centeredness came out with a violence. Claire told of the vacuum cleaner episode that morning: Mrs. Crocker had been cleaning under her bed when the vac stopped. They extracted a hairpin, but it still wouldn't go. They sent it to the Hockings for mending. The Hocking boy Roger came back with the machine and a pair of Claire's black bikini pants, underpants, I presume, which had been extracted from it. Her idols: Brigitte Bardot and Lolita. The sun filled the playroom over tea. Hilda & Vicky & Marjorie & Claire did not mix. I felt very partisan for the former. Marjorie left at quarter to six. Claire putting on her stylish white mackintosh. Marjorie had worn the usual buff or dun-colored cashmere sweater with a pleasant buff-and-black-squared skirt. Claire in a navy blue sweater. Her very thick legs.

APRIL 24

A new & fearsome strategy on the Smiths' part. Claire called up while we were embroiled with the curious blond Swedish lady journalist to ask if she could come and "read in our garden." I was aghast. It is one thing to ask to come around for a cup of tea, but to ask to come and lead a private life in our garden as if it were a public park is appalling. I was so fuming at the Swedish girl after Hilda & Vicky that I had a marvelous time saying how we had more company and were all sprawled out in the garden, so No. It was just as Ted said—if we get to know people too well here they will be using our garden as a place to come get a pleasant stroll & free tea. I had an intuitive fear the lot of them will come today & ask if they can have free run of the place as they are just about to leave & it "surely couldn't inconvenience us for two weeks." Later, Marjorie called. She wanted to tell Claire to come home. Claire is not with us, I said. Oh. This gave a new insight. Marjorie & Claire had arranged, before Marjorie "took her nap" (as Claire said she was doing when she phoned), that Claire should come to our garden & read, and anticipated no refusal. I had a suspicion that Claire had told her mother we wouldn't "let her come" in a rage & Marjorie had said: I'll settle them, I'll call & pretend I think you're there & get to the bottom of this. This is what I suspicioned. In any case, I had a beautiful chance to talk on about our fresh set of guests & Marjorie was forced to commiserate on my business. Now I can add the excuse of our having a lot of back work to do. To give the illusion of sweet loving charm while refusing. A marvelous art I must develop.

Anyhow, I vaguely said Claire *had* called about coming, but we had company again (What, *still!*) and she had said something about going over to the Bennetts'. She had actually said she would read in the Bennetts' field. This new tack I think was accelerated by Ted's picture & the rave writeup by Toynbee in this Sunday's *Observer*.

MAY 1

Claire came over to say goodbye, stocky & white & near to tears in a school blazer. She had been yelled at by her mother about the loss of a button & more or less driven out. Ted sat out a bit, talking, while I cut the long grass of the garden border with scissors. Then Ted went in to his study, saying: Goodbye, be seeing you. Very huffily Claire said: I don't know what you mean, I'm going back to school tomorrow, as if she expected us to extend some concrete invitation to back up the words. It's a manner of speaking, I said gently; we don't like to say goodbye. She sat with me, leafing through a copy of *Vogue* she had brought & giving a little monologue on each page, talked of "almond"-toed shoes, and the new round toe (I said I thought it was the old round toe) and how she had bought a blue beret in Exeter, and how wonderful Brigitte Bardot was, she had started so many styles. The clock struck six, and she left. Ted says he saw them all exiting in best clothes from the Bank House the next morning, to accompany Claire partway back to school & go on to Weston super Mare themselves for a few days.

May 6

Saw George coming up the back way. Took him into the front room, where he bounced Frieda on his lap (Hold Daddy, she cried, wriggling to get down and over to Ted) and passed the time of day. Very natty in gray suit, red silk scarf in pocket and red tie, as if a leashed flamboyance could now show itself since he was free of bank rules & respectability. He seemed lessened, deposed, slightly abashed by all his leisure.

May 7

The final farewell: dinner with Marjorie and Ruth at Burton Hall. I was feeling awful, with this crabby bacterial infection which made me want to rush out in agony to pee every few minutes, & felt I might dash home any minute. Marjorie all dolled up, new hairdo, new vibrant self full of stories about self, cutting Ruth off rudely every time she opened her mouth: obviously trying on a charming new nature in preparation for Richmond. Ruth's stammer bad. An indifferent dinner of steak & custard-fruit pudding. Marjorie in gray-and-white-striped spring suit and luster beads. Sat in lounge with old deaf woman. New bank manager had been at supper, but M said not a word. Story of selling their Ireland house, the flautist in the other part, the stain on the mantel, the girl lost her engagement ring there, but later found it in her pocket. We left at nine with a feeling of immense freedom. North Tawton, with the S's departure, an easier, much more restful place.

America! America!

Essay, 1963

I went to public schools—genuinely public. *Everybody* went: the spry, the shy, the podge, the gangler, the future electronic scientist, the future cop who would one night kick a diabetic to death under the mistaken impression he was a drunk and needed cooling off; the poor, smelling of sour wools and the urinous baby at home and polyglot stew; the richer, with ratty fur collars, opal birthstone rings and daddies with cars ("Wot does *your* daddy do?" "He don't woik, he's a bus droiver." Laughter). There it was—Education—laid on free of charge for the lot of us, a lovely slab of depressed American public. *We* weren't depressed, of course. We left that to our parents, who eked out one child or two, and slumped dumbly after work and frugal suppers over their radios to listen to news of the "home country" and a black-moustached man named Hitler.

Above all, we did feel ourselves American in the rowdy seaside town where I picked up, like lint, my first ten years of schooling—a great, loud cats' bag of Irish Catholics, German Jews, Swedes, Negroes, Italians and that rare, pure Mayflower dropping, somebody *English*.

On to this steerage of infant citizens the doctrines of Liberty and Equality were to be, through the free, communal schools, impressed. Although we could almost call ourselves Bostonian (the city airport with its beautiful hover of planes and silver blimps growled and gleamed across the bay), New York's skyscrapers were the icons on our "home room" walls, New York and the great green queen lifting a bedlamp that spelled out Freedom.

Every morning, hands on hearts, we pledged allegiance to the Stars and Stripes, a sort of aerial altarcloth over teacher's desk. And sang songs full of powder smoke and patriotics to impossible, wobbly, soprano tunes. One high, fine song, "For purple mountain majesties above the fruited plain," always made the scampi-size poet in me weep. In those days I couldn't have told a fruited plain from a mountain majesty and confused God with George Washington (whose lamblike granny-face shone down at us also from the schoolroom wall between neat blinders of white curls), yet warbled, nevertheless, with my small, snotty compatriots "America, America! God shed His grace on thee, and crown thy good with brotherhood from sea to shining sea."

The sea we knew something about. Terminus of almost every street, it buckled and swashed and tossed, out of its gray formlessness, china plates, wooden monkeys, elegant shells and dead men's shoes. Wet salt winds raked our playgrounds endlessly—those Gothic composites of gravel, macadam, granite and bald, flailed earth wickedly designed to bark and scour the tender knee. There we traded playing cards (for the patterns on the backs) and sordid stories, jumped clothes rope, shot marbles, and enacted the radio and comic book dramas of our day ("Who knows what evil lurks in the hearts of men? The Shadow knows—nyah, nyah, nyah!" or "Up in the sky, look! It's a bird, it's a plane, it's Superman!"). If we were destined for any special end —grooved, doomed, limited, fated, we didn't feel it. We beamed and sloshed from our desks to the dodge-ball dell, open and hopeful as the sea itself.

After all, we could be anybody. If we worked. If we studied hard enough. Our accents, our money, our parents didn't matter. Did not lawyers rise from the loins of coalheavers, doctors from the bins of dustmen? Education was the answer, and heaven knows how it came to us. Invisibly, I think, in the early days—a mystical infra-red glow off the thumbed multiplication tables, ghastly poems extolling October's bright blue weather, and a world of history that more or less began and ended with the Boston Tea Party—Pilgrims and Indians being, like the eohippus, prehistoric.

Later, the college obsession would seize us, a subtle, terrifying virus. Everybody had to go to *some* college or other. A business college, a junior college, a state college, a secretarial college, an Ivy League college, a pig farmers' college. The book first, then the work. By the time we (future cop and electronic brain alike) exploded into our prosperous, postwar high school, full-time guidance counselors jogged our elbows at ever-diminishing intervals to discuss motives, hopes, school subjects, jobs—and colleges. Excellent teachers showered onto us like meteors: Biology teachers holding up human brains, English teachers inspiring us with a personal ideological fierceness about Tolstoy and Plato, Art teachers leading us through the slums of Boston, then back to the easel to hurl public school gouache with social awareness and fury. Eccentricities, the perils of being *too* special, were reasoned and cooed from us like sucked thumbs.

The girls' guidance counselor diagnosed my problem straight off. I was just too dangerously brainy. My high, pure string of straight A's might, without proper extracurricular tempering, snap me into the void. More and more, the colleges wanted All-Round Students. I had, by that time, studied Machiavelli in Current Events class. I grabbed my cue.

Now this guidance counselor owned, unknown to me, a white-haired identical twin I kept meeting in supermarkets and at the dentist's. To this twin, I confided my widening circle of activities—chewing orange sections at the quarters of girls' basketball games (I had made the team), painting mammoth L'il Abners and Daisy Maes for class dances, pasting up dummies of the school newspaper at midnight while my already dissipated co-editor read out the jokes at the bottom of the columns of *The New Yorker*. The blank, oddly muffled expression of my guidance counselor's twin in the street did not deter me, nor did the apparent amnesia of her whitely efficient double in the school office. I became a rabid teenage pragmatist.

"Usage is Truth, Truth, Usage," I might have muttered, leveling my bobbysocks to match those of my schoolmates. There was no uniform, but there *was* a uniform—the pageboy hairdo, squeaky clean, the skirt and sweater, the "loafers," those scuffed copies of Indian moccasins. We even, in our democratic edifice, nursed two ancient relics of snobbism—two sororities: Subdeb and Sugar 'n' Spice. At the start of each

school year, invitation cards went out from old members to new girls
—the pretty, the popular, the in some way rivalrous. A week of initiation preceded our smug admittance to the cherished Norm. Teachers
preached against Initiation Week, boys scoffed, but couldn't stop it.

I was assigned, like each initiate, a Big Sister who systematically
began to destroy my ego. For a whole week I could wear no make-up,
could not wash, could not comb my hair, change clothes or speak to
boys. By dawn I had walked to my Big Sister's house and was making
her bed and breakfast. Then, lugging her intolerably heavy books, as
well as my own, I followed her, at a dog's distance, to school. On the
way she might order me to climb a tree and hang from a branch till
I dropped, ask a passer-by a rude question or stalk about the shops
begging for rotten grapes and moldy rice. If I smiled—showed, that is,
any sense of irony at my slavishness, I had to kneel on the public
pavement and wipe the smile off my face. The minute the bell rang to
end school, Big Sister took over. By nightfall I ached and stank; my
homework buzzed in a dulled and muzzy brain. I was being tailored
to an Okay Image.

Somehow it didn't take—this initiation into the nihil of belonging.
Maybe I was just too weird to begin with. What did these picked buds
of American womanhood do at their sorority meetings? They ate cake;
ate cake and catted about the Saturday night date. The privilege of
being anybody was turning its other face—to the pressure of being
everybody; ergo, no one.

Lately I peered through the plate-glass side of an American primary
school: child-size desks and chairs in clean, light wood, toy stoves and
minuscule drinking fountains. Sunlight everywhere. All the anar-
chism, discomfort and grit I so tenderly remembered had been, in a
quarter century, gentled away. One class had spent the morning on a
bus learning how to pay fares and ask for the proper stop. Reading (my
lot did it by age four off soapbox tops) had become such a traumatic
and stormy art one felt lucky to weather it by ten. But the children
were smiling in their little ring. Did I glimpse, in the First Aid cabinet,
a sparkle of bottles—soothers and smootheners for the embryo rebel,
the artist, the odd?

Charlie Pollard and the Beekeepers

From Notebooks, June 1962

JUNE 7

The midwife stopped up to see Ted at noon to remind him that the Devon beekeepers were having a meeting at six at Charlie Pollard's. We were interested in starting a hive, so dumped the babies in bed and jumped in the car and dashed down the hill past the old factory to Mill Lane, a row of pale orange stucco cottages on the Taw, which gets flooded whenever the river rises. We drove into the dusty, ugly paved parking lot under the gray peaks of the factory buildings, unused since 1928 and now only used for wool storage. We felt very new & shy, I hugging my bare arms in the cool of the evening, for I had not thought to bring a sweater. We crossed a little bridge to the yard where a group of miscellaneous Devonians were standing—an assortment of shapeless men in brown-speckled, bulgy tweeds, Mr. Pollard in white shirtsleeves, with his dark, nice brown eyes and oddly Jewy head, tan, balding, dark-haired. I saw two women, one very large, tall, stout, in a glistening aqua-blue raincoat, the other cadaverous as a librarian in a dun raincoat. Mr. Pollard glided toward us & stood for a moment on the bridge end, talking. He indicated a pile of hives, like white and green blocks of wood with little gables, & said we could have one, if we would like to fix it up. A small pale blue car pulled into the yard: the midwife. Her moony beam came at us through the windshield. Then the rector came pontificating across the bridge, & there was a silence that grew round him. He carried a curious contraption—a dark felt hat with a screen box built on under it, and cloth for a neckpiece under that. I thought the hat a clerical beekeeping hat, and that he must have made it for himself. Then I saw, on the grass, and in hands, everybody was holding a bee hat, some with netting of nylon, most with box screening, some with khaki round hats. I felt barer and barer. People became concerned. Have you no hat? Have you no coat? Then a dry little woman came up, Mrs. P, the secretary of the society, with tired, short blond hair. "I have a boiler suit." She went to her car and came back with a small white silk button-down smock, the sort pharmacist's assistants use. I put it on and buttoned it & felt more protected. Last year, said the midwife, Charlie Pollard's bees were bad-tempered and made everybody run. Everyone seemed to be waiting for someone. But then we all slowly filed after Charlie Pollard to his beehives. We threaded our way through neatly weeded allotment gardens, one with bits of tinfoil and a fan of black and white feathers on a string, very decorative, to scare the birds, and twiggy lean-tos over the plants. Black-eyed sweetpea-like blooms: broad beans, somebody said. The gray ugly backs of the factory. Then we came to a clearing, roughly scythed, with one hive, a double-brood hive, two layers. From this hive Charlie Pollard wanted to make three hives. I understood very little. The men gathered round the hive. Charlie Pollard started squirting smoke from a little funnel with a hand bellows attached to it round the entry at the bottom of the hive. "Too much smoke," hissed the large, blue-raincoated woman next to me. "What do you do if they sting?" I whispered, as the bees, now Charlie had lifted the top off the hive, were zinging out and dancing round as at the end of long elastics. (Charlie had produced a fashionable white straw Italian hat for me with a black nylon veil that collapsed perilously into my face in the least wind. The rector had tucked it into my collar, much to my surprise. "Bees always crawl up, never down," he said. I had drawn it down loose over my shoulders.) The woman said, "Stand behind me, I'll protect you." I did. (I had spoken to her husband earlier, a handsome, rather sarcastic man standing apart, silver hair, a military blue eye. Plaid tie, checked shirt, plaid vest, all different. Tweedy suit, navy blue beret. His wife, he had said, kept twelve hives & was the expert. The bees always stung him. His nose & lips, his wife later said.)

The men were lifting out rectangular yellow slides, crusted with bees, crawling, swarming. I felt prickles all over me, & itches. I had one pocket & was advised to keep my hands in this and not move. "See all the bees round the rector's dark trousers!" whispered the woman. "They don't seem to like white." I was grateful for my white smock. The rector was somehow an odd man out, referred to now and then by Charlie jestingly: "Eh, rector?" "Maybe they want to join his church," one man, emboldened by the anonymity of the hats, suggested.

The donning of the hats had been an odd ceremony. Their ugliness & anonymity very compelling, as if we were all party to a rite. They were brown or gray or faded green felt, mostly, but there was one white straw boater with a ribbon. All faces, shaded, became alike. Commerce became possible with complete strangers.

The men were lifting slides, Charlie Pollard squirting smoke, into another box. They were looking for queen cells—long, pendulous, honey-colored cells from which the new queens would come. The blue-coated woman pointed them out. She was from British Guiana, had lived alone in the jungle for eighteen years, lost £25 pounds on her first bees there—there had been no honey for them to eat. I was aware of bees buzzing and stalling before my face. The veil seemed hallucinatory. I could not see it for moments at a time. Then I became aware I was in a bone-stiff trance, intolerably tense, and shifted round to where I could see better. "Spirit of my dead father, protect me!" I arrogantly prayed. A dark, rather nice, "unruly"-looking man came up through the cut grasses. Everyone turned, murmured, "O Mr. Jenner, we didn't think you were coming."

This, then, the awaited expert, the "government man" from Exeter. An hour late. He donned a white boiler suit and a very expert bee hat —a vivid green dome, square black screen box for head, joined with yellow cloth at the corners, and a white neckpiece. The men muttered, told what had been done. They began looking for the old queen. Slide after slide was lifted, examined on both sides. To no avail. Myriads of crawling, creeping bees. As I understood it from my blue bee-lady, the first new queen out would kill the old ones, so the new queen cells were moved to different hives. The old queen would be left in hers. But they couldn't find her. Usually the old queen swarmed before the new queen hatched. This was to prevent swarming. I heard words like "supersede," "queen excluder" (a slatted screen of metal only workers could crawl through). The rector slipped away unnoticed, then the midwife. "He used too much smoke" was the general criticism of Charlie Pollard. The queen hates smoke. She might have swarmed earlier. She might be hiding. She was not marked. It grew later. Eight. Eight-thirty. The hives were parceled up, queen excluders put on. An old beamy brown man wisely jutted a forefinger as we left. "She's in that one." The beekeepers clustered around Mr. Jenner with questions. The secretary sold chances for a bee festival.

Friday, June 8

Ted & I drove down to Charlie Pollard's about nine tonight to collect our hive. He was standing at the door of his cottage in Mill Lane, the corner one, in white shirtsleeves, collar open, showing dark chest hairs & a white mail-knit undershirt. His pretty blond wife smiled & waved. We went over the bridge to the shed, with its rotovator, orange, resting at the end. Talked of floods, fish, Ash Ridge: the Taw flooded his place over & over. He was wanting to move up, had an eye on the lodge at Ash Ridge, had hives up there. His father-in-law had been head gardener when they had six gardeners. Told of great heaters to dry hay artificially & turn it to meal: two thousand, four thousand, the machines cost, were lying up there now, hardly used. He hadn't been able to get any more flood insurance once he had claimed. Had his rugs cleaned, but they were flat: you can live with them, I can't, he told the inspector. Had to have the upholstered sofa & chairs all redone at the bottom. Walked down the first step from the second floor one night & put his foot in water. A big salmon inhabited his reach of the Taw. "To be honest with you," he said, over & over. "To be honest with you." Showed us his big barny black offices. A honey ripener with a beautiful sweet-smelling, slow gold slosh of honey at the bottom. Loaned us a bee book. We loaded with our creaky old wood hive. He said if we cleaned it and painted it over Whitsun, he'd order a swarm of docile bees. Had showed us his beautiful red-gold Italian queen the day before, with her glossy green mark on the thorax, I think. He had made it. To see her the better. The bees were bad-tempered, though. She would lay a lot of docile bees. We said: Docile, be sure now, & drove home.

These few lines were typed at the top margin of the original MS:

Noticed: a surround of tall white cow parsley, pursy yellow gorse bloom, an old Christmas tree, white hawthorn, strong-smelling.

A Comparison

Essay, 1962

How I envy the novelist!

I imagine him—better say her, for it is the women I look to for a parallel—I imagine her, then, pruning a rosebush with a large pair of shears, adjusting her spectacles, shuffling about among the teacups, humming, arranging ashtrays or babies, absorbing a slant of light, a fresh edge to the weather, and piercing, with a kind of modest, beautiful X-ray vision, the psychic interiors of her neighbors—her neighbors on trains, in the dentist's waiting room, in the corner teashop. To her, this fortunate one, what is there that *isn't* relevant! Old shoes can be used, doorknobs, air letters, flannel nightgowns, cathedrals, nail varnish, jet planes, rose arbors and budgerigars; little mannerisms—the sucking at a tooth, the tugging at a hemline—any weird or warty or fine or despicable thing. Not to mention emotions, motivations—those rumbling, thunderous shapes. Her business is Time, the way it shoots forward, shunts back, blooms, decays and double-exposes itself. Her business is people in Time. And she, it seems to me, has all the time in the world. She can take a century if she likes, a generation, a whole summer.

I can take about a minute.

I'm not talking about epic poems. We all know how long *they* can take. I'm talking about the smallish, unofficial garden-variety poem. How shall I describe it?—a door opens, a door shuts. In between you have had a glimpse: a garden, a person, a rainstorm, a dragonfly, a heart, a city. I think of those round glass Victorian paperweights which I remember, yet can never find—a far cry from the plastic mass-productions which stud the toy counters in Woolworth's. This sort of paperweight is a clear globe, self-complete, very pure, with a forest or village or family group within it. You turn it upside down, then back. It snows. Everything is changed in a minute. It will never be the same in there—not the fir trees, nor the gables, nor the faces.

So a poem takes place.

And there is really so little room! So little time! The poet becomes an expert packer of suitcases:

> The apparition of these faces in the crowd;
> Petals on a wet black bough.

There it is: the beginning and the end in one breath. How would the novelist manage that? In a paragraph? In a page? Mixing it, perhaps, like paint, with a little water, thinning it, spreading it out.

Now I am being smug, I am finding advantages.

If a poem is concentrated, a closed fist, then a novel is relaxed and expansive, an open hand: it has roads, detours, destinations; a heart line, a head line; morals and money come into it. Where the fist excludes and stuns, the open hand can touch and encompass a great deal in its travels.

I have never put a toothbrush in a poem.

I do not like to think of all the things, familiar, useful and worthy things, I have never put into a poem. I did, once, put a yew tree in. And that yew tree began, with astounding egotism, to manage and order the whole affair. It was not a yew tree by a church on a road past a house in a town where a certain woman lived . . . and so on, as it might have been in a novel. Oh, no. It stood squarely in the middle of my poem, manipulating its dark shades, the voices in the churchyard, the clouds, the birds, the tender melancholy with which I contemplated it—everything! I couldn't subdue it. And, in the end, my poem was a poem about a yew tree. That yew tree was just too proud to be a passing black mark in a novel.

Perhaps I shall anger some poets by implying that the *poem* is proud. The poem, too, can include everything, they will tell me. And with far more precision and power than those baggy, disheveled and undiscriminate creatures we call novels. Well, I concede these poets their steamshovels and old trousers. I really *don't* think poems should be all that chaste. I would, I think, even concede a toothbrush, if the poem was a real one. But these apparitions, these poetical toothbrushes, are rare. And when they do arrive, they are inclined, like my obstreperous yew tree, to think themselves singled out and rather special.

Not so in novels.

There the toothbrush returns to its rack with beautiful promptitude and is forgot. Time flows, eddies, meanders, and people have leisure to grow and alter before our eyes. The rich junk of life bobs all about us: bureaus, thimbles, cats, the whole much-loved, well-thumbed catalog of the miscellaneous which the novelist wishes us to share. I do not mean that there is no pattern, no discernment, no rigorous ordering here.

I am only suggesting that perhaps the pattern does not insist so much.

The door of the novel, like the door of the poem, also shuts.

But not so fast, nor with such manic, unanswerable finality.

"Context"

Essay, 1962

The issues of our time which preoccupy me at the moment are the incalculable genetic effects of fallout and a documentary article on the terrifying, mad, omnipotent marriage of big business and the military in America—"Juggernaut, The Warfare State," by Fred J. Cook in a recent *Nation*. Does this influence the kind of poetry I write? Yes, but in a sidelong fashion. I am not gifted with the tongue of Jeremiah, though I may be sleepless enough before my vision of the apocalypse. My poems do not turn out to be about Hiroshima, but about a child forming itself finger by finger in the dark. They are not about the terrors of mass extinction, but about the bleakness of the moon over a yew tree in a neighboring graveyard. Not about the testaments of tortured Algerians, but about the night thoughts of a tired surgeon.

In a sense, these poems are deflections. I do not think they are an escape. For me, the real issues of our time are the issues of every time —the hurt and wonder of loving; making in all its forms—children, loaves of bread, paintings, buildings; and the conservation of life of all people in all places, the jeopardizing of which no abstract doubletalk of "peace" or "implacable foes" can excuse.

I do not think a "headline poetry" would interest more people any more profoundly than the headlines. And unless the up-to-the-minute poem grows out of something closer to the bone than a general, shifting philanthropy and is, indeed, that unicorn-thing—a real poem—it is in danger of being screwed up as rapidly as the news sheet itself.

The poets I delight in are possessed by their poems as by the rhythms of their own breathing. Their finest poems seem born all-of-a-piece, not put together by hand; certain poems in Robert Lowell's *Life Studies,* for instance; Theodore Roethke's greenhouse poems; some of Elizabeth Bishop and a very great deal of Stevie Smith ("Art is wild as a cat and quite separate from civilization").

Surely the great use of poetry is its pleasure—not its influence as religious or political propaganda. Certain poems and lines of poetry seem as solid and miraculous to me as church altars or the coronation of queens must seem to people who revere quite different images. I am not worried that poems reach relatively few people. As it is, they go surprisingly far—among strangers, around the world, even. Farther than the words of a classroom teacher or the prescriptions of a doctor; if they are very lucky, farther than a lifetime.

Rose and Percy B

From Notebooks, 1961/62

Retired Londoners, our nearest neighbors, live on the steep, rocky slant of our driveway, looking into our high side hedge through the small front windows. The cottage joined to the Watkins' cottage on the corner, joined in turn to the tiny white cottage of humpbacked Elsie fronting the street. A wreck when they bought it: hadn't been lived in for two years, all muck and falling plaster. They worked it to comfort all themselves. A telly (on hire purchase, almost paid off), a small back garden under our thatched cottage and strawberry patch, hidden by a dense screen of holly and bush there, and by a wattle fence and homemade garage on the drive side. Tiny rooms, bright, modernish. The typical British wallpaper—a pale beige embossed with faintly sheened white roses, the effect of cream scum patterns on weak tea. Starchy white curtains, good for peeking from behind. A stuffed, comfortable living-room suite. A fireplace glowing with coal and wood block. Pictures of the three daughters in wedding dress—an album of the model daughter. In modeling school they stole an expensive sweater her mother bought. Two grandsons, one from each other daughter. All daughters live in London. A side room full of gaudy satin materials the first day I came to visit, and a sewing machine on which Rose runs up mattress coverings for a firm in Okehampton in cerise and fuchsia shiny stuff with lurid sprawling patterns. Percy "care-takes" a firm one day a month. Upstairs, a pink bathroom, floors all sealed with new lino, flounces and mirrors and chrome. A new cooker in the kitchen (the other hire-purchase item), a cage of pistachio and pale blue budgies creaking and whistling, up a step from the living room.

First encounter: Rose brought a tray of tea for us and the workmen the day we moved in. A lively, youngish-looking woman, brimful of gabble, seeming to listen not to you, but to another, invisible person slightly to one side who is telling her something interesting and a bit similar, but much more compellingly. Her lightish brown hair, smooth face, plumping body. In her middle fifties? Percy seems twenty years older, very tall, spare, almost cadaverous. Wears a blue pea jacket. A weathered, humorous, wry face. Was a pub-keeper in London. South London. Oddly sensitive about Frieda and the baby. Asks very right questions. Sings to Frieda. Eye running, losing weight, no appetite, depressed after Christmas. Mrs. B caught Dr. Webb coming down from me one day. Got Percy a checkup. An X ray. He was coming out with others from their X rays but, unlike them, had no chart. "Where's your chart, Perce?" Oh, the nurse said, he's to come back for another after lunch. Now he is in Hawksmoor Chest Hospital in the hills in Bovey Tracy for a fortnight. Rose's ignorance—why a two-week checkup? Is it a checkup or a treatment? She says she will ask tomorrow when the G's drive her out for a visit. My startlement: these people ask nothing, they just "go to be treat" like mild cows.

Have been to church with Rose and Percy—the rector put me on to them. Percy the churchgoer. Rose not so much. They go every few weeks, sit in the same pew in the middle on the left. Rose's series of smart hats. She could be in her late thirties. Other encounters—to tea with them with Ted and Frieda. A smart tea—hot herring on toast, a plate of fancy teacakes, all sugar and frosting. Frieda flushed from the fire, shy enough to be good. Everybody barking at her to stay away from the huge blue-glazed eye and gold buttons of the telly in the corner, the great fancy silent companion, she burying her head in tears in the armchair cushion at the sharp voices, for what reason? Looked through album of all daughters—bright, lively, pretty, with handsomeish dark husbands. The model daughter fancily posed before a traditional wedding cake. The sideboard and telly and three-piece suite take up every inch of space. The cramped, steamy, cozy place. Then they came to tea with us. Percy much later. Rose dressed up but deprecating: "Ooh, look at these stockings, Sylvia," whipping up her skirt to reveal a shabbyish pair of thick stockings. "Percy said my suit had the seam open down the back when it came back from the cleaners, but no matter."

The last time Rose came to tea I had a big fancy sponge cake made with six eggs I had meant for the S's on Sunday, but they didn't come, George had stayed in bed. I broached it for Rose. She made a praising remark. Gobbled it. Seemed very nervous and flighty. Talked on about pensions—Percy had been ill one year and hadn't paid it, now their pension was forever cut short (she got 29s a week instead of the full 30s) and they couldn't pay up the year ("Oh," said the nasty official, "everybody would do that if we let them." And why not?). Shocking. How to get on on a pension. They rent their London house to one daughter. Can't buy much—not on hire purchase. It's all right to do that if you're young. After little more than half an hour, Rose jumped up to a knock at the back door. "That's Perce." A garbled excuse about going off with the G's somewhere. The G's (William's parents) very fancy, have, it seems, much money, a house on the hill, a brand-new car from their firm. I resentful. "You didn't mind my coming?" Her slippery eyes. She repeats everything I say to the G's. My repeating the rector's "We can see everything that goes on in your house" in innocence turning into a bad bedroom joke and getting repeated back to me by Mary G.

Met Percy on the street in front of the butcher's, his watery eyes in the lean face set somewhere in space. Told me he'd have to go into hospital for tests. I dropped in on Rose with a plate of absolutely indigestible "Black Walnut flavored" cupcakes from a Betty Crocker mix Mrs. S had dug out of her closet in the kitchen ("George and I never eat cakes and pies") and which seemed suspiciously ancient, but thought the sugary stuff would appeal to Percy, who ate a pound of jelly babies a week. Rang once, twice. A suspicious delay. Rose came to the door still shaking with tears. Frieda ran down from our gate and came in with me. I found myself saying "Take it easy, love," heartening nothings. "I'm so lonely," Rose wailed. Percy had gone into hospital Sunday. It was last Tuesday. "I know I've got the telly and things to do, look, I've just done a big washing, but you get so used to having them around the house." She burst into fresh tears. I put my arms around her, gave her a hug. "I've hardly eaten anything today, look, I'm writing Perce a letter . . ." She sniffed, showed a scrawled pencil message on the kitchen table. I ordered her to make tea, told her to come up for tea anytime. She wiped her face, peculiarly blanked out by her bare sorrows. Frieda fiddled with small ornaments, climbed the step in the kitchen and exclaimed over the birds. I left, in a hurry, to catch Marjorie S, who was coming to tea after her London weekend.

THURSDAY, FEBRUARY 15

Dropped by to see Rose and ask her if she could come to dinner this weekend. Had a lamb leg. Wanted to be kind, return the roast beef and gravy dinner she brought up when I had the baby a month ago, and the white knitted suit. Her vagueness. She retold the story of the doctor and Percy's eye. Flew on: how Percy had called up on the phone, asked for a sweater—he sat out on the balcony, had a nice room with only one other man. She was going to get the sweater in Exeter Friday, the G's were driving her to visit him Saturday. I asked her to dinner Sunday. She paused, looked vague, didn't know if she was going ("supposed to go") to dinner at the G's Sunday, couldn't afford to let them down, she depended on them for her rides to Percy (she drives, but not their own present car, it's too big). I told her a bit dryly that maybe she could find out and let me know. Aware of my impossibility as charitable worker—take my bloody offer and be grateful. She spoke of Ted's driving her to Percy Tuesday. I a bit dubious—what had he said? How far was the hospital from Exeter? She looked miffed —I said Ted had a dentist appointment; when were the hospital hours. Two to four. Well, would that give him time to shop and do errands and go to the dentist? I knew perfectly well Ted planned to go fishing early in the day and had no doubt thought he could drop her in the environs of the hospital for the day. She said she had no way of getting there (it being an intricate route). Her flightiness. Ted said he had told her he would drop her at Newton Abbot, where he had understood she could get a bus to the hospital. Her translation of this into his spending the day driving her and waiting for her. I told her to let us know if she could come to dinner, thinking she could well think about letting us down, too. Rose, a flighty, fickle, gossipy lady with a good enough heart.

Friday, February 16

A flying visit from Rose. Ted let her in and she came to the playroom, where we were typing opposite each other in piles of sprawled paper over the dull pewter pot of steaming tea. "My, isn't it lovely and warm." We urged her to have a cup of tea. She sat in the orange-striped deck chair. "My, isn't it hot." She was expecting a phone call from "the girls" (her daughters?). News: they asked for her permission to operate on Percy—her voice quavered. She couldn't see why, he was in no pain, if you operate like that it throws your system off some way, but "if it'll prolong his life." Ted pored hopelessly over maps of Exeter and Bovey Tracy, his day of fishing evaporating in face of the obvious impossibility of meeting Rose halfway. The prospect of Percy in hospital six weeks nudging us to sacrifice half a day—her kindness, our slowness. So he will take her to and from and forget the fishing. What is this "shadow" or "spot"? She visits him Saturday, has promised to find out all. Is it old scars, fresh scars? He is sixty-eight. She said she was going to G's on Sunday, but said she'd come to us on Monday for noon dinner. I have utterly forgot to describe what she wore: must train myself better, from head to toe.

February 21

Popped in on Rose, with Frieda, to get my application for Family Allowance witnessed. She and her daughter down from London at dinner at one. A handsome, lean girl with black short hair, a racing-horse body, a sharp nose and chin. Came in to boss mother, tell her how to sign form. Rose Emma B, Mrs. in parentheses. Blue eye shadow from train trip down. Percy operated on, to be operated on that night. Dropped by the next night, Feb. 22, for news—he had had part of his lung taken out, was resting comfortably. What was it? They didn't know(!), would find out Saturday when they went to visit him. They didn't want Rose to come visit him the first day. What was it? Betty: "Excuse me, I have a boil on my nose." The TV set blaring. Frieda cried, startled. Then fascinated. A closeup of a dump truck emptying rocks. "Ohhh."

April 17

A terrible thumping on our door about two o'clock. Ted and Frieda
and I were eating lunch in the kitchen. Do you suppose that's the mail?
I asked, thinking Ted might have won some fabulous prize. My words
were cut short by Rose's hysterical voice: "Ted, Ted, come quick, I
think Percy's had a stroke." We flung the door open, and there was
Rose B, wild-eyed, clutching her open blouse, which showed her slip,
and gabbling. "I've called the doctor," she cried, turning to rush back
to her cottage, Ted after her. I thought I would stay and wait, and then
something in me said, no, you must see this, you have never seen a
stroke or a dead person. So I went. Percy was in his chair in front of
the television set, twitching in a fearsome way, utterly gone off, mumbling over what I thought must be his false teeth, his eyes twitching
askew, and shaking as if pierced by weak electric shocks. Rose clutched
Ted. I stared from the doorway. The doctor's car drew immediately
up by the hedge at the bottom of the lane. He came very slowly and
ceremoniously, head seriously lowered, to the door. Ready to meet
death, I suppose. He said thank you, and we melted back to the house.
I have been waiting for this, I said. And Ted said he had, too. I was
seized by dry retching at the thought of that horrible mumbling over
false teeth. A disgust. Ted and I hugged each other. Frieda looked on
peacefully from her lunch, her big blue eyes untroubled and clear.
Later, we knocked. The elder Mrs. G was there, and the shambling
blond William. Rose said Percy was sleeping, and so he was, back to
us on the couch. He had had five strokes that day. One more, the doctor
said, and he would be gone. Ted went in later. Percy said Hello, Ted,
and asked after the babies.

He had been walking in the wind among our narcissi in his pea
jacket a few days before. He had a double rupture from coughing. The
sense his morale, his spirit, had gone. That he had given in with this.
Everybody, it seems, is going or dying in this cold, mean spring.

April 22, Easter Sunday

Ted and I were picking daffodils in the early evening. Rose had been
arguing with Percy, and I had discreetly let my picking lead me to the
hedge overlooking the lane in front of their house. I heard Rose saying

"You've got to take it easy, Perce," in a cross voice. Then she lowered it. Popped out and stood. Ted had sat Frieda and the baby and me in the daffodils to take pictures. "Sylvia," she yoohooed across. I did not answer immediately because Ted was taking the picture. "Sylvia!" "Just a minute, Rose." Then she asked if she could buy a bunch of daffodils. Ted and I knew she knew we would not ask for money. Dislike her scrounging to get something out of us. We brought by a bunch. Percy was sitting up in the bed made up in the living room for him after his stroke like a toothless bird, beaming a cracked smile, his cheeks bright pink like a baby's. As we went in, a couple in Easter outfits came up, she with a pink hat and a bunch of red, purple and pink anemones, he mustached and serious. She all dovey bosom and coos. They had kept the Fountains pub. Now they lived in The Nest (we've come home to roost!), that white cute cottage opposite the Ring o' Bells. She told me almost immediately that she was a Catholic and set up the altar in the Town Hall after the Saturday night dances. This meant her staying up late. A young girl waiting for a ride home had come up once and said "Pardon me, but I can't help thinking what a transformation, first it is a dance hall, and then it is all neatened up into a church," or some such. "Hubby isn't Catholic, but hubby waits up and helps me." How nice, I said, for hubbies to be so broadminded. Percy kept trying to say things in a vowelly mouthing, which Rose translated for us. "You can't raise a nation on fish alone" was one of the sayings.

APRIL 25

Stopped for a second to talk to Rose on my way up from bringing a load of daffodils to Elsie for the funeral of Nancy's mother-in-law this afternoon. We exchanged baby information: how Nicholas had been crying the past two days and might be teething ("Babies are so forward nowadays," says Rose) and how Percy had dressed himself and walked round to the back. Wasn't it wonderful. That's modern medicine, I said.

MAY 15

Heard a whooshing outside the gate as I came into the house with a load of clean laundry, and dashed to the big kitchen window to see who was trespassing. Old Percy, with fixed, mad blue eye and a rusty scythe, was attacking the "Japanese creeper" bambooey plant which had shot up green in the alley by the drive. I was outraged and scared. He had come over, beckoning in his sinister, senile way, a few days ago with a bag of fusty jelly babies for Frieda, which I immediately threw away, and warned me that this Japanese creeper was overtaking our field and we'd better cut it down. I told Ted Percy was cutting down the stalks and we flew out. Hey, Percy, leave off that, Ted said. I stood disapproving behind him, wiping my hands on a towel. Percy smiled foolishly, mumbled. Thought I was doing you a favor, he says. The scythe clattered out of his shaking hand onto the gravel. He had left a green mash of stalks, almost impossible to detach from the roots after his botched cutting. No sign of Rose. Had intuition she was hiding. She had come over a few days before to buy some daffodils for this hubby-loving Catholic who'd been helping her round the house. I thought I'd let her pay for these in earnest, as it was a gift. Why should I supply free gifts for other people to give? Said a bob a dozen. She looked stunned. Is that too much for you? I asked dryly. It obviously was. She must have expected further largesse. I told her that was what we charged everyone and picked her three dozen for her two bob while she sat over a cup of tea and minded Frieda. It had been pouring all day and I wore my Wellingtons. Now she has invited me down for a cup of tea today (May 17), and I feel sick about going because Percy makes me sick. I won't bring Frieda, I think. Rose told Ted yesterday that Percy goes "funny," has his left arm and side hang loose. Says she hopes the doctor will say something about this when Percy goes for the post-operation checkup.

MAY 17

Rose had popped out the day before and asked me for tea. I gardened heavily up to the church clock's striking four. Went down in my brown work pants. She all dressed up in a blue suit, freshly done dark brown hair (dyed?) and stockings riddled with runs. Raised her eyebrows at my wet knees. Percy not so bad, livelier, but his left hand goes dead and he seems always to be having turns. Saw she had four cups all ready, and herrings on toast, so ran up for Ted. His presence a relief. Rose mouthed about Percy's condition, very bad, she had to dress him, he took all her time. I had a revulsion at the cold herrings on cold toast, a feeling they took on a corruption from Percy. Discussing the cost of heating, admiring their new gas poker fixed in fireplace, we saw Mrs. G, resplendent in black furry Cossack cap, dragging the sullen, shaved-bob Miriam, age three in July, and exhibiting a flat silver ring and eating, as always and forever, a cellophane tube of colored sweets. I took this occasion to leave and attend to Nicholas (who was screaming on his back in the pram) and Frieda (crying upstairs). The G's, Herbert odd and sidelong and extinguished, came over, ostensibly to see Nicholas. Mrs. G said she thought I looked like Mary G's baby Joyce. I felt flattered. She thinks Ted looks just like her son William. Resemblances to loved ones the height of praise. Discussed William's new milk cow (cost about £75), the future of apples.

June 7

Well, Percy B is dying. That is the verdict. Poor old Perce, says everybody. Rose comes up almost every day. "Te-ed," she calls in her hysterical, throbbing voice. And Ted comes, from the study, the tennis court, the orchard, wherever, to lift the dying man from his armchair to his bed. He is very quiet afterward. He is a bag of bones, says Ted. I saw him in one "turn" or "do," lying back on the bed, toothless, all beakiness of nose and chin, eyes sunken as if they were not, shuddering and blinking in a fearful way. And all about the world is gold and green, dripping with laburnum and buttercups and the sweet stench of June. In the cottage the fire is on and it is a dark twilight. The midwife said Percy would go into a coma this weekend and then "anything could happen." The sleeping pills the doctor gives him don't work, says Rose. He is calling all night: Rose, Rose, Rose. It has happened so quickly. First Rose stopped the doctor in January when I had the baby for a look at Percy's running eye and a check on his weight loss. Then he was in hospital for lung X rays. Then in again for a big surgery for "something on the lung." Did they find him so far gone with cancer they sewed him up again? Then home, walking, improving, but oddly quenched in his brightness and his songs. I found a wrinkled white paper bag of dusty jelly babies in the car yesterday from Rose. Then his five strokes. Now his diminishing.

Everybody has so easily given him up. Rose looks younger and younger. Mary G set her hair yesterday. She felt creepy about it, left baby Joyce with me and came over in between rinses in her frilly apron, dark-haired, white-skinned, with her high, sweet child-voice. Percy looked terrible since she had seen him last, she said. She thought cancer went wild if it was exposed to the air. The general sentiment of townsfolk: doctors just experiment on you in hospital. Once you're in, if you're old, you're a goner.

JUNE 9

Met the rector coming out of his house-building site across the road. He turned up the lane to the house with me. I could feel his professional gravity coming over him. He read the notice on Rose's door as I went on up, then went round back. "Sylvia!" I heard Rose hiss behind me, and turned. She was pantomiming the rector's arrival and making lemon *moues* and rejecting motions with one hand, very chipper.

JULY 2

Percy B is dead. He died just at midnight, Monday, June 25th, and was buried Friday, June 29th, at 2:30. I find this difficult to believe. It all began with his eye watering, and Rose calling in the doctor, just after the birth of Nicholas. I have written a long poem, "Berck-Plage," about it. Very moved. Several terrible glimpses.

Ted had for some days stopped lifting Percy in and out of bed. He could not take his sleeping pills, or swallow. The doctor was starting to give him injections. Morphia? He was in pain when he was conscious. The nurse counted forty-five seconds between one breath and another. I decided to see him, I must see him, so went with Ted and Frieda. Rose and the smiling Catholic woman were lying on deck chairs in the yard. Rose's white face crumpled the minute she tried to speak. "The nurse told us to sit out. There's no more we can do. Isn't it awful to see him like this?" See him if you like, she told me. I went in through the quiet kitchen with Ted. The living room was full, still, hot with some awful translation taking place. Percy lay back on a heap of white pillows in his striped pajamas, his face already passed from humanity, the nose a spiraling, fleshless beak in thin air, the chin fallen in a point from it, like an opposite pole, and the mouth like an inverted black heart stamped into the yellow flesh between, a great raucous breath coming and going there with great effort like an awful bird, caught, but about to depart. His eyes showed through partly open lids like dissolved soaps or a clotted pus. I was very sick at this and had a bad migraine over my left eye for the rest of the day. The end, even of so marginal a man, a horror.

When Ted and I drove out to Exeter to catch the London train the following morning, the stone house was still, dewy and peaceful, the curtains stirring in the dawn air. He is dead, I said. Or he will be dead when we get back. He had died that night, Mother said over the phone, when I called her up the following evening.

Went down after his death, the next day, the 27th. Ted had been down in the morning, said Percy was still on the bed, very yellow, his jaw bound and a book, a big brown book, propping it till it stiffened properly. When I went down they had just brought the coffin and put him in. The living room where he had lain was in an upheaval—bed rolled from the wall, mattresses on the lawn, sheets and pillows washed and airing. He lay in the sewing room, or parlor, in a long coffin of orangey soap-colored oak with silver handles, the lid propped against the wall at his head with a silver scroll: Percy B, Died June 25, 1962. The raw date a shock. A sheet covered the coffin. Rose lifted it. A pale white, beaked face, as of paper, rose under the veil that covered the hole cut in the glued white cloth cover. The mouth looked glued, the face powdered. She quickly put down the sheet. I hugged her. She kissed me and burst into tears. The dark, rotund sister from London with purple eye circles deplored: They have no hearse, they have only a cart. Friday, the day of the funeral, hot and blue, with theatrical white clouds passing. Ted and I, dressed in hot blacks, passed the church, saw the bowler-hatted men coming out of the gate with a high, spider-wheeled black cart. They are going to call for the corpse, we said; we left a grocery order. The awful feeling of great grins coming onto the face, unstoppable. A relief; this is the hostage for death, we are safe for the time being. We strolled round the church in the bright heat, the pollarded green limes like green balls, the far hills red, just plowed, and one stooked with newly glittering wheat. Debated whether to wait out, or go in. Elsie, with her stump foot, was going in. Then Grace, Jim's wife. We went in. Heard priest meeting corpse at gate, incantating, coming close. Hair-raising. We stood. The flowery casket, nodding and flirting its petals, led up the aisle. The handsome mourners in black down to gloves and handbag, Rose, three daughters including the marble-beautiful model, one husband, Mrs. G and the Catholic, smiling, only not smiling, the smile in abeyance, suspended.

I hardly heard a word of the service, Mr. Lane for once quenched by the grandeur of ceremony, a vessel, as it should be.

Then we followed the funeral party after the casket out the side door to the street going up the hill to the cemetery. Behind the high black cart, which had started up, with the priest swaying in black and white, at a decorous pace, the funeral cars—one car, a taxi, then Herbert G, looking green and scared, in his big new red car. We got in with him. "Well, old Perce always wanted to be buried in Devon." You could see he felt he was next. I felt tears come. Ted motioned me to look at the slow, uplifted faces of children in the primary school yard, all seated on rest rugs, utterly without grief, only bland curiosity, turning after us. We got out at the cemetery gate, the day blazing. Followed the black backs of the women. Six bowler hats of the bearers left at the first yew bushes in the grass. The coffin on boards, words said, ashes to ashes—that is what remained, not glory, not heaven. The amazingly narrow coffin lowered into the narrow red earth opening, left. The women led round, in a kind of goodbye circle, Rose rapt and beautiful and frozen, the Catholic dropping a handful of earth, which clattered. A great impulse welled in me to cast earth also, but it seemed as if it might be indecent, hurrying Percy into oblivion. We left the open grave. An unfinished feeling. Is he to be left up there uncovered, all alone? Walked home over the back hill, gathering immense stalks of fuchsia foxgloves and swinging our jackets in the heat.

JULY 4

Saw Rose, in a borrowed black velour hat, letting herself into the house. She going to London, but will return in a week. She had been having her hair done, guiltily, a wave of tight curls. "I looked so awful." She had brought over two old books (one of which I am sure propped Percy's chin), a pile of buttons, thousands, that they had been going to put on cards and sell, an address stamp, also for home business, and a few notebooks: pitiable relics. I had passed once and seen two women, their hair tied from the dust in kerchiefs, on their knees in the parlor, sorting miscellaneous objects and walled in by upstanding vividly floral mattresses and bedsteads.

Rose said she heard a couple outside our house. "Oh, but it has a thatch and is much too big for us." She came out. Were they wanting a house? Yes, they were retiring from London and wanted a cottage. How strange, says Rose, I am wanting to sell this cottage. O it is just what we want, say the people. Now I wonder, will they come?

Day of Success

Story, 1960

Ellen was on her way to the bedroom with an armload of freshly folded diapers when the phone rang, splintering the stillness of the crisp autumn morning. For a moment she froze on the threshold, taking in the peaceful scene as if she might never see it again—the delicate rose-patterned wallpaper, the forest-green cord drapes she'd hemmed by hand while waiting for the baby to come, the old-fashioned four-poster inherited from a loving but moneyless aunt, and, in the corner, the pale pink crib holding sound-asleep six-month-old Jill, the center of it all.

Please don't let it change, she begged of whatever fates might be listening. *Let the three of us stay happy as this forever.*

Then the shrill, demanding bell roused her, and she stowed the pile of clean diapers on the big bed and went to pick up the receiver reluctantly, as if it were some small, black instrument of doom.

"Is Jacob Ross there?" inquired a cool, clear feminine voice. "Denise Kay speaking." Ellen's heart sank as she pictured the elegantly groomed red-headed woman at the other end of the wire. She and Jacob had been to lunch with the brilliant young television producer only a month before to discuss the progress of the play Jacob was working on—his first. Even at that early date, Ellen had secretly hoped Denise would be struck by lightning or spirited to Australia rather than have her thrown together with Jacob in the crowded, intimate days of rehearsal—author and producer collaborating on the birth of something wonderful, uniquely theirs.

"No, Jacob's not home at the moment." It occurred to Ellen, a bit guiltily, how easy it would be to call Jacob down from Mrs. Frankfort's flat for such an obviously important message. His finished script had been in Denise Kay's office for almost two weeks now, and she knew by the way he ran down the three flights of stairs each morning to meet the postman how eager he was to hear the verdict. Still, hadn't she promised to behave like a model secretary and leave his hours of writing time uninterrupted? "This is his wife, Miss Kay," she added, with perhaps unnecessary emphasis. "May I take a message, or have Jacob call you later?"

"Good news," Denise said briskly. "My boss is enthusiastic about the play. A bit odd, he thinks, but beautifully original, so we're buying it. I'm really thrilled to be the producer."

This is it, Ellen thought miserably, unable to see anything for the vision of that smooth-sheened coppery head bent with Jacob's dark one over a thick mimeographed script. *The beginning of the end.*

"That's wonderful, Miss Kay. I . . . I know Jacob will be delighted."

"Fine. I'd like to see him for lunch today, if I may, to talk about casting. We'll be wanting some name actors, I think. Could you possibly ask him to pick me up in my office about noon?"

"Of course . . ."

"Righto. Goodbye, then." And the receiver descended with a businesslike click.

Bewildered by an alien and powerful emotion, Ellen stood at the window, the confident, musical voice that could offer success casually as a bunch of hothouse grapes echoing in her ears. As her gaze lingered on the green square below, its patch-barked plane trees thrusting into the luminous blue sky above the shabby housefronts, a leaf, dull gold as a threepenny bit, let go and waltzed slowly to the pavement. Later in the day, the square would be loud with motorbikes and the shouts of children. One summer afternoon Ellen had counted twenty-five youngsters within view of her bench under the plane trees: untidy, boisterous, laughing—a miniature United Nations milling about the geranium-planted plot of grass and up the narrow, cat-populated alleys.

How often she and Jacob had promised themselves the legendary cottage by the sea, far from the city's petrol fumes and smoky railroad yards—a garden, a hill, a cove for Jill to explore, an unhurried, deeply savored peace!

"Just one play sale, darling," Jacob had said earnestly. "Then I'll know I can do it, and we'll take the risk." The risk, of course, was moving away from this busy center of jobs—odd jobs, part-time jobs, jobs Jacob could manage with relative ease while writing every spare minute—and depending solely on his chancy income from stories, plays and poems. Poems! Ellen smiled in spite of herself, remembering the gloomy, bill-harassed day before Jill's birth, just after they'd moved into the new flat.

She'd been down on her knees, laboriously slapping light gray lino paint on the depressing, chewed-up, hundred-year-old floorboards when the postman rang. "I'll go." Jacob laid down the saw he was using to cut bookshelf lengths. "You want to save yourself stairs, love." Ever since Jacob had begun sending manuscripts to magazines the postman, in his blue uniform, was a sort of possible magic godfather. Any day, instead of the disheartening fat manila envelopes and the impersonal printed rejection slips, there might be an encouraging letter from an editor or even . . .

"Ellen! Ellen!" Jacob took the steps two at a time, waving the opened airmail envelope. "I've done it! Isn't it beautiful!" And he dropped into her lap the pale blue, yellow-bordered check with the amazing amount of dollars in black and the cents in red. The glossy American weekly she'd addressed an envelope to a month before was delighted with Jacob's contribution. They paid a pound a line and Jacob's poem was long enough to buy—what? After giggling over the possibility of theater tickets, dinner in Soho, pink champagne, the cloud of common sense began to settle.

"You decide." Jacob bowed, handing her the check, frail and gay as a rare butterfly. "What does your heart desire?"

Ellen didn't need to think twice. "A pram," she said softly. "A great big beautiful pram with room enough for twins!"

Ellen toyed with the idea of saving Denise's message until Jacob came loping downstairs for lunch—too late to meet the attractive producer at her office—but immediately felt profoundly ashamed of herself. Any other wife would have called her husband to the phone excitedly, breaking all writing-schedule rules for this exceptional news, or at least rushed to him the minute she hung up, proud to be the bearer of such good tidings. *I'm jealous*, Ellen told herself dully. *I'm a regular jet-propelled, twentieth-century model of the jealous wife, small-minded and spiteful. Like Nancy Regan.* This thought pulled her up short, and she headed purposefully into the kitchen to brew herself a cup of coffee.

I'm just stalling, she realized wryly, putting the pot on the stove. Still, as long as Jacob remained unaware of Denise Kay's news, she felt, half-superstitiously, she would be safe—safe from Nancy's fate.

Jacob and Keith Regan had been schoolmates, served in Africa together, and come back to postwar London determined to avoid the subtle pitfalls of full-time bowler-hat jobs which would distract them from the one thing that mattered: writing. Now waiting for the water to boil, Ellen recalled those down-at-heel yet challenging months she and Nancy Regan had swapped budget recipes and the secret woes and worries of all wives whose husbands are unsalaried idealists, patching body and soul together by nightwatching, gardening, any odd job that happened to turn up.

Keith made the grade first. A play staged in an out-of-the-way theater catapulted through the hoop of please-see-it! reviews into the West End and kept going like some beautiful, lucky-star-guided missile to land smack in the middle of Broadway. That's all it took. And as at the wave of a wand, the beaming Regans were whisked from an unheated, cold-water flat and a diet of spaghetti and potato soup into the luxuriant green pastures of Kensington with a backdrop of vintage wines, sports cars, chic furs and, ultimately, the more somber decor of the divorce courts. Nancy simply couldn't compete—in looks, money, talent, oh, in anything that counted—with the charming blond leading lady who added such luster to Keith's play on its debut in the West End. From the wide-eyed adoring wife of Keith's lean years, she had lapsed gradually into a restless, sharp-tongued, cynical woman-about-town, with all the alimony she could want, but little else. Keith, of course, had soared out of their orbit. Still, whether out of pity or a sort of weatherproof affection, Ellen kept in touch with Nancy, who seemed to derive a certain pleasure from their meetings, as if through the Ross's happy, child-gifted marriage she could somehow recapture the best days of her own past.

Ellen set out a cup and saucer on the counter and was about to pour herself a large dose of scalding coffee when she laughed, ruefully, and reached for a second cup. *I'm not a deserted wife yet!* She arranged the cheap tin tray with care—table napkin, sugar bowl, cream pitcher, a sprig of gilded autumn leaves beside the steaming cups—and started up the steeply angled steps to Mrs. Frankfort's top-floor flat.

Touched by Jacob's thoughtfulness in lugging her coal buckets, emptying her trash bins and watering her plants when she visited her sister, the middle-aged widow had offered him the use of her flat during the day while she was at work. "Two rooms won't hold a writer, his wife and a bouncing baby! Let me contribute my mite to the future of world literature." So Ellen could let baby Jill creep and crow loud as she liked downstairs without fear of disturbing Jacob.

Mrs. Frankfort's door swung open at a touch of her fingertips, framing Jacob's back, his dark head and broad shoulders in the shaggy fisherman's sweater whose elbows she had mended more times than she liked to remember, bent over the spindly table littered with scrawled papers. As she poised there, holding her breath, Jacob raked his fingers absent-mindedly through his hair and creaked round in his chair. When he saw her, his face lit up, and she came forward smiling, to break the good news.

After seeing Jacob off, freshly shaven, combed and handsome in his well-brushed suit—his only suit—Ellen felt strangely let down. Jill woke from her morning nap, cooing and bright-eyed. "Dadada," she prattled, while Ellen deftly changed the damp diaper, omitting the customary game of peekaboo, her mind elsewhere, and put her to play in the pen.

It won't happen right away, Ellen mused, mashing cooked carrots for Jill's lunch. *Breakups seldom do. It will unfold slowly, one little telltale symptom after another like some awful, hellish flower.*

Propping Jill against the pillows on the big bed for her noon feed, Ellen caught sight of the tiny cut-glass vial of French perfume on the bureau, almost lost in the wilderness of baby-powder cans, cod-liver-oil bottles and jars of cotton wool. The few remaining drops of costly amber liquid seemed to wink at her mockingly—Jacob's one extravagance with the poem money left over from the pram. Why had she never indulged wholeheartedly in the perfume, instead of rationing it so cautiously, drop by drop, like some perishable elixir of life? A woman like Denise Kay must have a sizeable part of her salary earmarked: Delectable Scents.

Ellen was broodily spooning mashed carrot into Jill's mouth when the doorbell rang. *Darn!* She dumped Jill unceremoniously in her crib and made for the stairs. *It never fails.*

An unfamiliar, immaculately dressed man stood on the doorstep beside the clouded battalion of uncollected milk bottles. "Is Jacob Ross in? I'm Karl Goodman, editor of *Impact.*"

Ellen recognized, with awe, the name of the distinguished monthly which only a few days ago had accepted three of Jacob's poems. Uncomfortably aware of her carrot-spattered blouse and bedraggled apron, Ellen murmured that Jacob wasn't at home. "You took some poems of his!" she said shyly, then. "We were delighted."

Karl Goodman smiled. "Perhaps I should tell you what I've come for. I live nearby and happened to be home for lunch, so I thought I'd come round in person . . ."

Denise Kay had phoned *Impact* that morning to see if they couldn't arrange to publish part or all of Jacob's play in time to coincide with the performance. "I just wanted to make sure your husband wasn't committed to some other magazine first," Karl Goodman finished.

"No, I don't think he is." Ellen tried to sound calm. "In fact I know he's not. I'm sure he'd be happy to have you consider the play. There's a copy upstairs. May I get it for you . . . ?"

"That would be very kind."

As Ellen hurried into the flat, Jill's outraged wails met her. *Just a minute, love,* she promised. Snatching up the impressively fat manuscript she had typed from Jacob's dictation through so many hopeful teatimes, she started downstairs again.

"Thank you, Mrs. Ross." Abashed, Ellen felt Karl Goodman's shrewd eyes assess her, from the coronet of brown braids to the scuffed though polished tips of her flat walking shoes. "If we accept this, as I'm almost sure we shall, I'll have the check sent to you in advance."

Ellen flushed, thinking: *We're not that desperate. Not quite.* "That would be fine," she said.

Slowly she trudged upstairs to the shrill tune of Jill's cries. *Already I don't fit. I'm homespun, obsolete as last year's hemline. If I were Nancy, I'd grab that check the minute it dropped through the mail slot and be off to a fancy hairdresser's and top off the beauty treatment by cruising Regent Street in a cab loaded with loot.* But *I'm not Nancy,* she reminded herself firmly, and mustering a motherly smile, went in to finish feeding Jill. Thumbing through the smart fashion magazines in the doctor's office that afternoon, waiting for Jill's regular checkup, Ellen mused darkly on the gulf separating her from the self-possessed fur-, feather- and jewel-bedecked models who gazed back at her from the pages with astoundingly large, limpid eyes.

Do they ever start the day on the wrong foot? she wondered. *With a headache . . . or a heartache?* And she tried to imagine the fairytale world where these women woke dewy-eyed and pink-cheeked, yawning daintily as a cat does, their hair, even at daybreak, a miraculously intact turret of gold, russet, blue-black or perhaps lavender-tinted silver. They would rise, supple as ballerinas, to prepare an exotic breakfast for the man-of-their-heart—mushrooms and creamy scrambled eggs, say, or crabmeat on toast—trailing about a sparkling American kitchen in a foamy negligee, satin ribbons fluttering like triumphal banners . . .

No, Ellen readjusted her picture. They would, of course, have breakfast brought to them in bed, like proper princesses, on a sumptuous tray: crisp toast, the milky luster of frail china, water just off the boil for the orange-flower tea . . . And into the middle of this fabulous papier-mâché world the upsetting vision of Denise Kay insinuated itself. Indeed, she seemed perfectly at home there, her dark brown, almost black eyes profound under a ravishing cascade of coppery hair. *If only she were superficial, empty-headed.* Ellen was momentarily swamped by speculations unworthy of a resourceful wife. *If only . . .*

"Mrs. Ross?" The receptionist touched her shoulder, and Ellen snapped out of her daydream. *If only Jacob's home when I get back,* she changed her tack hopefully, *his feet up on the sofa, ready for tea, the same as ever . . .* And, hoisting Jill, she followed the efficient, white-uniformed woman into the doctor's consulting room.

Ellen unlatched the door with deliberate cheerfulness. Yet even as she crossed the threshold, Jill drowsing in her arms, she felt a wave of dismay. *He's not here . . .*

Mechanically she bedded Jill for her afternoon nap and started, with small heart, to cut out the pattern of a baby's nightgown she planned to run up on a neighbor's hand-wind sewing machine that evening.

The clear blue morning had betrayed its promise, she noticed. Looming clouds let their soiled parachute silks sag low above the small square, making the houses and sparse-leaved trees seem drabber than ever.

I love it here. Ellen attacked the warm red flannel with defiant snips. *Pouf to Mayfair, pouf to Knightsbridge, pouf to Hampstead . . .* She was snuffing out the silver spheres of luxury like so many pale dandelion clocks when the phone rang.

Red cloth, pins, tissue pattern pieces and scissors flew helter-skelter onto the rug as she scrambled to her feet. Jacob always called if he was held up somewhere, so she wouldn't worry. And at this particular moment, some token of his thoughtfulness, however small, would be more welcome than cool water to a waif in the desert.

"Hallo, darling!" Nancy Regan's cocky, theatrical voice vibrated across the wire. "How are things?"

"Fine," Ellen fibbed. "Just fine." She sat down on the edge of the chintz-covered trunk that doubled as wardrobe and telephone table to steady herself. No use hiding the news. "Jacob's just had his first play accepted."

"I know, I know."

"But how . . . ?" *How does she manage to pick up the least glitter of gossip? Like a professional magpie, a bird of ill-omen . . .*

"It was easy, darling. I ran across Jacob in the Rainbow Room tête-à-tête with Denise Kay. You know me. I couldn't resist finding out why the celebration. I didn't know Jacob went in for martinis, darling. Let alone redheads . . ."

A crawling prickle of misery, rather like gooseflesh, made Ellen go hot, then cold. In the light of Nancy's suggestive tone, even her worst dreads seemed naïve. "Oh, Jacob needs a change of scenery after all the work he's been doing." She tried to sound casual. "Most men take the weekend off, at least, but Jacob . . ."

Nancy's brittle laugh rang out. "Don't tell me! I'm the expert to end all experts when it comes to newly discovered playwrights. Are you going to have a party?"

"Party?" Then Ellen remembered the spectacular fatted calf the Regans had served up by way of commemorating their first really big check—friends, neighbors and strangers cramming the small, smoke-filled rooms, singing, drinking, dancing till night blued and the dawn sky showed pale as watered silk above the cockeyed chimney pots. If bottles with awe-inspiring labels and dozens of Fortnum and Mason chicken pies and imported cheeses and a soup plate of caviar were any measure of success, the Regans had cornered a lion's share. "No, no party, I think, Nancy. We'll be glad enough to have the gas and electric bills paid a bit in advance, and the baby's outgrowing her layette so fast . . ."

"Ellen!" Nancy moaned. "Where's your imagination?"

"I guess," Ellen confessed, "I just haven't got any."

"Excuse an old busybody, but you sound really blue, Ellen! Why don't you invite me round for tea? Then we can have one of our chats and you'll perk up in no time."

Ellen smiled wanly. Nancy was irrepressible, you had to say that for her. No one could accuse *her* of moping or wallowing in self-pity. "Consider yourself invited."

"Give me twenty minutes, darling."

"Now what you really should do, Ellen . . ." Stylish if a bit plump, in the dressy suit and fur toque, Nancy dropped her voice to a conspiratorial whisper and reached for her third cupcake. "Mmm," she murmured, "better than Lyons'. What you really should do," she repeated, "if you'll pardon me for being frank, is assert yourself." And she sat back with a triumphant expression.

"I don't quite see what you mean." Ellen bent over Jill, admiring the baby's clear gray eyes as she sipped her orange juice. It was getting on toward five, and still no word from Jacob. "What have I got to assert?"

"Your inner woman, of course!" Nancy exclaimed impatiently. "You need to take a good, long look at yourself in the mirror. The way I should have, before it was too late," she added grimly. "Men won't admit it, but they do want a woman to look *right*, really *fatale*. The right hat, the right hair color . . . Now's your chance, Ellen. Don't miss it!"

"I've never been able to afford a hairdresser," Ellen said lamely. *Jacob likes my hair long*, a small, secret voice protested. *He said so, when was it? Last week, last month . . .*

"Of course not," Nancy crooned. "You've been sacrificing all the expensive little feminine tricks for Jacob's career. But now he's arrived. You can go wild, darling. Simply wild."

Ellen entertained a brief vision of herself leaning seductively with priceless hunks of jewelry, green eye shadow heavy enough to astound

Cleopatra, one of the new pale lip colors, a coquettish feather cut complete with kiss curls . . . But she wasn't deceived—at least not for more than a few seconds. "I'm not the type."

"Oh, rubbish!" Nancy waved a ring-winking, vermilion-tipped hand that resembled, Ellen thought, a bright, predatory claw. "That's your trouble, Ellen. You've no self-confidence."

"You're wrong there, Nancy," Ellen returned with some spirit. "I've about two bobs' worth."

Nancy dumped a heaping spoon of sugar into her fresh cup of tea. "Shouldn't," she chided herself, and then rattled on without looking at Ellen, "I don't wonder if you're a tiny bit worried about Denise. She's a legend, one of those professional home wreckers. She specializes in family men."

Ellen felt her stomach lurch, as if she were on a boat in a gale. "Is she married?" she heard herself say. She didn't want to know. She wanted nothing more than to put her hands to her ears and flee into the comforting rose-patterned bedroom and find some outlet for the tears that were gathering to a hard lump in her throat.

"Married?" Nancy gave a dry little laugh. "She wears a ring, and that's covered a good deal. The current one—her third, I think—has a wife and three children. The wife won't hear of a divorce. Oh, Denise is a real career girl—she always manages to land a man with complications, so she never ends up drying dishes or wiping a baby's nose." Nancy's bright chatter slowed and began to run down, like a record, into an abyss of silence. "Pet!" she exclaimed, catching sight of Ellen's face. "You're as white as paper! I didn't mean to upset you—honestly, Ellen. I just figured you ought to know what you're up against. I mean, I was the last to know about Keith. In those days," and Nancy's wry smile didn't succeed in hiding the tremor in her voice, "I thought everybody had a heart of gold, everything was open and aboveboard."

"Oh, Nan!" Ellen laid an impulsive hand on her friend's arm. "We did have good times, didn't we!" But in her heart a new refrain sang itself over and over: *Jacob's not like Keith, Jacob's not like Keith . . .*

" 'The days of auld lang syne.' Huh!" With a delicate snort Nancy dismissed the past and began to draw on her admirably classic mauve gloves.

The moment the door closed on Nancy, Ellen started to behave in a curious and completely uncharacteristic fashion. Instead of putting on her apron and bustling about in the kitchen to prepare supper, she stowed Jill in her pen with a rusk and her favorite toys and disappeared into the bedroom to rummage through the bureau drawers with sporadic mutterings, rather like a female Sherlock Holmes on the scent of a crucial clue.

Why don't I do this every night? she was asking herself half an hour later as, flushed and freshly bathed, she slipped into the royal blue silk Japanese jacket she had been sent several Christmases ago by a footloose school friend circling the globe on a plump legacy, but never worn—an exquisite whispery, sapphire-sheened piece of finery that seemed to have no business whatsoever in her commonsensical world. Then she undid her coronet of braids and swept her hair up into a quite dashing impromptu topknot which she anchored precariously with a few pins. With a couple of tentative waltz steps she accustomed herself to her holiday pair of steep black heels and, as a final touch, doused herself thoroughly with the last drops of the French perfume. During this ritual, Ellen resolutely kept her eyes from lingering on the round moon face of the clock, which had already inched its short black hand past six. *Now all I have to do is wait . . .*

Breezing into the living room, she felt a sudden pang. *I've forgotton Jill!* The baby was sprawled sound asleep in the corner of her playpen, thumb in mouth. Gently Ellen picked up the warm little form and carried her into the bedroom.

They had a wonderful bathtime. Jill laughed and kicked until water flew all over the room, but Ellen hardly noticed, thinking how the baby's dark hair and serene gray eyes mirrored Jacob's own. Even when Jill knocked the cup of porridge out of her hand and onto her best black skirt she couldn't get really angry. She was spooning stewed plums into Jill's mouth when she heard the click of a key in the front door lock and froze. The day's fears and frustrations, momentarily brushed aside, swept back over her in a rush.

"Now that's what I like to see when I come home after a hard day!" Jacob leaned against the doorjamb, lit by a mysterious glow that didn't, somehow, seem to stem from martinis or redheads. "Wife and daughter waiting by the fireside to welcome the lord of the house . . ." Jill was, in fact, treating her father to a spectacular blue ear-to-ear smile, composed largely of stewed plums. Ellen giggled, and her desperate silent prayer of that morning appeared close to being granted when Jacob crossed the room in two strides and enveloped her, sticky plum dish and all, in a hearty bear hug.

"Mmm, darling, you smell good!" Ellen waited demurely for some mention of the French perfume. "A sort of marvelous homemade blend of Farex and cod liver oil. A new bedjacket too!" He held her tenderly at arm's length. "You look fresh from the tub with your hair up like that."

"Oooh!" Ellen shook herself free. "Men!" But her tone gave her away—Jacob obviously saw her as the wife and mother type, and she couldn't be better pleased.

"Seriously, love, I've a surprise."

"Isn't the play enough for one day?" Ellen asked dreamily, tilting her head to Jacob's shoulder and wondering why she didn't feel in the least like making a scene about his luncheon with Denise or his unexplained absence all the tedious, worrisome afternoon.

"I've been on the phone to the estate agent."

"Estate agent?"

"Remember that funny out-of-the-way little office we stopped at for a lark on our holiday in Cornwall, just before Jill came . . . ?"

"Ye-es." Ellen didn't dare let herself jump to conclusions.

"Well, he still has that place for sale . . . that cottage we rented overlooking the inlet. Want it?"

"*Want* it!" Ellen almost shouted.

"I sort of hoped you did, after the way you raved about the place last spring," Jacob said modestly. "Because I've arranged to make the down payment with the check Denise handed me at lunch."

For a second, the merest snag of foreboding caught at Ellen's heart. "Won't you have to stay around London for the play . . . ?"

Jacob laughed. "Not on your life! That Denise Kay is a career woman with a mind of her own—a regular diesel engine. Catch me crossing her path! Why, she's so high-powered she even fueled up on the martini she'd ordered for me when I told her I never touch the stuff on weekdays."

The phone, curiously muted, almost musical, interrupted him. Ellen bundled Jill into his arms for her goodnight lullaby and tucking-in and floated into the living room to answer.

"Ellen, darling." Nancy Regan's voice sounded giddy and thin as tinsel over a raucous background of jazz and laughter. "I've been racking my brain for what I could do to pep you up, and I've made you an appointment with my Roderigo for Saturday at eleven. It's amazing how an utterly new hairdo can raise your morale . . ."

"Sorry, Nan," Ellen said gently, "but I think you'd better cancel my appointment. I've news for you."

"News?"

"Braids are back in style this season, love—the latest thing for the country wife!"

The Fifteen-Dollar Eagle

Story, November 1959

There are other tattoo shops in Madigan Square, but none of them a patch on Carmey's place. He's a real poet with the needle and dye, an artist with a heart. Kids, dock bums, the out-of-town couples in for a beer put on the brakes in front of Carmey's, nose to the window, one and all. You got a dream, Carmey says, without saying a word, you got a rose on the heart, an eagle in the muscle, you got the sweet Jesus himself, so come in to me. Wear your heart on your skin in this life, I'm the man can give you a deal. Dogs, wolves, horses and lions for the animal lover. For the ladies, butterflies, birds of paradise, baby heads smiling or in tears, take your choice. Roses, all sorts, large, small, bud and full bloom, roses with name scrolls, roses with thorns, roses with Dresden-doll heads sticking up in dead center, pink petal, green leaf, set off smart by a lead-black line. Snakes and dragons for Frankenstein. Not to mention cowgirls, hula girls, mermaids and movie queens, ruby-nippled and bare as you please. If you've got a back to spare, there's Christ on the cross, a thief at either elbow and angels overhead to right and left holding up a scroll with "Mount Calvary" on it in Old

English script, close as yellow can get to gold.

Outside they point at the multicolored pictures plastered on Carmey's three walls, ceiling to floor. They mutter like a mob scene, you can hear them through the glass:

"Honey, take a looka those peacocks!"

"That's crazy, paying for tattoos. I only paid for one I got, a panther on my arm."

"You want a heart, I'll tell him where."

I see Carmey in action for the first time courtesy of my steady man, Ned Bean. Lounging against a wall of hearts and flowers, waiting for business, Carmey is passing the time of day with a Mr. Tomolillo, an extremely small person wearing a wool jacket that drapes his nonexistent shoulders without any attempt at fit or reformation. The jacket is patterned with brown squares the size of cigarette packs, each square boldly outlined in black. You could play tick-tack-toe on it. A brown fedora hugs his head just above the eyebrows like the cap on a mushroom. He has the thin, rapt, triangular face of a praying mantis. As Ned introduces me, Mr. Tomolillo snaps over from the waist in a bow neat as the little moustache hairlining his upper lip. I can't help admiring this bow because the shop is so crowded there's barely room for the four of us to stand up without bumping elbows and knees at the slightest move.

The whole place smells of gunpowder and some fumey antiseptic. Ranged along the back wall from left to right are: Carmey's worktable, electric needles hooked to a rack over a Lazy Susan of dye pots, Carmey's swivel chair facing the show window, a straight customer's chair facing Carmey's chair, a waste bucket, and an orange crate covered with scraps of paper and pencil stubs. At the front of the shop, next to the glass door, there is another straight chair, with the big placard of Mount Calvary propped on it, and a cardboard file drawer on a scuffed wooden table. Among the babies and daisies on the wall over Carmey's chair hang two faded sepia daguerreotypes of a boy from the waist up, one front view, one back. From the distance he seems to be wearing a long-sleeved, skintight black lace shirt. A closer look shows he is stark naked, covered only with a creeping ivy of tattoos.

In a jaundiced clipping from some long-ago rotogravure, these Oriental men and women are sitting cross-legged on tasseled cushions, back to the camera and embroidered with seven-headed dragons, mountain ranges, cherry trees and waterfalls. "These people have not a stitch of clothing on," the blurb points out. "They belong to a society in which tattoos are required for membership. Sometimes a full job costs as much as $300." Next to this, a photograph of a bald man's head with the tentacles of an octopus just rounding the top of the scalp from the rear.

"Those skins are valuable as many a painting, I imagine," says Mr. Tomolillo. "If you had them stretched on a board."

But the Tattooed Boy and those clubby Orientals have nothing on Carmey, who is himself a living advertisement of his art—a schooner in full sail over a rose-and-holly-leaf ocean on his right biceps, Gypsy Rose Lee flexing her muscled belly on the left, forearms jammed with hearts, stars and anchors, lucky numbers and name scrolls, indigo edges blurred so he reads like a comic strip left out in a Sunday rainstorm. A fan of the Wild West, Carmey is rumored to have a bronco reared from navel to collarbone, a thistle-stubborn cowboy stuck to its back. But that may be a mere fable inspired by his habit of wearing tooled leather cowboy boots, finely heeled, and a Bill Hickock belt studded with red stones to hold up his black chino slacks. Carmey's eyes are blue. A blue in no way inferior to the much-sung about skies of Texas.

"I been at it sixteen years now," Carmey says, leaning back against his picturebook wall, "and you might say I'm still learning. My first job was in Maine, during the war. They heard I was a tattooist and called me out to this station of Wacs . . ."

"To tat*too* them?" I ask.

"To tattoo their numbers on, nothing more or less."

"Weren't some of them *scared?*"

"Oh, sure, sure. But some of them came back. I got two Wacs in one day for a tattoo. Well, they hemmed. And they hawed. 'Look,' I tell them, 'you came in the other day and you knew which one you wanted, what's the trouble?' "

" 'Well, it's not what we want but where we want it,' one of them pipes up. 'Well, if that's all it is you can trust me,' I say. 'I'm like a doctor, see? I handle so many women it means nothing.' 'Well, I want three roses,' this one says: 'one on my stomach and one on each cheek of my butt. So the other one gets up courage, you know how it is, and asks for one rose . . ."

"Little ones or big ones?" Mr. Tomolillo won't let a detail slip.

"About like that up there." Carmey points to a card of roses on the wall, each bloom the size of a Brussels sprout. "The biggest going. So I did the roses and told them: 'Ten dollars off the price if you come back and show them to me when the scab's gone.'"

"Did they come?" Ned wants to know.

"You bet they did." Carmey blows a smoke ring that hangs wavering in the air a foot from his nose, the blue, vaporous outline of a cabbage rose.

"You wanta know," he says, "a crazy law? I could tattoo you anywhere," he looks me over with great care, "anywhere at all. Your back. Your rear." His eyelids droop, you'd think he was praying. "Your breasts. Anywhere at all but your face, hands and feet."

Mr. Tomolillo asks: "Is that a *Fed*eral law?"

Carmey nods. "A Federal law. I got a blind." He juts a thumb at the dusty-slatted venetian blind drawn up in the display window. "I let that blind down, and I can do privately any part of the body. Except face, hands and feet."

"I bet it's because they *show*," I say.

"Sure. Take in the Army, at drill. The guys wouldn't look right. Their faces and hands would stand out, they couldn't cover up."

"However that may be," Mr. Tomolillo says, "I think it is a shocking law, a totalitarian law. There should be a freedom about personal adornment in any democracy. I mean, if a lady *wants* a rose on the back of her hand, I should think . . ."

"She should *have* it," Carmey finishes with heat. "People should have what they want, regardless. Why, I had a little lady in here the other day." Carmey levels the air with the flat of his hand not five feet from the floor. "So high. Wanted Calvary, the whole works, on her back, and I gave it to her. Eighteen hours it took."

I eye the thieves and angels on the poster of Mount Calvary with some doubt. "Didn't you have to shrink it down a bit?"

"Nope."

"Or leave off an angel?" Ned wonders. "Or a bit of the foreground?"

"Not a bit of it. A thirty-five-dollar job in full color, thieves, angels, Old English—the works. She went out of the shop proud as punch. It's not every little lady's got all Calvary in full color on her back. Oh, I copy photos people bring in, I copy movie stars. Anything they want, I do it. I've got some designs I wouldn't put up on the wall on account of offending some of the clients. I'll show you." Carmey opens the cardboard file drawer on the table at the front of the shop. "The wife's got to clean this up," he says. "It's a terrible mess."

"Does your wife help you?" I ask with interest.

"Oh, Laura, she's in the shop most of the day." For some reason Carmey sounds all at once solemn as a monk on Sunday. I wonder, does he use her for a come-on: Laura, the Tattooed Lady, a living masterpiece, sixteen years in the making. Not a white patch on her, ladies and gentlemen—look all you want to. "You should drop by and keep her company, she likes talk." He is rummaging around in the drawer, not coming up with anything, when he stops in his tracks and stiffens like a pointer.

This big guy is standing in the doorway.

"What can I do for you?" Carmey steps forward, the maestro he is.

"I want that eagle you showed me."

Ned and Mr. Tomolillo and I flatten ourselves against the side walls to let the guy into the middle of the room. He'll be a sailor out of uniform in his peajacket and plaid wool shirt. His diamond-shaped head, width all between the ears, tapers up to a narrow plateau of cropped black hair.

"The nine-dollar or the fifteen?"

"The fifteen."

Mr. Tomolillo sighs in gentle admiration.

The sailor sits down in the chair facing Carmey's swivel, shrugs out of his peajacket, unbuttons his right shirt cuff and begins slowly to roll up the sleeve.

"You come right in here," Carmey says to me in a low, promising voice, "where you can get a good look. You've never seen a tattooing before." I squinch up and settle on the crate of papers in the corner at the left of Carmey's chair, careful as a hen on eggs.

Carmey flicks through the cardboard file again and this time digs out a square piece of plastic. "Is this the one?"

The sailor looks at the eagle pricked out on the plastic. Then he says: "That's right," and hands it back to Carmey.

"Mmmm," Mr. Tomolillo murmurs in honor of the sailor's taste.

Ned says: "That's a fine eagle."

The sailor straightens with a certain pride. Carmey is dancing round him now, laying a dark-stained burlap cloth across his lap, arranging a sponge, a razor, various jars with smudged-out labels and a bowl of antiseptic on his worktable—finicky as a priest whetting his machete for the fatted calf. Everything has to be just so. Finally he sits down.

The sailor holds out his right arm and Ned and Mr. Tomolillo close in behind his chair, Ned leaning over the sailor's right shoulder and Mr. Tomolillo over his left. At Carmey's elbow I have the best view of all.

With a close, quick swipe of the razor, Carmey clears the sailor's forearm of its black springing hair, wiping the hair off the blade's edge and onto the floor with his thumb. Then he anoints the area of bared flesh with vaseline from a small jar on top of his table. "You ever been tattooed before?"

"Yeah." The sailor is no gossip. "Once." Already his eyes are locked in a vision of something on the far side of Carmey's head, through the walls and away in the thin air beyond the four of us in the room.

Carmey is sprinkling a black powder on the face of the plastic square and rubbing the powder into the pricked holes. The outline of the eagle darkens. With one flip, Carmey presses the plastic square powder-side against the sailor's greased arm. When he peels the plastic off, easy as skin off an onion, the outline of an eagle, wings spread, claws hooked for action, frowns up from the sailor's arm.

"Ah!" Mr. Tomolillo rocks back on his cork heels and casts a meaning look at Ned. Ned raises his eyebrows in approval. The sailor allows himself a little quirk of the lip. On him it is as good as a smile.

"Now," Carmey takes down one of the electric needles, pitching it rabbit-out-of-the-hat, "I am going to show you how we make a nine-dollar eagle a fifteen-dollar eagle."

He presses a button on the needle. Nothing happens.

"Well," he sighs, "it's not working."

Mr. Tomolillo groans. "Not again?"

Then something strikes Carmey and he laughs and flips a switch on the wall behind him. This time when he presses the needle it buzzes and sparks blue. "No connection, that's what it was."

"Thank heaven," says Mr. Tomolillo.

Carmey fills the needle from a pot of black dye on the Lazy Susan. "This same eagle," Carmey lowers the needle to the eagle's right wing-tip, "for nine dollars is only black and red. For fifteen dollars you're going to see a blend of four colors." The needle steers along the lines laid by the powder. "Black, green, brown and red. We're out of blue at the moment or it'd be five colors." The needle skips and backtalks like a pneumatic drill but Carmey's hand is steady as a surgeon's. "How I *love* eagles!"

"I believe you *live* on Uncle Sam's eagles," says Mr. Tomolillo.

Black ink seeps over the curve of the sailor's arm and into the stiff, stained butcher's-apron canvas covering his lap, but the needle travels on, scalloping the wing feathers from tip to root. Bright beads of red are rising through the ink, heart's-blood bubbles smearing out into the black stream.

"The guys complain," Carmey singsongs. "Week after week I get the same complaining: What have you got new? We don't want the same type eagle, red and black. So I figure out this blend. You wait. A solid color eagle."

The eagle is losing itself in a spreading thundercloud of black ink. Carmey stops, sloshes his needle in the bowl of antiseptic, and a geyser of white blooms up to the surface from the bowl's bottom. Then Carmey dips a big, round cinnamon-colored sponge in the bowl and wipes away the ink from the sailor's arm. The eagle emerges from its hood of bloodied ink, a raised outline on the raw skin.

"Now you're gonna see something." Carmey twirls the Lazy Susan till the pot of green is under his thumb and picks another needle from the rack.

The sailor is gone from behind his eyes now, off somewhere in Tibet, Uganda or Barbados, oceans and continents away from the blood drops jumping in the wake of the wide green swaths Carmey is drawing in the shadow of the eagle's wings.

About this time I notice an odd sensation. A powerful sweet perfume is rising from the sailor's arm. My eyes swerve from the mingling red and green and I find myself staring intently into the waste bucket by my left side. As I watch the calm rubble of colored candy wrappers, cigarette butts and old wads of muddily stained Kleenex, Carmey tosses a tissue soaked with fresh red onto the heap. Behind the silhouetted heads of Ned and Mr. Tomolillo the panthers, roses and red-nippled ladies wink and jitter. If I fall forward or to the right, I will jog Carmey's elbow and make him stab the sailor and ruin a perfectly good fifteen-dollar eagle, not to mention disgracing my sex. The only alternative is a dive into the bucket of bloody papers.

"I'm doing the brown now," Carmey sings out a mile away, and my eyes rivet again on the sailor's blood-sheened arm. "When the eagle heals, the colors will blend right into each other, like on a painting."

Ned's face is a scribble of black India ink on a seven-color crazy-quilt.

"I'm going . . . ." I make my lips move, but no sound comes out.

Ned starts toward me but before he gets there the room switches off like a light.

The next thing is, I am looking into Carmey's shop from a cloud with the X-ray eyes of an angel and hearing the tiny sound of a bee spitting blue fire.

"The blood get her?" It is Carmey's voice, small and far.

"She looks all white," says Mr. Tomolillo. "And her eyes are funny."

Carmey passes something to Mr. Tomolillo. "Have her sniff that." Mr. Tomolillo hands something to Ned. "But not too much."

Ned holds something to my nose.

I sniff, and I am sitting in the chair at the front of the shop with Mount Calvary as a backrest. I sniff again. Nobody looks angry, so I have not bumped Carmey's needle. Ned is screwing the cap on a little flask of yellow liquid. Yardley's smelling salts.

"Ready to go back?" Mr. Tomolillo points kindly to the deserted orange crate.

"Almost." I have a strong instinct to stall for time. I whisper in Mr. Tomolillo's ear, which is very near to me, he is so short, "Do *you* have any tattoos?"

Under the mushroom brim of his fedora Mr. Tomolillo's eyes roll heavenward. "My gracious, no! I'm only here to see about the springs. The springs in Mr. Carmichael's machine have a way of breaking in the middle of a customer."

"How annoying."

"That's what I'm here for. We're testing out a new spring now, a much heavier spring. You know how distressing it is when you're in the dentist's chair and your mouth is full of what-not . . ."

"Balls of cotton and little metal siphons . . . ?"

"Precisely. And in the middle of this the dentist turns away," Mr. Tomolillo half-turns his back in illustration and makes an evil, secretive face, "and buzzes about in the corner for ten minutes with the machinery, you don't know what." Mr. Tomolillo's face smooths out like linen under a steam iron. "That's what I'm here to see about, a stronger spring. A spring that won't let the customer down."

By this time I am ready to go back to my seat of honor on the orange crate. Carmey has just finished with the brown and in my absence the inks have indeed blended into one another. Against the shaven skin, the lacerated eagle is swollen in tri-colored fury, claws curved sharp as butcher's hooks.

"I think we could redden the eye a little?"

The sailor nods, and Carmey opens the lid on a pot of dye the color of tomato ketchup. As soon as he stops working with the needle, the sailor's skin sends up its blood beads, not just from the bird's black outline now, but from the whole rasped, rainbowed body.

"Red," Carmey says, "really picks things up."

"Do you save the blood?" Mr. Tomolillo asks suddenly.

"I should think," says Ned, "you might well have some arrangement with the Red Cross."

"With a blood bank!" The smelling salts have blown my head clear as a blue day on Monadnock. "Just put a little basin on the floor to catch the drippings."

Carmey is picking out a red eye on the eagle. "We vampires don't share our blood." The eagle's eye reddens but there is now no telling blood from ink. "You never heard of a vampire do that, did you?"

"Nooo . . ." Mr. Tomolillo admits.

Carmey floods the flesh behind the eagle with red and the finished eagle poises on a red sky, born and baptized in the blood of its owner.

The sailor drifts back from parts unknown.

"Nice?" With his sponge Carmey clears the eagle of the blood filming its colors the way a sidewalk artist might blow the pastel dust from a drawing of the White House, Liz Taylor or Lassie-Come-Home.

"I always say," the sailor remarks to nobody in particular, "when you get a tattoo, get a good one. Nothing but the best." He looks down at the eagle, which has begun in spite of Carmey's swabbing to bleed again. There is a little pause. Carmey is waiting for something and it isn't money. "How much to write Japan under that?"

Carmey breaks into a pleased smile. "One dollar."

"Write Japan, then."

Carmey marks out the letters on the sailor's arm, an extra flourish to the J's hook, the loop of the P, and the final N, a love letter to the eagle-conquered Orient. He fills the needle and starts on the J.

"I under*stand,*" Mr. Tomolillo observes in his clear, lecturer's voice, "Japan is a center of tattooing."

"Not when *I* was there," the sailor says. "It's banned."

"Banned!" says Ned. "What for?"

"Oh, they think it's *bar*barous nowadays." Carmey doesn't lift his eyes from the second A, the needle responding like a broken-in bronc under his masterly thumb. "There are operators, of course. Sub rosa.

There always are." He puts the final curl on the N and sponges off the wellings of blood which seem bent on obscuring his artful lines. "That what you wanted?"

"That's it."

Carmey folds a wad of Kleenex into a rough bandage and lays it over the eagle and Japan. Spry as a shopgirl wrapping a gift package he tapes the tissue into place.

The sailor gets up and hitches into his peajacket. Several schoolboys, lanky, with pale, pimply faces, are crowding the doorway, watching. Without a word the sailor takes out his wallet and peels sixteen dollar bills off a green roll. Carmey transfers the cash to his wallet. The schoolboys fall back to let the sailor pass into the street.

"I hope you didn't mind my getting dizzy."

Carmey grins. "Why do you think I've got those salts so close at hand? I have big guys passing out cold. They get egged in here by their buddies and don't know how to get out of it. I got people getting sick to their ears in that bucket."

"She's never got like that before," Ned says. "She's seen all sorts of blood. Babies born. Bull fights. Things like that."

"You was all worked up." Carmey offers me a cigarette, which I accept, takes one himself, and Ned takes one, and Mr. Tomolillo says no-thank-you. "You was all tensed, that's what did it."

"How much is a heart?"

The voice comes from a kid in a black leather jacket in the front of the shop. His buddies nudge each other and let out harsh, puppy-barks of laughter. The boy grins and flushes all at once under his purple stipple of acne. "A heart with a scroll under it and a name on the scroll."

Carmey leans back in his swivel chair and digs his thumbs into his belt. The cigarette wobbles on his bottom lip. "Four dollars," he says without batting an eye.

"Four dollars?" The boy's voice swerves up and cracks in shrill disbelief. The three of them in the doorway mutter among themselves and shuffle back and forth.

"Nothing here in the heart line under three dollars." Carmey doesn't kow-tow to the tight-fisted. You want a rose, you want a heart in this life, you pay for it. Through the nose.

The boy wavers in front of the placards of hearts on the wall, pink, lush hearts, hearts with arrows through them, hearts in the center of buttercup wreaths. "How much," he asks in a small, craven voice, "for just a name?"

"One dollar." Carmey's tone is strictly business.

The boy holds out his left hand. "I want Ruth." He draws an imaginary line across his left wrist. "Right here . . . so I can cover it up with a watch if I want to."

His two friends guffaw from the doorway.

Carmey points to the straight chair and lays his half-smoked cigarette on the Lazy Susan between two dye pots. The boy sits down, schoolbooks balanced on his lap.

"What happens," Mr. Tomolillo asks of the world in general, "if you choose to change a name? Do you just cross it off and write the next above it?"

"You could," Ned suggests, "wear a watch over the old name so only the new name showed."

"And then another watch," I say, "over that, when there's a third name."

"Until your arm," Mr. Tomolillo nods, "is up to the shoulder with watches."

Carmey is shaving the thin scraggly growth of hairs from the boy's wrist. "You're taking a lot of ragging from somebody."

The boy stares at his wrist with a self-conscious and unsteady smile, a smile that is maybe only a public substitute for tears. With his right hand he clutches his schoolbooks to keep them from sliding off his knee.

Carmey finishes marking R-U-T-H on the boy's wrist and holds the needle poised. "She'll bawl you out when she sees this." But the boy nods him to go ahead.

"Why?" Ned asks. "Why should she bawl him out?"

" 'Gone and got yourself tattooed!' " Carmey mimics a mincing disgust. " 'And with just a name! Is *that* all you think of me?'—She'll be wanting roses, birds, butterflies . . ." The needle sticks for a second and the boy flinches like a colt. "And if you *do* get all that stuff to please her—roses . . ."

"Birds and butterflies," Mr. Tomolillo puts in.

". . . she'll say, sure as rain at a ball game: 'What'd you want to go and spend all that *money* for?' " Carmey whizzes the needle clean in the bowl of antiseptic. "You can't beat a woman." A few meager blood drops stand up along the four letters—letters so black and plain you

can hardly tell it's a tattoo and not just inked in with a pen. Carmey
tapes a narrow bandage of Kleenex over the name. The whole operation lasts less than ten minutes.

The boy fishes a crumpled dollar bill from his back pocket. His
friends cuff him fondly on the shoulder and the three of them crowd
out the door, all at the same time, nudging, pushing, tripping over
their feet. Several faces, limpet-pale against the window, melt away as
Carmey's eye lingers on them.

"No wonder he doesn't want a heart, that kid, he wouldn't know
what to do with it. He'll be back next week asking for a Betty or a
Dolly or some such, you wait." He sighs, and goes to the cardboard file
and pulls out a stack of those photographs he wouldn't put on the wall
and passes them around. "One picture I would like to get," Carmey
leans back in the swivel chair and props his cowboy boots on a little
carton, "the butterfly. I got pictures of the rabbit hunt. I got pictures
of ladies with snakes winding up their legs and into them, but I could
make a lot of sweet dough if I got a picture of the butterfly on a
woman."

"Some queer kind of butterfly nobody wants?" Ned peers in the
general direction of my stomach as at some high-grade salable parch-
ment.

"It's not what, it's where. One wing on the front of each thigh. You
know how butterflies on a flower make their wings flutter, ever so
little? Well, any move a woman makes, these wings look to be going
in and out, in and out. I'd like a photograph of that so much I'd
practically do a butterfly for free."

I toy, for a second, with the thought of a New Guinea Golden, wings
extending from hipbone to kneecap, ten times life size, but drop it fast.
A fine thing if I got tired of my own skin sooner than last year's sack.

"Plenty of women *ask* for butterflies in that particular spot," Carmey goes on, "but you know what, not one of them will let a photograph be taken after the job's done. Not even from the waist down.
Don't imagine I haven't asked. You'd think everybody over the whole
United States would recognize them from the way they carry on when
it's even mentioned."

"Couldn't," Mr. Tomolillo ventures shyly, "the wife oblige? Make
it a little family affair?"

Carmey's face skews up in a pained way. "Naw." He shakes his head,
his voice weighted with an old wonder and regret. "Naw, Laura won't

hear of the needle. I used to think the idea of it'd grow on her after a bit, but nothing doing. She makes me feel, sometimes, what do I see in it all. Laura's white as the day she was born. Why, she *hates* tattoos."

Up to this moment I have been projecting, fatuously, intimate visits with Laura at Carmey's place. I have been imaging a lithe, supple Laura, a butterfly poised for flight on each breast, roses blooming on her buttocks, a gold-guarding dragon on her back and Sinbad the Sailor in six colors on her belly, a woman with Experience written all over her, a woman to learn from in this life. I should have known better.

The four of us are slumped there in a smog of cigarette smoke, not saying a word, when a round, muscular woman comes into the shop, followed closely by a greasy-haired man with a dark, challenging expression. The woman is wrapped to the chin in a woolly electric-blue coat; a fuchsia kerchief covers all but the pompadour of her glinting blond hair. She sits down in the chair in front of the window regardless of Mount Calvary and proceeds to stare fixedly at Carmey. The man stations himself next to her and keeps a severe eye on Carmey too, as if expecting him to bolt without warning.

There is a moment of potent silence.

"Why," Carmey says pleasantly, but with small heart, "here's the wife now."

I take a second look at the woman and rise from my comfortable seat on the crate at Carmey's elbow. Judging from his watchdog stance, I gather the strange man is either Laura's brother or her bodyguard or a low-class private detective in her employ. Mr. Tomolillo and Ned are moving with one accord toward the door.

"We must be running along," I murmur, since nobody else seems inclined to speak.

"Say hello to the people, Laura," Carmey begs, back to the wall. I can't help but feel sorry for him, even a little ashamed. The starch is gone out of Carmey now, and the gay talk.

Laura doesn't say a word. She is waiting with the large calm of a cow for the three of us to clear out. I imagine her body, death-lily-white and totally bare—the body of a woman immune as a nun to the eagle's anger, the desire of the rose. From Carmey's wall the world's menagerie howls and ogles at her alone.

The Fifty-ninth Bear

Story, September 1959

By the time they arrived, following the map of the Grand Loop in the brochure, a dense mist shrouded the rainbow pools; the parking lot and the boardwalks were empty. Except for the sun, already low above the violet hills, and the sun's image, red as a dwarf tomato lodged in the one small space of water visible, there was nothing to see. Still, enacting as they were a ritual of penance and forgiveness, they crossed the bridge over the scalding river. On either side, ahead and behind, columns of steam mushroomed above the surface of the pools. Veil after veil of whiteness raveled across the boardwalk, erasing at random patches of the sky and the far hills. They moved slowly, enclosed by a medium at once intimate and insufferable, the sulfurous air warm and humid on their faces, on their hands and bare arms.

Norton dallied then, letting his wife drift on ahead. Her slender, vulnerable shape softened, wavered, as the mists thickened between them. She withdrew into a blizzard, into a fall of white water; she was nowhere. What hadn't they seen? The children squatting at the rim of the paintpots, boiling their breakfast eggs in rusty strainers; copper

pennies winking up from cornucopias of sapphire water; the thunderous gushers pluming, now here, now there, across a barren ocher-and-
oyster-colored moonscape. She had insisted, not without her native
delicacy, on the immense, mustard-yellow canyon where, halfway
down to the river, hawks and the shadows of hawks looped and hung
like black beads of fine wire. She had insisted on the Dragon's Mouth,
that hoarse, booming spate of mud-clogged water; and the Devil's
Cauldron. He had waited for her habitual squeamishness to turn her
away from the black, porridgy mass that popped and seethed a few
yards from under her nose, but she bent over the pit, devout as a
priestess in the midst of those vile exhalations. And it was Norton,
after all, bare-headed in the full noon sun, squinting against the salt-
white glare and breathing in the fumes of rotten eggs, who defaulted,
overcome by headache. He felt the ground frail as a bird's skull under
his feet, a mere shell of sanity and decorum between him and the dark
entrails of the earth where the sluggish muds and scalding waters had
their source.

To top it off, someone had stolen their desert water bag, simply
pinched it from the front fender of the car while they were being
elbowed along by the midday crowds on the boardwalk. Anybody
might have done it: that man with a camera, that child, that Negress
in the pink sprigged dress. Guilt diffused through the crowd like a
drop of vermilion dye in a tumbler of clear water, staining them all.
They were all thieves; their faces were blank, brutish or sly. Disgust
curdled in Norton's throat. Once in the car, he slumped down, closed
his eyes, and let Sadie drive. A cooler air fanned his temples. His hands
and feet seemed to be lifting, elongating, pale and puffed with a
dreamy yeast. Like a vast, luminous starfish he drifted, awash with
sleep, his consciousness fisted somewhere there, dark and secret as a
nut.

"Fifty-six," Sadie said.

Norton opened his eyes; they stung and watered as though someone
had scoured them with sand while he drowsed. It was a fine bear,
black-furred and compact, purposefully skirting the edge of the forest.
To left and right, the tall, mottled boles of pines speared skyward,
spreading out, far overhead, their dark thatch of needles. Although the
sun stood high, only a few splinters of light pierced the cool, blue-black
mass of the trees. The bear-counting started as a game on their first day
in the park, and continued still, five days later, long after they stopped

listing license plates from different states and noticing when the mile-
age showed four, or five, or six identical figures in a row. Perhaps it
was the bet that kept it going.

Sadie bet ten dollars on seeing fifty-nine bears by the end of their
stay. Norton had set his figure carelessly at seventy-one. In secret, he
hoped Sadie would win. She took games seriously, like a child. Losing
wounded her, she was so trusting; and above all, she trusted her luck.
Fifty-nine was Sadie's symbol of plenitude. For Sadie there were never
"hundreds of mosquitoes," or "millions," or even "a great many," but
always fifty-nine. Fifty-nine bears, she predicted breezily, without a
second thought. Now that they were so close to that total—having
numbered grandfather bears, mother bears and cubs, honey-colored
bears and black bears, brown bears and cinnamon bears, bears up to
their middles in trash cans, bears begging at the roadside, bears swimming the river, bears nosing around the tents and trailers at suppertime—they might well stick at fifty-nine bears. They were leaving the
park the next day.

Away from the boardwalks, the spiels of rangers, the popular mar-
vels, Norton revived a little. His headache, withdrawn to the far edge
of awareness, circled and stalled there like a thwarted bird. As a boy,
Norton had developed, quite by himself, a method of intense prayer
—not to any image of God, but to what he liked to think of as the
genius of a place, the fostering spirit of an ash grove, or a shore line.
What he prayed for was, in one guise or another, a private miracle: he
contrived to be favored, by the sight of a doe, say, or the find of a lump
of water-polished quartz. Whether his will merely coincided with
circumstance, or really did force tribute, he could not be sure. Either
way, he had a certain power. Now, lulled by the putter of the car, and
feigning sleep, Norton began to will toward him all the animals of the
forest—the fog-colored, delicately striated antelope, the lumbering,
tousled buffalo, the red foxes, the bears. In his mind's eye he saw them
pause, startled, as by some alien presence, in their deep thickets and
noonday retreats. He saw them, one by one, turn and converge toward
the center where he sat, fiercely, indefatigably willing the movement
of each hoof and paw.

"Elk!" Sadie exclaimed, like a voice out of the depths of his head. The
car swerved to a halt at the side of the road. Norton came to with a
start. Other cars were pulling up beside them and behind them. Tim-
orous as Sadie was, she had no fear of animals. She had a way with

them. Norton had come upon her once, feeding a wild stag blueberries out of her hand, a stag whose hooves could, in one blow, have dashed her to the ground. The danger simply never occurred to her.

Now she hurried after the men in shirt-sleeves, the women in cotton print dresses, the children of all ages, who were crowding to the verge of the road as to the scene of an astounding accident. The shoulder dropped steeply to a clearing in a thick growth of pines. Everybody carried a camera. Twirling dials, waving light meters, calling to relatives and friends above for fresh rolls of film, they plunged over the slope in a wave, slipping, lapsing, half-falling, in an avalanche of rust-colored pine needles and loose turf. Great-eyed, kingly under the burden of their spreading, dark-scalloped antlers, the elk knelt in the damp green bottom of the little valley. As the people came charging and crying toward them, they rose with a slow, sleepy amazement and moved off, unhurried and detached, into the pathless wood beyond the clearing. Norton stood on the top of the slope with a quiet, insular dignity. He ignored the people about him, disgruntled now, and barging about noisily in the underbrush. In his mind he was forming an apology to the elk. He had meant well.

"I didn't even have time for a shot," Sadie was saying at his elbow. "It was pitch-dark down there anyway, I guess." Her fingers closed on the bare flesh of his upper arm, soft-tipped as limpets. "Let's go see that pool. The one that comes to a boil every fifteen minutes."

"You go," Norton said. "I have a headache, a touch of sunstroke, I think. I'll sit and wait for you in the car."

Sadie did not answer, but she ground the car into gear with an unmistakable wantonness, and Norton knew he had disappointed her.

A short while later, with a sense of approaching storm, Norton watched Sadie stalk away from the car in the peaked straw hat with the red ribbon bow under the chin, her underlip set, pink and glistening, in a grieved pout. Then she passed, with the line of other tourists, over the glaring white horizon.

Often, in daydreams, Norton saw himself in the role of a widower: a hollow-cheeked, Hamletesque figure in somber suits, given to standing, abstracted, ravaged by casual winds, on lonely promontories and at the rail of ships, Sadie's slender, elegant white body embalmed, in a kind of bas-relief, on the central tablet of his mind. It never occurred to Norton that his wife might outlive him. Her sensuousness, her simple pagan enthusiasms, her inability to argue in terms of anything but her immediate emotions—this was too flimsy, too gossamery a stuff to survive out from under the wings of his guardianship.

As he had guessed, Sadie's jaunt on her own was anything but satisfactory. The pool boiled up, right enough, a perfectly lovely shade of blue, but a freakish shift in wind flung the hot steam in her face and nearly scalded her to death. And somebody, some boy or group of boys, had spoken to her on the boardwalk and spoiled the whole thing. A woman could never be alone in peace; a solitary woman was a walking invitation to all sorts of impudence.

All this, Norton knew, was a bid for his company. But since the incident of the water bag, a revulsion for the crowds of tourists had been simmering at the base of his skull. When he thought of going out into the mobs again, his fingers twitched. He saw himself, from a great distance, from Olympus, pushing a child into a steaming pool, punching a fat man in the belly. His headache stabbed back out of the blue like a vulture's beak.

"Why don't we leave the rest till tomorrow," he said. "Then I'd feel up to walking round with you."

"Today's our last *day.*"

Norton couldn't think of an answer to that.

It was only when they passed the fifty-seventh bear that he realized how upset Sadie was. The bear lay stretched into the road ahead of them, a ponderous brown Sphinx occupying a pool of sunlight. Sadie could not have missed seeing him: she had to pull out into the left lane to get round, but she set her lips and said nothing, accelerated, and shot them past a bend in the road. She was driving recklessly now. When they came to the junction near the great rainbow pools, she drove by so fast that a group of people about to cross the road jumped back in alarm, and the ranger with them yelled out angrily, "Hey, slow down there!" A few hundred yards beyond the junction Sadie began to cry. Her face puckered up and her nose reddened; tears streamed into the corners of her mouth and over her chin.

"Pull up," Norton ordered at last, taking the reins in hand. The car bumped off onto the shoulder of the road, bucked once or twice, and stalled. Sadie collapsed like a rag doll over the steering wheel.

"I didn't ask anything else," she sobbed vaguely. "All I asked was the pools and the springs."

"Look," Norton said, "I know what's the matter with us. It's about two o'clock, and we've been driving around six hours without a bite."

Sadie's sobs quieted. She let him untie her straw hat and stroke her hair.

"We'll go along to Mammoth Junction," Norton went on, as if he were telling a soothing bedtime story, "and we'll have hot soup and sandwiches, and see if there's any mail, and we'll climb all the hot springs and stop at all the pools going back. How's that?"

Sadie nodded. He felt her hesitate for a second. Then she blurted, "Did you see the *bear?*"

"Of course I saw the bear," Norton said, hiding a smile. "How many is that, now?"

"Fifty-seven."

With the waning of the sun's force, the pleasant, pliable shape of Sadie's waist in the crook of his arm, Norton felt a new benevolence toward humanity bloom in him. The irritable flame at the base of his skull cooled. He started the car with a firm, complacent mastery.

Now Sadie strolled, well fed and at peace, a few yards ahead of him, invisible, swathed in a mist, but surely his as a lamb on a leash. Her innocence, her trustfulness, endowed him with the nimbus of a protecting god. He fathomed her, enclosed her. He did not see, or did not care to see, how her submissiveness moved and drew him, nor how now, through the steaming, suffocating baths of mist, she led him, and he followed, though the rainbows under the clear water were lost.

By the time they completed their circuit of the boardwalk, the sun had gone under the hills and the tall pines walled the deserted road with shadow. As he drove, a touch of uneasiness made Norton glance at the gas gauge. The white pointer registered empty. Sadie must have seen it, too, for in the obscure, fading light she was watching him.

"Do you think we'll make it?" she asked, with a curious vibrancy.

"Of course," Norton said, although he was not at all sure. There were no gas stations until they got to the lake, and that stretch would take over an hour. The tank had a reserve, of course, but he had never tested it, never let it run below a quarter full. The upset with Sadie must have taken his mind off the gauge. They could so easily have filled up at Mammoth Junction. He switched on the high beams, but even then the little cave of light moving ahead of them seemed no match for the dark battalions of surrounding pines. He thought how pleasant it would be, for a change, to see the beams of another car close behind him, reflected in the rear-view mirror. But the mirror brimmed with darkness. For one craven, irrational moment, Norton felt the full weight of the dark: it bore down on top of his skull, pressed in upon him from all sides, brutally, concentratedly, as if intent to crush the frail, bone-plated shell that set him apart.

Working to moisten his lips, which had gone quite dry, Norton started to sing against the dark, something he had not done since childhood.

> You wanderin' boys of Liverpool
> I'll have you to beware
> When you go a-huntin'
> With your dog, your gun, your snare . . .

The plaintive cadences of the song deepened the loneliness of the night around them.

> One night as I lay on my bunk
> A dreamin' all alone . . .

Suddenly, like a candle in a draft, Norton's memory flickered. The words of the song blacked out. But Sadie took it up:

> I dreamt I was in Liverpool
> Way back in Marylebone . . .

They finished in unison:

> With my true love beside me
> And a jug of ale in hand
> And I woke quite broken-hearted
> Lying off Van Diemen's land.

Forgetting the words disturbed Norton: he had known them by heart, surely as his name. His brain felt to be going soft.

In half an hour of driving they passed no landmark they recognized, and the pointer of the gas gauge was dipping well below empty. Norton found himself listening to the tenuous whirring of the motor as to the breathing of a dear, moribund relative, his ears cocked for the break in continuity, the faltering, the silence.

"Even if we make this," Sadie said once, with a taut little laugh, "there will be two more bad things. There'll be a trailer parked in our car space and a bear waiting at the tent."

At last the lake loomed before them, a radiant, silvery expanse beyond the dark cone-shapes of the pines, reflecting the stars and the ruddy, newly risen moon. A flash of white crossed the headlights as a stag galloped off into the brush. The faint, dry reverberation of the stag's hooves consoled them, and the sight of the open water. Across the lake, a tiny crownlet of lights marked the shops of the camp center. Twenty minutes later they were driving into the lit gas station, laughing like giddy adolescents. The engine died five yards from the pump.

Norton hadn't seen Sadie so gay since the start of their trip. Sleeping out, even in state parks, among the other tents and trailers, unnerved her. One evening when he had walked off along the lake shore for a few moments, leaving her to finish up the supper dishes, she had become hysterical—run down to the shore with her dishtowel, waving and calling, the blue shadows thickening around her like water, until he heard her and turned back. But now the safely-passed scare of darkness, the empty tank and the unpeopled road was affecting her like brandy. Her exhilaration bewildered him; he shouldered the burden of her old cautions, her rabbitish fears. As they drove into the campground and around D-loop to their site, Norton's heart caught. Their tent was gone. Then, flushing at his own foolishness, he saw that the tent was merely hidden behind the long, balloon shape of an unfamiliar aluminum trailer which had moved in on them.

He swung the car into the parking space behind the trailer. The headlights fixed on a dark, mounded shape a few yards from their tent. Sadie gave a low, exultant laugh. "Fifty-eight!"

Distracted by the bright lights, or the noise of the engine, the bear backed away from the garbage can. Then, at a cumbersome lope, it vanished into the maze of darkened tents and trailers.

Usually Sadie did not like to cook supper after dark, because the food smells attracted animals. Tonight, though, she went to the camp ice chest and took out the pink fillets of lake trout they caught the day before. She fried them, with some cold boiled potatoes, and steamed a few ears of corn. She even went through the ritual of mixing Ovaltine by the yellow beam of their flashlight and cheerfully heated water for the dishes.

To make up for the loss of the water bag and his carelessness about the gas tank, Norton was especially scrupulous about cleaning up. He wrapped the remains of the fried fish in wax paper and stored it in the back seat of the car, along with a bag of cookies, some fig newtons and the ice chest. He checked the car windows and locked the doors. The trunk of the car was packed with enough canned and dry goods to last

them two months; he made sure that was locked. Then he took the
bucket of soapy dishwater and scrubbed down the wooden table and
the two benches. Bears only bothered messy campers, the rangers said
—people who littered food about or kept food in their tents. Every
night, of course, the bears traveled throughout the camp, from garbage
can to garbage can, foraging. You couldn't stop that. The cans had
metal lids and were set deep in the ground, but the bears were sly
enough to flip up the tops and scoop out the debris, rummaging
through wax paper and cardboard cartons for stale breadcrusts, bits of
hamburgers and hotdogs, jars with honey or jam still glued to the sides,
all the prodigal leavings of campers without proper iceboxes or storage
bins. In spite of the strict rules, people fed the bears, too—lured them
with sugar and crackers to pose in front of the camera, even shoved
their children under the bear's nose for a more amusing shot.

In the furred, blue moonlight, the pines bristled with shadow. Norton imagined the great, brutish shapes of the bears padding there, in
the heart of the black, nosing for food. His headache was bothering
him again. Together with the headache, something else beat at the
edge of his mind, tantalizing as the forgotten words to a song: some
proverb, some long-submerged memory he fished for but could not
come by.

"Norton!" Sadie hissed from within the tent.

He went to her with the slow, tranced gestures of a sleepwalker,
zipping the canvas door with its inset window of mosquito netting
behind him. The sleeping bag had taken warmth from her body, and
he crawled in beside her as into a deep nest.

The crash woke him. He dreamed it first, the tearing smash, the after-
shattering tinkle of glass, then woke, with a deadly clear head, to hear
it going on still, a diminished cascade of bells and gongs.

Beside him Sadie lay taut. The breath of her words caressed his ear.
"My bear," she said, as if she had called it up out of the dark.

After the crash the air seemed unnaturally quiet. Then Norton
heard a scuffling in the vicinity of the car. A bumping and clattering
set in, as if the bear were bowling cans and tins down an incline. It's
got into the trunk, Norton thought. It's going to rip open all our stews
and soups and canned fruits and sit there all night, gorging. The vision
of the bear at their stores infuriated him. The bear was somehow at
the root of the filched water bag, the empty gas tank, and, as if that

were not enough, he would eat them out of two months' supplies in a single night.

"Do something." Sadie huddled down into the nest of blankets. "Shoo him away." Her voice challenged him, yet his limbs were heavy.

Norton could hear the bear snuffling and padding along beside the tent. The canvas luffed like a sail. Gingerly, he climbed out of the sleeping bag, reluctant to leave the dark, musky warmth. He peered through the netting of the door. In the blue drench of moonlight he could see the bear hunched at the left rear window of the car, shoving its body through a gap where the glass should have been. With a crackle, like the fisting of a ball of paper, the bear brought out a little bundle of straw and trailing ribbons.

A surge of anger beat up in Norton's throat. The damn bear had no right to his wife's hat, mangling it like that. The hat belonged to Sadie as indissolubly as her own body, and there was the bear, ravaging it, picking it apart in a horrid, inquisitive way.

"You stay here," Norton said. "I'm going to drive that bear off."

"Take the light. That'll scare it."

Norton felt for the cold, cylindrical shape of the flashlight on the floor of the tent, unzipped the door, and stepped out into the pale blur of moonlight. The bear had managed to get the fried fish out of the bottom of the car now, and stood reared, preoccupied, fumbling with the wax paper wrappings. The remains of Sadie's hat, a grotesque crumple of straw, lay at its feet.

Norton aimed the beam of the flashlight straight at the bear's eyes. "Get out of here, you," he said.

The bear did not move.

Norton took a step forward. The shape of the bear towered against the car. Norton could see, in the glare of the light, the jagged teeth of glass around the hole gaping in the car window. "Get out . . ." He held the light steady, moving forward, willing the bear to be gone. At any moment the bear should break and run. "Get out . . ." But there was another will working, a will stronger, even, than his.

The darkness fisted and struck. The light went out. The moon went out in a cloud. A hot nausea flared through his heart and bowels. He struggled, tasting the thick, sweet honey that filled his throat and oozed from his nostrils. As from a far and rapidly receding planet, he heard a shrill cry—of terror, or triumph, he could not tell.

It was the last bear, her bear, the fifty-ninth.

The Daughters
of Blossom Street

Story, 1959

As it turns out, I don't need any hurricane warnings over the seven A.M. news-and-weather to tell me today will be a bad day. First thing when I come down the third-floor hall of the Clinics Building to open up the office I find a pile of patients' records waiting for me just outside the door, punctual as the morning paper. But it is a thin pile, and sure as Thursday's a full day with us, I know I'll have to spend a good half hour phoning every station in the Record Room to chase those missing records down. Already, so early in the morning, my white eyelet blouse is losing starch, and I can feel a little wet patch spreading under each arm. The sky outside is low, thick, and yellow as hollandaise. I shove open the one window in the office to change the air; nothing happens. Everything hangs still, heavier than wet laundry in a basement. Then I cut the string around the record folders and, staring up at me from the cover of the top record, I see stamped in red ink: DEAD. DEAD. DEAD.

I try to make the letters out to read DEAF, only it doesn't work. Not that I'm superstitious. Even though the ink is smeared rusty as blood on the cover of the case history, it simply means Lillian Ulmer is Dead, and Number nine-one-seven-oh-six canceled in the Record Room's active file for once and forever. Grim Billy at Station Nine has mixed the numbers up again, meaning me no harm. Still and all, with the sky so dark, and the hurricane rumbling up the coast, closer every time I turn around, I feel Lillian Ulmer, rest her soul, has started my day off on the wrong foot.

When my boss Miss Taylor comes in, I ask why they don't burn the records of the people gone to Blossom Street to save room in the files. But she says they often keep the records around a bit, if the disease is interesting, in case there might be a statistical survey of patients who lived or died with it.

It was my friend Dotty Berrigan in Alcoholic Clinic told me about Blossom Street. Dotty took it on herself to show me around the hospital when I first signed on as Secretary in Adult Psychiatric, she being right down the hall from me and we sharing a lot of cases.

"You must have a lot of people dead here every day," I said.

"You bet," she said. "And all the accidents and beatings-up you could want from the South End coming into Emergency Ward steady as taxes."

"Well, where do they keep them, the dead ones?" I didn't want suddenly by mistake to walk into a room of people laid out or cut up, and it seemed only too easy at that point for me to get lost in the numberless levels of corridors in the greatest general hospital in the world.

"In a room off Blossom Street, I'll show you where. The doctors never say anyone *died* in so many words, you know, because of making the patients morbid. They say: 'How many of yours went to Blossom Street this week?' And the other guy'll say: 'Two.' Or 'Five.' Or however many. Because the Blossom Street exit's where the bodies get shipped off to the funeral parlors to be fixed up for burying."

You can't beat Dotty. She's a regular mine of information, having to go about, as she does, checking for alcoholics in Emergency Ward and comparing notes with the doctors on duty in Psychiatric Ward, not to mention her dating various members of the hospital staff, even a surgeon once, and another time a Persian intern. Dotty is Irish—

shortish, and a little plump, but she dresses to make the best of it: always something blue—heaven blue to match her eyes, and these snug black jumpers she runs off herself from *Vogue* patterns, and high pumps with the spindly steel heels.

Cora, in Psychiatric Social Service down the hall from Dotty and me, is nowhere near the person Dotty is—pushing forty, you can tell it by the pleats around her eyes, even if she does keep her hair red, thanks to these colored rinses. Cora lives with her mother, and to hear her talk you'd think she was a green teenager. She had three of the girls in Nerve Clinic over her place one night, for bridge and supper, and stuck the casserole into the oven with the frozen raspberry tarts and wondered an hour later why they weren't warm, when all the time she hadn't thought to turn the oven on. Cora keeps taking these bus trips to Lake Louise and these cruises to Nassau on her vacations to meet Mr. Right, but all she ever meets is girls from Tumor Clinic or Amputee Clinic and every one of them on the selfsame mission.

Anyhow, the third Thursday of the month being the day we have our Secretaries' Meeting in the Hunnewell Room on the second floor, Cora calls for Dotty and the two of them call for me, and we click-clack in our heels down the stone stairs and into this really handsome room, dedicated, as it says on a bronze plaque over the door, to a Dr. Augustus Hunnewell in 1892. The place is full of glass cases crammed with old-fashioned medical instruments, and the walls are covered with faded, reddish-brown tintypes of Civil War doctors, their beards bushy and long as the beards of the Smith Brothers on those cough-drop packets. Set in the middle of the room, and stretching almost from wall to wall, is a great, dark, oval walnut-wood table, legs carved in the shape of lions' legs, only with scales instead of fur, and the whole top polished so you can see your face in it. Around this table we sit smoking and talking, waiting for Mrs. Rafferty to come in and start the meeting.

Minnie Dapkins, the tiny white-haired receptionist in Skin, is handing around pink and yellow referral slips. "Is there a Dr. Crawford in Nerve?" she asks, holding up a pink slip.

"Dr. Crawford!" Mary Ellen in Nerve bursts out laughing, her black bulk jiggling like a soft aspic in the flowered print dress. "He's dead six, seven years. Who wants him?"

Minnie purses her mouth to a tight pink bud. "A patient *said* she had

Dr. Crawford," she returns coldly. Minnie can't stand disrespect for the dead. She's been working at the hospital since she was married in the Depression and just got her Twenty-five Year Silver Service Pin at a special ceremony at the Secretaries' Christmas Party last winter, but the story goes she hasn't cracked a joke about a patient or a dead person in all her time. Not like Mary Ellen, or Dotty, or even Cora, who isn't above seeing the humor in a situation.

"What are you girls going to do about the hurricane?" Cora asks Dotty and me in a low voice, leaning across the table to dab off her cigarette ash in the glass ash tray with the hospital seal showing through the bottom. "I'm worried blue about my car. That motor gets wet in a sea breeze, it stops dead."

"Oh, it won't hit till after we're well through work," Dotty says, casual as usual. "You'll make it home."

"I still don't like the look of the sky." Cora wrinkles her freckled nose as if she smelled something bad.

I don't much like the look of the sky either. The room has been darkening steadily since we came in, until we are now all sitting in a kind of twilight, smoke drifting up from our cigarettes and hanging its pall in the already dense air. For a minute no one says anything. Cora seems to have spoken out loud everybody's secret worry.

"Well, well, well, what's the *mat*ter with us, girls! We're gloomy as a funeral!" The electric lights in the four copper lamp bowls overhead flash on, and, almost magically, the room brightens, shutting the stormy sky off in the distance where it belongs, harmless as a painted stage backdrop. Mrs. Rafferty steps up to the head of the table, her silver bangles making a cheerful music on each arm, her pendant earrings, exact replicas, in miniature, of stethoscopes, bouncing gaily from her plump earlobes. With an agreeable flurry she sets her notes and papers down on the table, her tinted blonde chignon gleaming under the lights like a cap of mail. Even Cora can't be sour-faced in front of such professional sunniness. "We'll get our affairs cleared up in a jiffy and then I've told one of the girls to send in the coffee machine and we'll have a little pick-me-up." Mrs. Rafferty glances around the table, absorbing, with a gratified smile, the exclamations of good feeling.

"Give her credit," Dotty mutters in my ear. "The old girl ought to market it."

Mrs. Rafferty starts out with one of her jolly scoldings. Mrs. Rafferty is really a buffer. A buffer between us and the hierarchies of Administration, and a buffer between us and the doctors, with their odd, endless follies and foibles, their illegible handwriting ("I've seen better in *kind*ergarten myself," Mrs. Rafferty is reported to have said), their childlike inability to paste prescriptions and reports on the right page in the patients' record books, and so on. "Now, girls," she says, raising one finger playfully, "I'm having all sorts of complaints about the daily statistics. Some of them are coming down without the Clinic stamp or date." She pauses, to let the enormity of this sink in. "Some aren't added correctly. Some"—another pause—"aren't coming down at *all*." I lower my eyes and try to will away the blush I feel rising to heat my cheeks. The blush is not for myself, but for my boss, Miss Taylor, who confided to me shortly after my arrival that, to be perfectly open and aboveboard, she *hates* statistics. Our patients' interviews with the staff psychiatrists often run over the Clinic's official closing time, and of course Miss Taylor can't get the statistics turned in downstairs every night unless she's going to be more of a martyr to the office than she is anyway. "Enough said, girls."

Mrs. Rafferty glances down at her notes, bends to make a check mark with her red pencil, and straightens, easy as a reed. "Another thing. Record Room says they're getting a lot of calls for records you already have on hand in your hold boxes, and they're simply in*fur*iated down there . . ."

"Infuriated is right," Mary Ellen groans good-naturedly, rolling her eyes so for a minute nothing but the whites are showing. "That guy what's-his-name at Station Nine acts like we shouldn't call in at all anyhow."

"Oh, that's *Billy*," says Minnie Dapkins.

Ida Kline and a couple of the other girls from the typing pool in the first basement titter among themselves, and then hush up.

"I guess you girls all know by now," Mrs. Rafferty sends a meaning smile around the table, "Billy's got troubles of his own. So let's not be too hard on him."

"Isn't he seeing somebody in your clinic?" Dotty asks me in a whisper. I just have time to nod, when Mrs. Rafferty's clear green eye silences us like an ice bath.

"I've got a complaint myself, Mrs. Rafferty," Cora puts in, taking advantage of the interruption. "What's going *on* down there at Admissions, I wonder? I tell our patients to come in an hour early for appointments with the girls in Social Service, so they'll have plenty of time to get through the line downstairs and pay the cashier and all, and that's *still* not early enough. They call up frantic from downstairs, ten minutes late already, and say the line's not moving for half an hour, and the Social Service girls on my end are waiting too, so what should I do in a case like that?"

Mrs. Rafferty's eyes drop, for the briefest moment, to her notes, as if she had the answer to Cora's question outlined there. She seems almost embarrassed. "Some of the other girls have complained of that too, Cora," she says finally, looking up. "We're short a girl at Admissions, so it's a terrible job to do all the processing . . ."

"Can't they *get* a guhl?" Mary Ellen asks boldly. "I mean, what's holding them up?"

Mrs. Rafferty exchanges a quick look with Minnie Dapkins. Minnie rubs her pale, papery hands together and licks at her lips in that rabbity way she has. Outside the open windows a small wind has suddenly risen, and it sounds as if it is beginning to rain, though it is probably only the rustle and scrape of papers starting to blow about down in the street. "I guess I may as well come straight out and *tell* everybody," Mrs. Rafferty says then. "Some of you know already, Minnie here knows, the reason we're holding up filling that position is . . . Emily Russo. You tell them, Minnie."

"Emily Russo," Minnie announces with funereal awe, "has got *cancer.* She's in this hospital right now. I want to tell you, anybody who knows her, she might like company. She still can have visitors on account of she's got no kin to stand by . . ."

"Gee, I didn't know that," Mary Ellen says slowly. "That's a shame."

"It was the last cancer check showed it up," says Mrs. Rafferty. "She's just hanging on by a *thread.* Those new drugs help with the pain, of course. The only thing is, sick as she is, Emily's *count*ing on coming back to her job. She *loves* that job, it's been her life these forty years, and Dr. Gilman doesn't want to tell her the hard facts as to how she isn't ever going back for fear of giving her a shock and all. Everybody who comes in to see her, she asks, 'Is the job filled yet? Have they got anybody yet down in Admissions?' The minute that job's filled Emily'll think it's her own death warrant, plain and simple."

"How about a substitute?" Cora wants to know. "You could say whoever-it-was was pinch-hitting, sort of."

Mrs. Rafferty shakes her smooth, gilded head. "No, Emily's to the point she wouldn't believe it, she'd think we were just jollying her along. People in her state get *aw*fully keen. We can't risk that. I go down to Admissions myself, when I can, and lend a hand. It's only," her voice drops, sober as an undertaker's, "a little while now, Dr. Gilman says."

Minnie looks about to cry. The whole meeting is in a worse state than when Mrs. Rafferty walked in, everybody bowing their heads over their cigarettes or picking away at their nail polish. "Now, now, girls, don't take on so," Mrs. Rafferty says, with a bright, rallying glance round. "Emily couldn't be in a better place for care, I'm sure we'll all agree, and Dr. Gilman is like a relative to her, she's known him these ten years. And you can go visit her, she'd love that . . ."

"How about flowers?" Mary Ellen puts in. There is a general murmur of approval. Every time anybody in our group gets sick, or engaged, or married, or a baby (though that is a lot rarer than the rest) or a Service Award, we chip in and send flowers, or a suitable gift, and cards. This is the first terminal case I've been in on, though; if I do say so, the girls couldn't have been sweeter about it.

"How about pink, something cheerful?" Ida Kline suggests.

"A wreath, why not?" a recently engaged little typist from the pool says softly. "A big pink wreath, carnations maybe."

"Not a *wreath*, girls!" Mrs. Rafferty groans. "With Emily so touchy, not a *wreath*, for heaven's sake!"

"A vase, then," says Dotty. "The nurses are always complaining about no vases. A real nice vase, maybe from the hospital gift shop, they have these im*por*ted vases, and a mixed bouquet in the vase from the hospital florist's."

"Now that is a very good idea, Dorothy." Mrs. Rafferty sounds relieved. "That's much more the type of thing. How many of you girls agree on a vase with a mixed bouquet?" Everybody, including the little typist, raises their hands. "Now I'll just put you in charge of that, Dorothy," Mrs. Rafferty says. "Leave your contributions with Dorothy, girls, before you go, and we'll send around a card this afternoon for everyone to sign."

The meeting breaks up then, everybody talking to everybody else, and some of the girls are already digging dollar bills out of their bags and shoving them across the table at Dotty.

"Quiet!" Mrs. Rafferty calls out. "Quiet, please, one more *min*ute, girls!" In the hush that follows, the siren of a nearing ambulance raises and lets fall its banshee wail, passing under our windows, fading around the corner, and ceasing at last at the Emergency Ward entrance. "I meant to tell you. About the *hurr*icane, girls, in case you were wondering what the procedure is. The latest bulletin from the Head Office says things may start blowing up around noon, but you're not to *wor*ry. Keep calm. Business as usual" (amused laughter from the typing pool) "and above all don't show any con*cern* you may have over the hurricane to the patients. They'll be nervous enough without that. Those of you who live far out, if it's too bad, can stay over in the hospital tonight. Cots are being set up in the halls of the Clinics Building, and we have the third floor all marked out for you girls, barring any emergency."

At this point, the swinging doors open with a bump, and a nurse walks in pushing the coffee maker on a metal food cart. Her rubber-soled shoes creak as though she was stepping on live mice. "Meeting adjourned," says Mrs. Rafferty. "Coffee, everyone."

Dotty draws me away from the crush around the coffee urn. "Cora's bound to have coffee, but that stuff's so bitter I can't stomach it. And in paper cups, yet." Dotty makes a little grimace of distaste. "Why don't you and me go blow this money on a vase and flowers for Miss Emily right here and now."

"Okay." Leaving the room with Dotty, I notice she is walking with short choppy strides. "Say, what's with you? You don't *want* to buy a vase?"

"It's not a *vase* I mind, it's the thought of that old lady up there being fed all this soft soap. She's going to die, she should have decent time to get used to the idea, see a priest, not hear everything's finesy-winesy." Dotty started taking a novitiate, she told me once, before she knew what the world was about, only, she said, she could no more keep her eyes down and her hands folded neatly in her sleeves or her tongue still than she could stand on her head and recite the Greek alphabet backwards. Every now and then, though, I feel her convent training showing through, like the sheen of her fair skin under the pink and peach-colored powder she uses.

"You should have been a missionary," I say. By this time we are up to the gift shop, a spiffy bandbox of a place, with fancy goods stacked from floor to ceiling—fluted vases, breakfast cups enameled with hearts and flowers, wedding-dress dolls and china bluebirds, gilt-edged card decks, cultured pearls, all you can think of, and every bit of it priced too high for anybody but a loving relative with his mind on something besides his pocketbook. "She's better off not knowing," I add, since Dotty doesn't say anything.

"I've got half a mind to *tell* her." Dotty picks up a big purple bubble-glass vase with a wide ruffle of glass around the rim and glares at it. "This we-know-better-than-you-do business around here gives me the creeps every so often. I sometimes think if there *weren't* any cancer check-ups or any National Diabetes Weeks with booths in the hall for you to test your own sugar, there wouldn't be so much cancer or diabetes, if you see what I mean."

"Now you're talking like those Christian Science types," I say. "And by the way, I think that vase is too loud for an old lady like Miss Emily."

Dotty gives me an odd little smile, takes the vase up to the saleslady at the counter and plonks down six dollars for it. Now instead of keeping to the kitty money she has left over after blowing most of it on the vase, Dotty adds a couple of dollars of her own, and, I must admit, so do I, without much prodding on her part. When the florist next door comes up, rubbing his hands and looking equally ready for congratulations or condolences, to ask what we want, a dozen long-stem roses, or maybe a bachelor's-button and baby's-breath corsage with silver ribbon, Dotty holds out the purple bubble-glass vase. "Something of everything, buster. Fill her up."

The florist peers at Dotty, one side of his mouth skipping up in a little smile, the other side waiting until he can be sure she's just josh-ing him. "Come on, come on." Dotty thumps the vase up and down the glass counter, causing the florist to wince and rapidly relieve her of it. "Like I said. Tea roses, carnations, some of those whatyama-callums . . ."

The florist's eyes follow Dotty's finger. "Gladioluses," he supplies in a pained tone.

"Gladolus. Some of them, different colors—red, orange, yellow, you know. And a couple of those purple irises . . ."

"Ah, they'll match the vase," the florist says, starting to get into the spirit of the thing. "*And* an assortment of anemones?"

"That too," Dotty says. "Except it sounds like a rash."

We are out of the florist's in short order, through the covered passageway between the Clinics Building and the hospital proper, and up on an elevator to Miss Emily's floor, Dotty bearing the purple vase jammed with this bouquet.

"Miss Emily?" Dotty whispers as we tiptoe into the four-bed ward. A nurse glides out from behind the curtains drawn around the bed in the far corner by the window.

"Shh." She puts her fingers to her lips and points back at the curtains. "In there. Don't stay too long."

Miss Emily is sunk back into the pillows, her eyes open and filling most of her face, her hair spread out in a gray fan on the pillow round her head. Bottles of all sorts are on the medicine table, on the floor under the bed, and hung up around the bed. Thin rubber tubes lead off from a couple of the bottles, one tube disappearing under the bed covers and one tube going right up into Miss Emily's left nostril. There is no sound in the room but the dry rustle of Miss Emily's breathing, no motion but the faint heave of the sheet over her chest and the air bubbles sending up their rhythmic silver balloons in one of these bottles of fluid. In the unhealthy storm-light from the window Miss Emily looks like a wax dummy, except for her eyes, which fix on us. I can almost feel them burning into my skin, they are so keen.

"We brought these flowers, Miss Emily." I point to the enormous multicolored vaseful of hothouse blooms Dotty is setting down on the medicine table. The table is so small she first has to clear away all the jars and glasses and pitchers and spoons onto the bottom shelf to make room.

Miss Emily's eyes slide to this heap of flowers. Something flickers there. I feel I am watching two candles at the end of a long hall, two pinpoint flames blowing and recovering in a dark wind. Outside the window the sky is blacker than a cast-iron skillet.

"The girls sent them." Dotty takes Miss Emily's inert, waxen hand from where it lies on the coverlet. "The card'll be up later, everybody's signing it, only we didn't want to wait with the flowers."

Miss Emily tries to speak. A faint hiss and rattle escape her lips, no words you can make out.

Still, Dotty seems to know what she means. "The job is there, Miss Emily," she says, spacing her words clear and slow, the way you explain things to a very young child. "They're holding it open." The selfsame words Mrs. Rafferty would use, I thought wonderingly. Only Mrs. Rafferty would add something to spoil it: You'll be up and around in a jiffy, Miss Emily, don't you fret. Or, You'll be getting your Gold Fifty Year Service Bracelet yet, Miss Emily, just you wait and see. The queer thing is, Dotty doesn't give any impression of twisting the facts into a fib. She is telling the honest truth, saying: Everybody is flying around like chickens with their heads off in Admissions, Miss Emily, because they want you to know you aren't replaceable. Not so soon, not so fast.

Miss Emily lets the lids droop over her eyes. Her hand goes limp in Dotty's palm, and she sighs, a sigh that passes with a shudder through her whole body.

"She knows," Dotty says to me as we leave Miss Emily's bed. "She knows now."

"But you didn't *tell* her. Not in so many words."

"Whaddayou think I am?" Dotty is indignant. "No heart or something? Say," she breaks off suddenly, as we step out of the doorway into the hall, "who's that?"

A lean, slight figure is propped up against the wall in the empty corridor a short way down from Miss Emily's door. As we approach, the figure flattens back against the wall, as if it could by some miracle become part of the pale, green-painted plaster material and vanish from sight. In the dim corridor, the electric lights give the effect of early nightfall.

"Billy *Moni*han!" Dotty exclaims. "What in the name of goodness are *you* doing here?"

"Wuh-wuh-waiting," Billy manages to squeak, his face flushing a painful shade of red under the crimson overlay of pimples and boils. He is a very short boy, almost as short as Dotty, and extremely thin, although he has attained his full growth and has nothing more to expect in that line. His long black hair is slicked back with some sort of redolent hair oil and shows the furrows of a comb drawn recently through the glossed, patent-leather surface.

"Just what," Dotty straightens to her full height, and in her heels she has the edge on Billy, "do you think you're doing hanging around up here?"

"Juh-just . . . wuh-waiting." Billy ducks his head to avoid Dotty's gimlet eye. He seems to be making an effort to swallow his tongue so as to be beyond all communication whatsoever.

"You should be trotting up records from Record Room in the Clinics Building right this minute," Dotty says. "You don't know Miss

Emily from Adam, you leave Miss Emily alone, hear?"

A weird, indecipherable gurgle escapes from Billy's throat. "Shuh-shuh-she suh-said I cuh-could come," he gets out then.

Dotty gives a sharp, exasperated snort. Still, something in Billy's eye makes her turn away and leave him to his devices. By the time the elevator stops for us, Billy has melted, pimples, slick hair, stutter, and all, into Miss Emily's room.

"I don't like that boy, that boy's a regular," Dotty pauses for the right word, "a regular *vul*ture. There's something funny with him these days, let me tell you. He hangs around that Emergency Ward entrance, you'd think the Lord God himself was supposed to come in that door and announce Judgment Day."

"He's seeing Dr. Resnik in our place," I say, "only I haven't got any of the audiograph records on him to type up yet, so I don't know. Did it come on sudden, this vulture business?"

Dotty shrugs. "All I know is, he scared Ida Kline sick in the typing pool last week, telling her some story or other about a woman came into Skin Clinic all purple and swollen fat as an elephant in a wheelchair with this tropical disease. Ida couldn't eat her lunch for thinking of it. They've got a name for it, these people who hang around bodies and all. Nega . . . negafills. They get real bad, they start digging up bodies right out of the graveyard."

"I was doing an intake report on a woman yesterday," I say. "She sounds something like that. Couldn't believe her little girl had died, kept seeing her around, at church services, in the grocery store. Visited the graveyard day in, day out. One day, she says, the little girl comes to see her, dressed in this white lace smock, and says not to worry, she's in heaven and well taken care of, doing just fine."

"I wonder," Dotty says. "I wonder how do you cure that?"

From the hospital cafeteria where we are sitting around one of the big tables over dessert and signing Miss Emily's Get-Well-Quick card, I can see the rain swatting in long lines against the windows overlooking the garden court. Some wealthy lady had the court built and filled up with grass and trees and flowers so the doctors and nurses could have something prettier than brick walls and gravel to look at while they ate. Now the windows are streaming so you can't even see the color green through the sheets of water.

"You girls going to stay over?" Cora's voice is wobbly as the jello she is spooning up. "I mean, I don't know what to *do* with Mother home alone. What if the lights go out, she might break a hip hunting around for candles in the cellar in the dark, and the roof shingles are none too good, they leak through the attic even if it's just a shower . . ."

"You stay, Cora," Dotty says with decision. "You try going home in *this* soup, you'll be drowned silly. You call up home tomorrow morning, you'll find your mother happy as a cricket with the storm blowing itself out a hundred miles away up Maine someplace."

"Look!" I say, partly to distract Cora. "Here's Mrs. Rafferty just come in with her tray. Let's get her to sign." Before any of us can wave, Mrs. Rafferty spots us and comes over, a white sloop in full sail, her stethoscope earrings bobbing on either side of a face that means nothing but bad news.

"Girls," she says, seeing the card lying open there on the table in front of us, "girls, I don't like to be the bearer of sad tidings, but I have to tell you that card won't be needed."

Cora turns the color of putty under her freckles, a spoonful of strawberry jello suspended halfway to her mouth.

"Emily Russo passed away not an hour ago." Mrs. Rafferty bows her head for a second, and lifts it with a certain fortitude. "It's all for the *best*, girls, you know that as well as I do. She passed on easy as could be, so don't let it get you down now. We've got," she nods her head briskly at the blind, streaming panes, "other people to think of."

"Was Miss Emily," Dotty asks, stirring cream into her coffee with an odd absorption, "was Miss Emily *alone* at the last?"

Mrs. Rafferty hesitates. "No, Dorothy," she says then. "No. She was *not* alone. Billy Monihan was with her when she passed on. The nurse on duty says he seemed *very* affected by it, very moved by the old lady. He said," Mrs. Rafferty adds, "he said to the nurse Miss Emily was his aunt."

"But Miss Emily doesn't have any brothers or sisters," Cora protests. "Minnie told us. She doesn't have *any*body."

"Be that as it may," Mrs. Rafferty seems eager to close the subject, "be that as it may, the boy was very moved. Very moved by the whole thing."

With it raining cats and dogs, and a wind blowing to flatten the city itself, no patients come into the office all that afternoon. Nobody, that is, except old Mrs. Tomolillo. Miss Taylor has just gone out to get two cups of coffee at the dispenser down the hall when Mrs. Tomolillo walks in on me, furious and wet as a witch in her black wool year-round dress, waving a soggy lump of papers. "Where's Dr. Chrisman, Dr. Chrisman, I want to know."

The soggy lump of papers turns out to be Mrs. Tomolillo's own record book, which patients are never under any circumstances allowed to get hold of. It is a fine mess, the red, blue and green ink entries of the numerous doctors in the numerous clinics Mrs. Tomolillo frequents blurring into a wild rainbow, dripping colored beads of water and ink even as I take it from her hands. "Lies, lies, lies," Mrs. Tomolillo hisses at me, so I can't get a word in. "Lies."

"What lies, Mrs. Tomolillo?" I ask then, in a clear, loud voice, for Mrs. Tomolillo is notably hard of hearing, although she refuses to learn to operate an aid. "I'm sure Dr. Chrisman . . ."

"Lies, lies he's written in that book. I am a good woman, my husband dead. You let me just get my hands on that man, I'll teach him lies . . ."

I glance quickly out into the hall. Mrs. Tomolillo is flexing her strong fingers in an alarming fashion. A man on crutches, one pants leg empty and folded up in a neat tuck at the hip, is swinging along past the door. After him comes an aide from Amputee Clinic, lugging a pink artificial leg and half an artificial torso. Mrs. Tomolillo quiets at the sight of the little procession. Her hands fall to her sides, losing themselves in the folds of her voluminous black skirt.

"I'll tell Dr. Chrisman, Mrs. Tomolillo. I'm sure there's been some mistake, don't you get upset." Behind my back, the window rattles in its frame as if some great drafty giant out there is trying to shoulder into the light. The rain is striking the pane now with the force of pistol cracks.

"Lies . . ." Mrs. Tomolillo hisses, but more placidly, rather like a kettle just coming off the boil. "You tell him."

"I'll tell him. Oh, Mrs. Tomolillo . . ."

"Yes?" She pauses in the doorway, black and portentous as one of the Fates, caught in a squall of her own making.

"Where shall I tell Dr. Chrisman the record book came from?"

"Down there in that room," she says simply. "That room where all the books are. I ask for it, they give it to me."

"I see." The number on Mrs. Tomolillo's record, printed in indelible ink, reads nine-three-six-two-five. "I see, I see. Thank you, Mrs. Tomolillo."

The Clinics Building, big as it is, founded solid on concrete and built of brick and stone, seems shaken to its roots as Dotty and I cross through the first floor halls and down the passageway to the cafeteria in the main hospital for a hot supper. We can hear the sirens, loud and faint, in and around the city—fire engines, ambulances, police wagons. The Emergency Ward parking lot is jammed with ambulances and private cars pouring in from the outlying towns—people with heart attacks, people with collapsed lungs, people with galloping hysteria. And to top it off, there is a power failure, so we have to feel our way along the walls in the semi-dark. Everywhere doctors and interns are snapping out orders, nurses gliding by white as ghosts in their uniforms, and stretchers with people bundled on them—groaning, or crying, or still—being rolled this way and that. In the middle of it all, a familiar shape darts past us and down a flight of unlit stone steps leading to the first and second basements.

"Isn't that him?"

"Him who?" Dotty wants to know. "I can't see a thing in this pitch, I should get glasses."

"Billy. From the Record Room."

"They must be having him whip up records on the double for the emergency cases," Dotty says. "They need all the extra hands they can get when things are thick as this."

For some reason I can't bring myself to tell Dotty about Mrs. Tomolillo. "He's not such a bad kid," I find myself saying, in spite of what I know about Mrs. Tomolillo, and Emily Russo, and Ida Kline and the elephant woman.

"Not bad," Dotty says, ironically. "If you happen to like vampires."

Mary Ellen and Dotty are sitting cross-legged on one of the cots in the third-floor annex, trying to play social solitaire by the light of a purse flashlight somebody has dug up, when Cora comes flying down the hall toward the row of us propped in the cots.

Dotty lays a red nine on a black ten. "You get hold of your mother? The roof still on at your place?"

In the pale, luminous circle cast by the flashlight, Cora's eyes are wide, wet around the edges.

"Say," Mary Ellen leans toward her, "you haven't heard anything bad? You're as white as a sheet, Cora."

"It's not . . . it's not my *mother*," Cora brings out. "The lines are down, I couldn't even get through. It's that boy, that *Billy* . . ."

Everybody is very quiet all of a sudden.

"He was running up and down these *stairs,*" Cora says, her voice so teary you'd think she was talking about her kid brother or something. "Up and down, up and down with these records, and no lights, and he's in such a hurry he's skipping two, three steps. And he *fell.* He fell a whole flight . . ."

"Where is he?" Dotty asks, slowly putting down her hand of cards. "Where is he now?"

"Where *is* he?" Cora's voice rises an octave. "Where is he, he's dead."

It's a funny thing. The minute those words are out of Cora's mouth, everybody forgets how little Billy was, and how really ridiculous-looking, with that stammer and that awful complexion. With all this worry about the hurricane, and nobody able to get through to their folks, memory throws a kind of halo around him. You'd think he'd laid down and died for the whole bunch of us sitting there on those cots.

"He wouldn't of died," Mary Ellen observes, "if he hadn't been helping out other folks."

"Seeing how things are," Ida Kline puts in, "I'd like to take back what I said about him the other day, about him and that woman with the elephant sickness. He didn't know what a bad stomach I've got or anything."

Only Dotty is silent.

Mary Ellen turns out the flashlight then, and everybody takes off their dresses in the dark and lies down. Dotty climbs into the cot at the far end of the row, next to mine. All along the corridor you can hear the rain, quieted now, drumming steadily against the panes. After a while the sound of regular breathing is rising from most of the cots.

"Dotty," I whisper. "Dotty, you awake?"

"Sure," Dotty whispers back. "I've got asomnia like nobody's business."

"So, Dotty, what do you think?"

"You want to know what I think?" Dotty's voice seems wafted to my ears from a small, invisible point in a great darkness. "I think that boy's a lucky boy. For once in his life he's got sense. For once in his life, I think that boy's going to be a hero."

And what with the newspaper stories, and the church ceremonies, and the Posthumous Gold Medal awarded by the Hospital Director to Billy's parents after the storm is blown over, I have to give Dotty credit. She's right. She's absolutely right.

Sweetie Pie and
the Gutter Men

Story, May 1959

Waiting on the front doorstep of the unfamiliar house for someone
to answer the bell and listening to the shrill, musical intonation of
children's voices from the open window upstairs, Myra Wardle
remembered how little she had cared for Cicely Franklin (then
Cicely Naylor) at college. In those days she had tolerated Cicely—
few of the other girls did—as a well-meaning, if prudish and provincial, classmate. Clearly, that same bare tolerance on Myra's part must
have mellowed in Cicely's mind over the subsequent eight years to a
facsimile of friendship. How else to explain Cicely's note, their one
communication in all that time, turning up in the Wardles' mailbox?
"Come see our new house, our two little girls and cocker puppy,"
Cicely had written in her large, schoolmarmish hand on the back of
an engraved card announcing the opening of Hiram Franklin's obstetrical practice.

The card itself, until she'd discovered Cicely's note on the reverse side, gave Myra an unpleasant moment. Why should a new obstetrician in town (Myra hadn't recognized Cicely's husband's name) be sending her an engraved announcement unless to suggest, with the utmost subtlety, that the Wardles were not fulfilling their duty to the community, to the human race? Myra Wardle, after five years of marriage, had no children. It was not, she explained, in answer to the delicate queries of relatives and friends, because she couldn't have them, or because she didn't want them. It was simply because her husband Timothy, a sculptor, insisted that children tied one down too much. And the Wardles' relatives and friends, saddled with children, with the steady jobs, the mortgaged houses, the installment-plan station wagons and washing machines that form such an inevitable part of parenthood in the suburbs, couldn't have been in more gratifying agreement.

Myra pressed the doorbell again, faintly annoyed that Cicely should keep her waiting so long on the unshaded step in the humid August afternoon. The children's voices continued, a clear, sweetly discordant babble from the second-floor window. A woman's voice sounded among them now, a low counterpoint to the slenderly spun treble. Myra tried the handle of the screen door to get at the front-door knocker, but the screen door seemed hooked from within. Unwilling to raise her voice, to shout upstairs as if Cicely were a back-fence neighbor, she rapped loudly with her knuckles on the doorjamb. A bit of paint flaked off into the dry, sepia-colored shrubbery. The whole place looked in bad shape. White paint peeling away in blistered swatches, shutters down, stacked haphazardly at the end of the yard, the house had a curiously lashless, albino expression—rather, Myra thought, resembling Cicely's own. For a moment she wondered if Cicely meant her to go away under the illusion that the bell didn't work. Then she heard the voices receding from the window. Footsteps clattered on a staircase in the depths of the house. The front door swung inward.

"Well, Myra." It was Cicely's voice, the same prosy Midwestern accent, the trace of a lisp lending a touch of primness. Shading her eyes against the glare of the white shingles, Myra peered through the screen, unable to make out much of anything in the dark well of the hall. Cicely opened the screen door then, and came out onto the step, carrying a chubby blond child in her arms. A thin, lively girl of about four followed her, looking at Myra with frank interest. Flat-chested, her complexion pallid even in summer, Cicely still wore her wan blond hair crimped tight, like a doll's wig.

"You weren't sleeping, were you?" Myra said. "Is this a bad time?"

"Oh, no. Alison had just woken Millicent up anyway." Behind the tortoiseshell-rimmed glasses, Cicely's pale eyes shifted slightly to a point somewhere beyond Myra's right shoulder. "Let's go out and sit under the beech tree in the back. It's always coolest there."

Striped canvas chairs and child-size wicker chairs stood in a circle in the dense, russet-blue shade of the great tree whose comprehensive boughs arched over half of the small yard. A rubber wading pool, a swing, a metal slide, a wooden seesaw and a yellow sandbox crowded the children's play area. Cicely set Millicent on her feet beside the wading pool. The child paused, teetering slightly, her plump belly rounding out over her pink seersucker pants like a smooth-skinned fruit. Alison jumped immediately into the pool and sat down hard; the water splashed up in a fine sheet of spray, dousing her close-cropped hair.

Cicely and Myra pulled up two canvas chairs and sat some little distance from the children. "Now, Alison," Cicely said, rehearsing what was evidently an old lesson, "you can wet yourself and the toys, and the grass, but you mustn't wet Millicent. Let Millicent wet herself."

Alison did not seem to hear. "The water's *cold*," she told Myra, widening her gray-blue eyes in emphasis.

"Cud," Millicent echoed. Squatting beside the pool, she made gentle churning motions in the water with her hand.

"I often wonder if linguistic ability is hereditary," Cicely said, lowering her voice out of range of the children's hearing. "Alison spoke complete sentences at eleven months. She's amazingly word-conscious. Millicent mispronounces everything."

"Why, how do you mean?" Myra had a private pact with herself to "bring people out." She began by imagining herself a transparent vase, clearer than crystal—almost, in fact, invisible. (She had read somewhere that a certain school of actors pretended they were empty glasses when studying a new role.) In this way—purged of any bias, any individual color tint—Myra became the perfect receptacle for confidences. "How do you mean, 'word-conscious'?"

"Oh, Alison makes an *effort* to learn words. She works on changing her vocabulary. Once, for instance, I overheard her talking to herself in the playroom. 'Daddy will fix it,' she said. Then she corrected herself: 'No, Daddy will *repair* it.' But Millicent's hopeless . . ."

"Perhaps Alison subdues her?" Myra suggested. "Often when one child talks a lot, the other turns inward, develops a sort of secret personality all her own. Millicent may, don't you think, one day simply come out with a complete sentence?"

Cicely shook her head. "I'm afraid there's little chance of that. When we were in Akron, visiting Mother, Millicent learned to say 'Nana' and 'Daddy' quite clearly. Ever since we moved up here, though, she's confused the two. She comes out with 'Nada,' some weird combination like that. And she says 'goggy' for 'doggy' and so on."

"Ah, but that's quite natural, isn't it? Quite common?" Myra's fingers twiddled at the leaves of a low branch of the beech tree near the arm of her chair. Already she had shredded several of the glossy, reddish-black leaves with her nails. "Don't most children substitute some letters for others that way?"

"I suppose," Cicely said, her attention diverted momentarily by the children chattering and dabbling in the wading pool, "it's common enough."

"Why, I remember when *I* was a child," Myra said, "I couldn't pronounce 'l' for some reason. I used to say 'Night! Night!' when I wanted the hall light left on. This confused the women who used to baby-sit for me no end."

Cicely smiled, and Myra, heartened, was inspired to ad-lib. "I believe I also alienated a certain Aunt Lily from the family. She wouldn't accept Mother's explanation of my foible with 'l's. She insisted I'd overheard her called Aunt Ninny by my parents."

Cicely shook with dry, silent laughter. In her starched middy blouse, her beige Bermuda shorts and her flat brown walking shoes with the scalloped flaps over the ties, Cicely was undeniably plain, even dowdy. She possessed none of the fruity buxomness of the harassed working-class mothers Myra ran into in Woolworth's or the A & P. Then, a bit guilty about her brief lapse from impersonal glassiness, Myra steered the conversation toward Hiram and his obstetrical practice. With some relief, she became transparent, crystalline, again. But as Cicely talked on about the difficulties of starting an obstetrical practice in a strange town, Myra fell into a reverie of her own. Cicely's words faded away like the words of a television announcer after the sound track is shut off. Suddenly Myra felt a warm silkiness graze her ankle. She glanced down. The black cocker puppy lay stretched out under her chair, eyes shut, his tongue a scrap of pink felt lolling at the corner of his mouth.

". . . the Chamber of Commerce letters were mostly silly," Cicely was saying. "All about population, industry, things like that. Some of the towns had too many obstetricians. Some had none . . ."

"Why wouldn't a town without any be a good place to start?"

Obligingly, Cicely launched into a detailed account of the animosity kindled in the hearts of general practitioners when an obstetrician invaded their town and stole away their clients by his specialty. "Then Dr. Richter wrote from here. He said there was a good opening, and a man was already thinking about moving in, so Hiram had better hurry if he wanted to come . . ."

At that moment, Cicely was interrupted. Millicent lay on her stomach in the wading pool, howling and spitting water, her round face twisted into an image of outrage.

"She must have fallen," Myra found herself saying, although she was reasonably sure Alison had pushed her sister into the water.

Cicely jerked up from her chair and went to pick Millicent out of the pool.

"Can you open this?" Coolly ignoring Millicent's cries, Alison handed Myra a black-enameled can with holes punched in the screw top. "It's stuck."

"I can try." The can felt oddly heavy. Myra wondered for a moment if she was reading her own suppressed pleasure into Alison's eyes—pleasure at the sight of plump, white-skinned Millicent whining on the grass, rubbing at her wet sunsuit pants, stained a deep crimson from the water. "What's *in* here?"

"Cake mix."

Myra tried to loosen the screw-top, but the can, glistening with wet, slithered around in her grasp. The lid would not budge. With a sense of mild chagrin, she handed the can back to Alison. She felt a little as if she had failed to pass a test of some sort. "I can't do a thing with it."

"Daddy will open the can when he comes home from the office." Cicely paused by Myra's chair, Millicent bundled under her arm. "I'm going in to make us some lemonade and change Millicent. Want to see the house?"

"Sure." Myra's hands were uncomfortably wet and gritty, even sore, from her efforts with the can. Taking a Kleenex from her purse, she dabbed at her palms. From the back steps of the house she glanced over at Alison, framed by the greenery around the wading pool. "What's in that can, anyway?" With a small beech twig, Alison was prodding the stomach of the sleepy cocker puppy. "It's heavy as lead."

"Oh," Cicely shrugged and gave Millicent a little jounce in her arms, "sand from the sandbox and water from the wading pool, I guess."

The interior of the Franklins' house smelled of varnish and turpentine, and the white-painted walls gave off a surgical light. An upright piano, a few armchairs upholstered in vague pastels, and a mauve sofa stood, desolate as rocks on a prairie, on the bare, freshly shellacked floor of the living room. The linoleum in the dining room, playroom and kitchen, patterned with inordinately large black and white squares, suggested a modernized Dutch painting—bereft, however, of the umber and ocher patinas of polished wood, the pewter and brass highlights, and the benevolent pear and cello shapes which enrich the interiors of a Vermeer.

Cicely opened the icebox and took out a frost-covered can of lemonade concentrate. "Do you mind?" She handed Myra a can opener. "I'll just run up and change Millicent."

While Cicely was upstairs, Myra opened the can, poured the contents into an aluminum pitcher, and measured four cans of cold water into the lemonade base, stirring the mixture with a spoon she found in the sink. The sunlight glancing off the white enamel and chrome surfaces of the kitchen appliances made her feel dazed, far off.

"All set?" Cicely chirruped from the doorway. Millicent beamed in her arms, dressed in a clean pair of seersucker pants, exactly like the pink ones, only blue.

Carrying the aluminum pitcher of lemonade and four red plastic cups, Myra drifted after Cicely and Millicent toward the little oasis of chairs in the dark shade of the beech tree.

"Do you want to pour?" Cicely set Millicent on the lawn and dropped into her canvas chair. Alison wandered over to them from the wading pool, her short, sandy hair slicked back like an otter's.

"Oh, I'll let you do it." Myra handed Cicely the pitcher and the cups. With a curious, nerveless languor, she watched Cicely start to pour out the lemonade. The tree leaves, and the sun falling through the leaves in long pencils of light, went out of focus for a moment in a dappled green-and-gold blur. Then a quick flash caught her eye.

Alison had, in plain view, given Millicent a sudden, rough shove, tumbling her to the ground. There was a second of silence, expectant as the brief interval between the flash of lightning and the thunder crack, and then Millicent howled from the grass.

Cicely placed the pitcher and the cup she was filling on the ground beside her chair, got up, and lifted the sobbing Millicent to her lap. "Alison, you've made a mistake." Cicely's tone was remarkably cool, Myra thought. "You know we don't hit people in this house."

Alison, wary, a small foxy creature at bay, stood her ground, her eyes flickering from Myra to Cicely and back again. "She wanted to sit in *my* chair."

"We don't hit people in any case." Cicely smoothed Millicent's hair. When the child's sobs had quieted, she set Millicent in one of the small wicker chairs and poured her a cup of lemonade. Alison, without a word, stared at Myra while waiting her turn, took the cup Cicely gave her, and returned to her chair. Her steady look made Myra uneasy. She felt the child expected something of her, some sign, some pledge.

The silence deepened, punctuated only by the irregular sound of four people sipping lemonade—the children, loud and unselfconscious, the grown-ups more discreet. Except for this tenuous noise, the silence surrounded them like a sea, lapping at the solid edges of the afternoon. At any moment, Myra thought, the four of them might become fixed, forever speechless and two-dimensional—waxlike figures in a faded photograph. "Has Hiram had any patients yet?" With an effort she broke the gathered stillness.

"Oh, Hiram's joined the charity ward in the hospital for the month of August." Cicely tilted her cup of lemonade and drained it. "Of course, he doesn't get paid for ward cases, but he's had four deliveries already this month."

"Four!" A vision of babies in pink and blue bassinets loomed in Myra's mind—three hundred and sixty-five babies in three-hundred and sixty-five bassinets—each baby a perfect replica of the others, all lined up in a ghostly alley of diminishing perspective between two mirrors. "Why, that's about one a day!"

"That's about the average for this town. Hiram hasn't really had any patients of his own yet, any private patients. Still, a woman walked into his office yesterday, out of the blue. She asked for an appointment for today. I don't know how she heard of Hiram, maybe from the announcement in the paper."

"What sort of anesthesia does Hiram use?" Myra asked suddenly.

"Well, that depends . . ." Cicely's own frankness demanded that she answer, but she was withdrawing, Myra could tell, into that blithe evasiveness of so many mothers when questioned point-blank about childbirth by childless women.

"I just meant," Myra said hastily, "there seem to be different schools of thought. I've heard some mothers talk about caudal anesthesia. Something that deadens the pain, but still lets you see the baby born . . .?"

"Caudal anesthesia." Cicely sounded a trifle scornful. "That's what Dr. Richter uses in *all* his cases. That's why he's so popular."

Myra started to laugh, but behind the sheen of her glasses Cicely looked dubious. "It only seems so amusing," Myra explained, "to raise your popularity rating by the kind of anesthesia you use." Still, Cicely did not appear to see the joke.

"Perhaps . . ." Myra dropped her voice, with a cautious glance at Alison, who was sucking up the dregs of her lemonade. "Perhaps I'm so interested because I had an experience myself, once, years ago, seeing a baby born."

Cicely's eyebrows rose. "How ever did you do that? Was it a relative? They don't let people, you know . . ."

"No relative." Myra gave Cicely a slight, wry smile. "It happened in my . . . salad days. In college, when I was dating medical students, I went to lectures on sickle-cell anemia, watched them cut up cadavers. Oh, I was a regular Florence Nightingale."

Alison got up at this point and went over to the sandbox just behind Myra's chair. Millicent was kneeling by the wading pool, swirling a fallen beech leaf in the water.

"That's how I got into the hospital to watch a delivery in the charity ward. Camouflaged in a white uniform and a white mask, of course. Actually, it must have been about the time I knew you, when you were a senior and I was a sophomore." As she spoke, hearing her own voice, stilted, distant, as on an old record, Myra remembered with sudden clarity the blind, mushroom-colored embryos in the jars of preserving fluid, and the four leather-skinned cadavers, black as burnt turkey, on the dissecting tables. She shuddered, touched by a keen chill in spite of the hot afternoon. "This woman had some drug, invented by a man, I suppose, as all those drugs are. It didn't stop her feeling the pain, but made her forget it right afterwards."

"There are lots of drugs like that," Cicely said. "You forget the pain in a sort of twilight sleep."

Myra wondered how Cicely could be so calm about forgetting pain. Although erased from the mind's surface, the pain was there, some-where, cut indelibly into one's quick—an empty, doorless, windowless corridor of pain. And then to be deceived by the waters of Lethe into coming back again, in all innocence, to conceive child after child! It was barbarous. It was a fraud dreamed up by men to continue the human race; reason enough for a woman to refuse childbearing alto-gether. "Well," Myra said, "this woman was yelling a good deal, and moaning. That kind of thing leaves its impression. They had to cut into her, I remember. There seemed to be a great deal of blood . . ."

From the sandbox Alison's voice began to rise in a shrill monologue, but Myra, intent on her own story, did not bother to distinguish the child's words. "The third-year man delivering the baby kept saying, 'I'm going to drop it, I'm going to drop it' in a kind of biblical chant . . ." Myra paused, staring through the red-dark scrim of beech leaves without seeing them, acting out once again her part in the remem-bered play, a part after which all other parts had somehow dwindled, palled.

". . . and she goes upstairs in the attic," Alison was saying. "She gets splinters in her feet." Myra checked a sudden impulse to slap the child. Then the words caught her interest. "She pokes people's eyes on the sidewalk. She pulls off their dresses. She gets diarrhea in the *night* . . ."

"Alison!" Cicely yelped. "You be quiet now! You know better than that."

"Just who's she talking about?" Myra let her story of the blue baby lapse back, unfinished, into the obscure fathoms of memory from which it had risen. "Some neighborhood child?"

"Oh," Cicely said with some irritation, "it's her *doll.*"

"Sweetie Pie!" Alison shouted.

"And what else does Sweetie Pie do?" Myra asked, countering Cicely's move to quiet the child. "I used to have a doll myself."

"She climbs on the roof." Alison jumped into her wicker chair and squatted on the seat, frog-fashion. "She knocks down the gutter men."

"*Gutter* men?"

"The painters took the gutters off the porch roof this morning," Cicely explained. "Tell Mrs. Wardle," she ordered Alison in the clear, socially constructive tones of a Unitarian Sunday-school teacher, "how you *helped* the painters this morning."

Alison paused, fingering her bare toes. "I packed their things up. One was named Neal. One was named Jocko."

"I don't know what I'm going to *do* with Mr. Grooby." Cicely turned to Myra, pointedly leaving Alison out. "This morning he came to start painting at six-thirty."

"Six-thirty!" Myra said. "Why on earth?"

"And left at ten-thirty. He's got a heart condition, so he works all morning and fishes all afternoon. Each morning he's come earlier and earlier. Eight-thirty was all right, but *six*-thirty! I don't know what it'll be tomorrow."

"Sunup, at that rate," Myra said. "I guess," she added thoughtlessly, "you must be kept pretty much occupied just being a mother." She hadn't meant to say "just," which sounded disparaging, but there it was. Lately Myra had started wondering about babies. Young as she was, and happily married, she felt something of a maiden aunt among the children of her relatives and friends. Lately, too, she had taken to tearing off low-hanging leaves or tall grass heads with a kind of wanton energy, and to twisting her paper napkin into compact pellets at the table, something she hadn't done since childhood.

"Morning, noon, and night," Cicely said with an air, Myra thought, of noble martyrdom. "Morning, noon, and night."

Myra glanced at her watch. It was close to four-thirty. "I guess," she said, "I ought to be running along now." She would be staying on till suppertime, if she wasn't careful, out of sheer inertia.

"No need to go," Cicely said, but she rose from her chair, idly dusting off the seat of her Bermudas.

Myra tried to think of a good excuse to see her to the gate. It was too early to be preparing dinner, too late to plead last-minute shopping downtown. Her life all at once seemed excessively spacious. "I must go, anyway."

As Myra turned, she noticed a dark blue car pulling up outside the unpainted picket gate that closed the driveway and backyard off from the street. It would be Hiram Franklin, whom Myra had met only once or twice eight years ago at college. Already Cicely and the children were receding from her, behind the glass window of some heartless nonstop express, secure in their rosily lit, plush compartment, arranging themselves in loving attitudes about the young man of medium height now unlatching the gate. Millicent started, with uneven steps, toward her father. "Daddy!" Alison shouted from the sandbox.

Hiram walked toward the women. As he approached, Millicent caught him about the knees, and Hiram bent to pick her up. "She's her daddy's girl," Cicely said.

Myra waited, the smile stiffening on her face as it did when she had to hold still for a photographer. Hiram looked very young to be an obstetrician. His eyes, a hard, clear blue, bordered by black lashes, gave him a slightly glacial expression.

"Myra Smith Wardle, Hiram," Cicely said. "An old college friend you should remember."

Hiram Franklin nodded at Myra. "Whom I should remember, but do not, unfortunately." His words were less an apology for forgetfulness than a firm denial of any prior acquaintance.

"I'm just going." Cicely's alliance with Hiram, powerful and immediate, shut out everything else. Some women were like that with their husbands, Myra thought—overly possessive, not wishing to share them, even for a moment. The Franklins would be wanting to talk about family matters, about the woman who had made the office appointment out of the blue for that afternoon. "Bye now."

"Bye, Myra. Thanks for coming." Cicely made no move to accompany Myra to the gate. "Bring Timothy over sometime."

"I will," Myra called back from halfway across the lawn. "If I can ever wean Timothy from the chisel."

At last the bunched shrubbery at the corner of the house shut out the Franklins' family portrait of togetherness. Myra felt the late afternoon heat wearing into the crown of her head and into her back. Then she heard footsteps thudding behind her.

"Where's your car?" Alison stood on the ragged grass strip between sidewalk and the street, detached, willfully or for some other reason, from the family group in the yard.

"I don't have one. Not with me." Myra paused. The street and sidewalk were deserted. With an odd sense of entering into a conspiracy with the child, she bent toward Alison and dropped her voice to a whisper. "Alison," she said, "what do you do to Sweetie Pie when she is *very* bad?"

Alison scuffed her bare heel in the weed-grown grass and looked up at Myra with a strange, almost shy, little smile. "I hit her." She hesitated, waiting for Myra's response.

"Fine," Myra said. "You hit her. What else?"

"I throw her up in the sky," Alison said, her voice taking on a faster rhythm. "I knock her down. I spank her and spank her. I bang her eyes in."

Myra straightened. A dull ache started at the base of her spine, as if a bone, once broken and mended, were throbbing into pain again. "Good," she said, wondering why she felt at such a loss. "Good," she repeated, with little heart. "You keep on doing that."

Myra left Alison standing in the grass and began to walk up the long, sun-dazzled street toward the bus stop. She turned only once, and saw the child, small as a doll in the distance, still watching her. But her own hands hung listless and empty at her sides, like hands of wax, and she did not wave.

The Shadow

Story, January 1959

The winter the war began I happened to fall in the bad graces of the
neighborhood for biting Leroy Kelly on the leg. Even Mrs. Abrams
across the street, who had an only son in technical college and no
children our age, and Mr. Greenbloom, the corner grocer, chose sides:
they were all for the Kellys. By rights, I should have been let off easy
with a clear verdict of self-defense, yet this time, for some reason, the
old Washington Street ideals of fairness and chivalry didn't seem to
count.

In spite of the neighborhood pressure, I couldn't see apologizing
unless Leroy and his sister Maureen apologized too, since they started
the whole thing. My father couldn't see my apologizing at all, and
mother lit into him about this. From my listening post in the hall I
tried to catch the gist of it, but they were having hot words off the
point, all about aggression, and honor, and passive resistance. I waited
a full fifteen minutes before I realized the problem of my apology was
the last thing in their heads. Neither of them brought it up to me

afterwards, so I guessed my father had won, the way he won about church.

Every Sunday, Mother and I set out for the Methodist church, passing the time of day, often as not, with the Kellys or the Sullivans, or both, on their way to eleven o'clock mass at St. Brigid's. Our whole neighborhood flocked to one church or another; if it wasn't church, it was synagogue. But Mother never could persuade my father to come with us. He pottered around at home, in the garden when the weather was fair, in his study when it wasn't, smoking and correcting papers for his German classes. I imagined he had all the religion he needed and didn't require weekly refills the way Mother did.

Give or take, my mother couldn't get enough of preaching. She was always after me to be meek, merciful, and pure in heart: a real peacemaker. Privately, I figured Mother's sermon about "winning" by not fighting back worked only if you were a fast runner. If you were being sat on and pummeled, it served less purpose than a paper halo, as proved by my skirmish with Maureen and Leroy.

The Kellys lived next door to us in a turreted, yellow frame house with a sagging verandah and orange and purple panes in the window on the stair landing. For convenience, my mother classed Maureen as my best friend, although she was over a year younger than I and a grade behind me in school. Leroy, just my age, was a lot more interesting. He had built a whole railroad village in his room on top of a large plywood table, which left barely enough space for his bed and the crystal set he was working on. "Believe It or Not, by Ripley" clippings and drawings of green men with grasshopper antennae and ray guns, cut out of the several science fiction magazines he subscribed to, covered the walls. He had a lead on moon rockets. If Leroy could make a radio with earphones that tuned in on regular programs like "The Shadow" and "Lights Out," he might well be inventing moon rockets by the time he got to college, and I favored moon rockets a lot more than dolls with open-and-shut glass eyes who wah-wahed if you held them upside down.

Maureen Kelly was one for the dolls. Everybody called her cute as a button. Petite, even for a girl of seven, Maureen had soulful brown eyes and natural ringlets that Mrs. Kelly coaxed around her fat, sausage finger every morning with a damp brush. Maureen also had a trick of making her eyes go suddenly teary and guileless, a studied imitation, no doubt, of the picture of St. Theresa of the Child Jesus pinned up over her bed. When she didn't get her way, she simply raised those brown eyes to heaven and yowled. "Sadie Shafer, what are you *doing* to poor Maureen?" Somebody's mother, toweling her hands, flour-whitened, or wet from the dishpan, would appear in a doorway or at a window, and not a hundred straight-talking Girl Scout witnesses from around the block could convince her I wasn't plaguing Maureen above and beyond all human feeling. Just because I was big for my age, I came in for all the scoldings going. I didn't think I deserved it; no more than I deserved the full weight of blame for biting Leroy.

The facts of the fight were clear enough. Mrs. Kelly had gone down to Greenbloom's to get some gelatin for one of those jiggly, plastic salads she was always making, and Maureen and I were sitting by ourselves on the couch in the Kellys' den, cutting out the last of the wardrobe for her Bobbsey Twin paper dolls.

"Let me use the big scissors now." Maureen gave a delicate, put-upon sigh. "I'm tired of mine, they make such little snips."

I didn't look up from the sailor suit I was trimming for the boy Bobbsey. "Oh, you know your mother won't let you use these," I said reasonably. "They're her best sewing scissors, and she said you can't use them until you're bigger."

It was then that Maureen put down her stub-ended Woolworth scissors and started to tickle me. Tickling made me have hysterics, and Maureen knew it.

"Don't be *silly*, Maureen!" I stood up out of reach on the narrow scatter rug in front of the couch. Probably nothing more would have happened if Leroy hadn't come in at that moment.

"Tickle her! Tickle her!" Maureen shouted, bouncing up and down on the couch. Why Leroy responded as he did I found out several days later. Before I could dart past him and through the door, he had whisked the scatter rug from under my feet and was sitting on my stomach while Maureen squatted beside me, tickling, craven pleasure written all over her face. I squirmed; I shrieked. As far as I could see, there was no escape. Leroy had my arms pinioned and Maureen wasn't anywhere in range of my wild kicks. So I did the one thing I was free to do. I twisted my head and sank my teeth in the bare space of skin just above Leroy's left sock, which, I had time to notice, smelled of mice, and held on until he let go of me. He fell to one side, roaring. At that moment Mrs. Kelly walked in the front door.

The Kellys told certain neighbors my bite drew blood, but Leroy confessed to me, after the excitement died down and we were speaking to each other again, that the only sign he had been bitten was a few purplish teeth marks, and these turned yellow and faded in a day or two. Leroy had learned the scatter-rug trick from a Green Hornet comic book he later loaned me, pointing out the place where the Green Hornet, at bay, the spy's gun a few feet from his nose, asks humbly to pick up a cigarette he has just dropped and please, may he enjoy his last smoke on earth. The spy, carried away by his certain triumph and neglecting to notice he is standing at the end of a narrow scatter rug, says, with fatal smugness, "Off corss!" A deep knee bend, a flick of the wrist, and the Green Hornet has the rug out from under the spy, the spy's gun in his hand, and the spy flat on the floor, his word balloon crammed with asterisks and exclamation points. Maybe I'd have done the same thing if I'd had Leroy's chance. If the scatter rug hadn't been under my feet, Leroy would have no doubt scorned Maureen's silly screams and both of us coolly walked out on her. Still, however such breakdown of cause and effect may illumine a sequence of events, it doesn't alter the events.

That Christmas we did not get our annual fruit cake from Mrs. Abrams; the Kellys got theirs. Even after Leroy and Maureen and I had come to terms, Mrs. Kelly didn't start up the Saturday morning coffee hours with my mother which she had broken off the week of our quarrel. I continued to go to Greenbloom's for comics and candy, but there, too, the neighborhood cold front was apparent. "A little something to sharpen the teeth, eh?" Mr. Greenbloom lowered his voice, although there was no one else in the shop. "Brazil nuts, almond rock, something tough?" His sallow, square-jowled face with the purple-pouched black eyes didn't crinkle up in the familiar smile but remained stiff and heavy, a creased, lugubrious mask. I had an impulse to burst out, "It wasn't my fault. What would you have done? What would you have had me do?" as if he had challenged me directly about the Kellys, when, of course, he had done nothing of the sort. Rack on rack of the latest gaudily covered comic books—Superman, Wonder

Woman, Tom Mix and Mickey Mouse—swam in a rainbowed blur before my eyes. I fingered a thin dime, extorted as early allowance, in my jacket pocket, yet I didn't have the heart to choose among them. "I-I think I'll come back later." Why I felt compelled to explain my each move so apologetically I didn't know.

From the first, I thought the issue of my quarrel with the Kellys a pure one, uncomplicated by any flow of emotion from sources outside it—whole and self-contained as those globed, red tomatoes my mother preserved at the end of every summer in airtight Mason jars. Though the neighbors' slights seemed to me wrong, even strangely excessive —since they included my parents as well as myself—I never doubted that justice, sooner or later, would right the balance. Probably my favorite radio programs and comic strips had something to do with my seeing the picture so small, and in such elementary colors.

Not that I wasn't aware of how mean people can be.

"Who knows what evil lurks in the hearts of men?" the nasal, sardonic voice of the Shadow asked rhetorically every Sunday afternoon. "The Shadow knows, heh, heh, heh, heh." Each week Leroy and I studied our lesson: somewhere innocent victims were being turned into rats by a vicious, experimental drug, burned on their bare feet with candles, fed to an indoor pool of piranha fish. Gravely, in Leroy's room or my own, behind shut doors, or in whispers at recess on some patch of the playground, we shared our accumulating evidence of the warped, brutish emotions current in the world beyond Washington Street and the precincts of the Hunnewell School.

"You know what they do with prisoners in Japan," Leroy told me one Saturday morning soon after Pearl Harbor. "They tie them to these stakes on the ground over these bamboo seeds, and when it rains the bamboo shoot grows right up through their back and hits the heart."

"Oh, a little shoot couldn't do that," I objected. "It wouldn't be strong enough."

"You've seen the concrete sidewalk in front of the Sullivans', haven't you—all funny cracks in it, bigger and bigger every day? Just take a look what's pushing up under there." Leroy widened his pale, owl eyes significantly. "Mushrooms! Little, soft-headed mushrooms!"

The sequel to the Shadow's enlightening comment on evil was, of course, his farewell message: "The weed of crime bears *bitter* fruit.

Crime does *not* pay." On his program it never did; at least never for more than twenty-five minutes at a stretch. We had no cause to wonder: *Will* the good people win? Only: *How?*

Still, the radio programs and the comic books were a hard-won concession; I knew Mother would put her foot down once and for all at my seeing a war movie ("It's not good to fill the child's mind with that trash, things are bad enough"). When, without her knowledge, I saw a Japanese prison-camp film by the simple device of going to Betty Sullivan's birthday party, which included treating ten of us to a double feature and ice cream, I had some second thoughts about Mother's wisdom. Night after night, as if my shut eyelids were a private movie screen, I saw the same scene come back, poisonous, sulphur-colored: the starving men in their cells, for days without water, reached, over and over again, through the bars toward the audibly trickling fountain in the center of the prison yard, a fountain at which the slant-eyed guards drank with sadistic frequency and loud slurps.

I didn't dare to call Mother or to tell her of my dream, though this would have relieved me greatly. If she found out about my harassed nights, it would be the end of any movies, comic books, or radio programs that departed from the sugary fables of the Singing Lady, and such a sacrifice I was not prepared to make.

The trouble was, in this dream, my sure sense of eventual justice deserted me: the dream incident had lost its original happy ending—the troops of the good side breaking into the camp, victorious, to the cheers of the movie audience and the near-dead prisoners. If a familiar color—the blue of Winthrop Bay, and the sky over it, or the green of grass, trees—suddenly vanished from the world and left a pitch-black gap in its place, I could not have been more bewildered or appalled. The old, soothing remedy "It's not true, it's only a dream" didn't seem to work anymore, either. The hostile, brooding aura of the nightmare seeped out, somehow, to become a part of my waking landscape.

The peaceful rhythm of classes and play periods at the Hunnewell School was broken often now by the raucous, arbitrary ringing of the air raid alarm. With none of the jostling and whispering we indulged in during fire drills, we would take up our coats and pencils and file down the creaking stairs into the school basement, where we crouched in special corners according to our color tags and put our pencils between our teeth so, the teachers explained, the bombs wouldn't make us bite our tongues. Some of the children in the lower grades always started to cry; it was dark in the cellar, the cold stone bleakly lit by one bare bulb in the ceiling. At home, my parents sat a great deal by the radio, listening, with serious faces, to the staccato briefs of the newscasters. And there were the sudden, unexplained silences when I came within hearing, the habit of gloom, relieved only by a false cheer worse than the gloom itself.

Prepared as I was for the phenomenon of evil in the world, I was not ready to have it expand in this treacherous fashion, like some uncontrollable fungus, beyond the confines of half-hour radio programs, comic book covers, and Saturday afternoon double features, to drag out past all confident predictions of a smashing-quick finish. I had an ingrained sense of the powers of good protecting me: my parents, the police, the FBI, the President, the American Armed Forces, even those symbolic champions of Good from a cloudier hinterland—the Shadow, Superman, and the rest. Not to mention God himself. Surely, with these ranked round me, circle after concentric circle, reaching to infinity, I had nothing to fear. Yet I was afraid. Clearly, in spite of my assiduous study of the world, there was something I had not been told; some piece to the puzzle I did not have in hand.

My speculations about this mystery came into focus that Friday when Maureen Kelly hurried to catch up with me on the way to school. "My mother says it's not your fault for biting Leroy," she called out in clear, saccharine tones. "My mother says it's because your father's German."

I was astounded. "My father is not German!" I retorted when I had my breath back. "He's . . . he's from the Polish Corridor."

The geographical distinction was lost on Maureen. "He's German. My mother says so," she insisted stubbornly. "Besides, he doesn't go to church."

"How could it be my father's fault?" I tried another tack. "My father didn't bite Leroy. I did." This wanton involving of my father in a quarrel Maureen had started in the first place made me furious, and a little scared. At recess I saw Maureen in a huddle with some of the other girls.

"Your father's German," Betty Sullivan whispered to me in art period. I was designing a civil defense badge, a white lightning bolt bisecting a red-and-blue-striped field on the diagonal, and I didn't look up. "How do you know he's not a spy?"

I went home straight after school, determined to have it out with Mother. My father taught German at the city college, right enough, but that didn't make him any less American than Mr. Kelly or Mr. Sullivan or Mr. Greenbloom. He didn't go to church, I had to admit. Still, I could not see how this or his teaching German had the slightest relation to my row with the Kellys. I only saw, confusedly, that by biting Leroy I had, in some obscure, roundabout way, betrayed my father to the neighbors.

I walked slowly in through the front door and out to the kitchen. There was nothing in the cookie jar except two stale gingersnaps left over from the last week's batch. "Ma!" I called, heading for the stairs. "Ma!"

"Here, Sadie." Her voice sounded muffled and echoey, as if she were calling to me from the far end of a long tunnel. Although the winter afternoon light died early on these shortest days, no lamps were lit in the house. I took the steps two at a time.

Mother was sitting in the big bedroom by the graying window. She looked small, almost shrunken, in the great wing chair. Even in that wan light I could tell her eyes were raw-rimmed, moist at the corners.

Mother didn't act the least bit surprised when I told her what Maureen had said. Nor did she try to sweeten things with her usual line about how Maureen didn't know any better, being so little, and how I ought to be the generous one, forgive and forget.

"Daddy *isn't* German, the way Maureen said," I asked, to make sure, "is he?"

"In one way," my mother took me by surprise, "he is. He is a German citizen. But, in another way, you are right—he isn't German the way Maureen said."

"He wouldn't hurt anybody!" I burst out. "He'd fight for us, if he had to!"

"Of course he would. You and I know that." Mother did not smile. "And the neighbors know it. In wartime, though, people often become frightened and forget what they know. I even think your father may have to go away from us for a while because of this."

"To be drafted? Like Mrs. Abrams' boy?"

"No, not like that," Mother said slowly. "There are places out West for German citizens to live in during the war so people will feel safer about them. Your father has been asked to go to one of those."

"But that's not fair!" How Mother could sit there and coolly tell me my father was going to be treated like some German spy made my flesh creep. "It's a mistake!" I thought of Maureen Kelly, Betty Sullivan, and the kids at school: what would they say to this? I thought, in rapid succession, of the police, the FBI, the President, the United States Armed Forces. I thought of God. "God won't let it happen!" I cried, inspired.

Mother gave me a measured look. Then she took me by the shoulders and began to talk very fast, as if there were something vital she had to get settled with me before my father came home. "Your father's going away *is* a mistake, it *is* unfair. You must never forget that, no matter what Maureen or anybody says. At the same time, there is nothing we can do about it. It's government orders, and there is nothing we can do about them . . ."

"But you said God . . ." I protested feebly.

Mother overrode me. "God will let it happen."

I understood, then, that she was trying to give me the piece to the puzzle I had not possessed. The shadow in my mind lengthened with the night blotting out our half of the world, and beyond it; the whole globe seemed sunk in darkness. For the first time the facts were not slanted Mother's way, and she was letting me see it.

"I don't think there is any God, then," I said dully, with no feeling of blasphemy. "Not if such things can happen."

"Some people think that," my mother said quietly.

Johnny Panic and
the Bible of Dreams

Story, December 1958

Every day from nine to five I sit at my desk facing the door of the office and type up other people's dreams. Not just dreams. That wouldn't be practical enough for my bosses. I type up also people's daytime complaints: trouble with mother, trouble with father, trouble with the bottle, the bed, the headache that bangs home and blacks out the sweet world for no known reason. Nobody comes to our office unless they have troubles. Troubles that can't be pinpointed by Wassermanns or Wechsler-Bellevues alone.

Maybe a mouse gets to thinking pretty early on how the whole world is run by these enormous feet. Well, from where I sit, I figure the world is run by one thing and this one thing only. Panic with a dog-face, devil-face, hag-face, whore-face, panic in capital letters with no face at all—it's the same Johnny Panic, awake or asleep.

When people ask me where I work, I tell them I'm Assistant to the Secretary in one of the Out-Patient Departments of the Clinics Building of the City Hospital. This sounds so be-all end-all they seldom get around to asking me more than what I do, and what I do is mainly type up records. On my own hook though, and completely under cover, I am pursuing a vocation that would set these doctors on their ears. In the privacy of my one-room apartment I call myself secretary to none other than Johnny Panic himself.

Dream by dream I am educating myself to become that rare character, rarer, in truth, than any member of the Psychoanalytic Institute, a dream connoisseur. Not a dream stopper, a dream explainer, an exploiter of dreams for the crass practical ends of health and happiness, but an unsordid collector of dreams for themselves alone. A lover of dreams for Johnny Panic's sake, the Maker of them all.

There isn't a dream I've typed up in our record books that I don't know by heart. There isn't a dream I haven't copied out at home into Johnny Panic's Bible of Dreams.

This is my real calling.

Some nights I take the elevator up to the roof of my apartment building. Some nights, about three A.M. Over the trees at the far side of the park the United Fund torch flare flattens and recovers under some witchy invisible push and here and there in the hunks of stone and brick I see a light. Most of all, though, I feel the city sleeping. Sleeping from the river on the west to the ocean on the east, like some rootless island rockabying itself on nothing at all.

I can be tight and nervy as the top string on a violin, and yet by the time the sky begins to blue I'm ready for sleep. It's the thought of all those dreamers and what they're dreaming wears me down till I sleep the sleep of fever. Monday to Friday what do I do but type up those same dreams. Sure, I don't touch a fraction of them the city over, but page by page, dream by dream, my Intake books fatten and weigh down the bookshelves of the cabinet in the narrow passage running parallel to the main hall, off which passage the doors to all the doctors' little interviewing cubicles open.

I've got a funny habit of identifying the people who come in by their dreams. As far as I'm concerned, the dreams single them out more than any Christian name. This one guy, for example, who works for a ball-bearing company in town, dreams every night how he's lying on his back with a grain of sand on his chest. Bit by bit this grain of sand grows bigger and bigger till it's big as a fair-sized house and he can't draw breath. Another fellow I know of has had a certain dream ever since they gave him ether and cut out his tonsils and adenoids when he was a kid. In this dream he's caught in the rollers of a cotton mill, fighting for his life. Oh, he's not alone, although he thinks he is. A lot of people these days dream they're being run over or eaten by machines. They're the cagey ones who won't go on the subway or the elevators. Coming back from my lunch hour in the hospital cafeteria I often pass them, puffing up the unswept stone stairs to our office on the fourth floor. I wonder, now and then, what dreams people had before ball bearings and cotton mills were invented.

I've a dream of my own. My one dream. A dream of dreams.

In this dream there's a great half-transparent lake stretching away in every direction, too big for me to see the shores of it, if there are any shores, and I'm hanging over it, looking down from the glass belly of some helicopter. At the bottom of the lake—so deep I can only guess at the dark masses moving and heaving—are the real dragons. The ones that were around before men started living in caves and cooking meat over fires and figuring out the wheel and the alphabet. Enormous isn't the word for them; they've got more wrinkles than Johnny Panic himself. Dream about these long enough and your feet and hands shrivel away when you look at them too closely. The sun shrinks to the size of an orange, only chillier, and you've been living in Roxbury since the last ice age. No place for you but a room padded soft as the first room you knew of, where you can dream and float, float and dream, till at last you actually are back among those great originals and there's no point in any dreams at all.

It's into this lake people's minds run at night, brooks and gutter trickles to one borderless common reservoir. It bears no resemblance to those pure sparkling-blue sources of drinking water the suburbs guard more jealously than the Hope diamond in the middle of pine woods and barbed fences.

It's the sewage farm of the ages, transparence aside.

Now the water in this lake naturally stinks and smokes from what dreams have been left sogging around in it over the centuries. When you think how much room one night of dream props would take up for one person in one city, and that city a mere pinprick on a map of the world, and when you start multiplying this space by the population of the world, and that space by the number of nights there have been since the apes took to chipping axes out of stone and losing their hair, you have some idea what I mean. I'm not the mathematical type: my head starts splitting when I get only as far as the number of dreams going on during one night in the State of Massachusetts.

By this time, I already see the surface of the lake swarming with snakes, dead bodies puffed as blowfish, human embryos bobbing around in laboratory bottles like so many unfinished messages from the great I Am. I see whole storehouses of hardware: knives, paper cutters, pistons and cogs and nutcrackers; the shiny fronts of cars looming up, glass-eyed and evil-toothed. Then there's the spider-man and the webfooted man from Mars, and the simple, lugubrious vision of a human face turning aside forever, in spite of rings and vows, to the last lover of all.

One of the most frequent shapes in this backwash is so commonplace it seems silly to mention it. It's a grain of dirt. The water is thick with these grains. They seep in among everything else and revolve under some queer power of their own, opaque, ubiquitous. Call the water what you will, Lake Nightmare, Bog of Madness, it's here the sleeping people lie and toss together among the props of their worst dreams, one great brotherhood, though each of them, waking, thinks himself singular, utterly apart.

This is my dream. You won't find it written up in any casebook. Now the routine in our office is very different from the routine in Skin Clinic, for example, or in Tumor. The other clinics have strong similarities to each other; none are like ours. In our clinic, treatment doesn't get prescribed. It is invisible. It goes right on in those little cubicles, each with its desk, its two chairs, its window and its door with the opaque glass rectangle set in the wood. There is a certain spiritual purity about this kind of doctoring. I can't help feeling the special privilege of my position as Assistant Secretary in the Adult Psychiatric Clinic. My sense of pride is borne out by the rude invasions of other clinics into our cubicles on certain days of the week for lack of space elsewhere: our building is a very old one, and the facilities have not expanded with the expanding needs of the time. On these days of overlap the contrast between us and the other clinics is marked.

On Tuesdays and Thursdays, for instance, we have lumbar punctures in one of our offices in the morning. If the practical nurse chances to leave the door of the cubicle open, as she usually does, I can glimpse the end of the white cot and the dirty yellow-soled bare feet of the patient sticking out from under the sheet. In spite of my distaste at this sight, I can't keep my eyes away from the bare feet, and I find myself glancing back from my typing every few minutes to see if they are still there, if they have changed their position at all. You can understand what a distraction this is in the middle of my work. I often have to reread what I have typed several times, under the pretense of careful proofreading, in order to memorize the dreams I have copied down from the doctor's voice over the audiograph.

Nerve Clinic next door, which tends to the grosser, more unimaginative end of our business, also disturbs us in the mornings. We use their offices for therapy in the afternoon, as they are only a morning clinic, but to have their people crying, or singing, or chattering loudly in Italian or Chinese, as they often do, without break for four hours at a stretch every morning, is distracting to say the least.

In spite of such interruptions by other clinics, my own work is advancing at a great rate. By now I am far beyond copying only what comes after the patient's saying: "I have this dream, Doctor." I am at the point of re-creating dreams that are not even written down at all. Dreams that shadow themselves forth in the vaguest way, but are themselves hid, like a statue under red velvet before the grand unveiling.

To illustrate. This woman came in with her tongue swollen and stuck out so far she had to leave a party she was giving for twenty friends of her French-Canadian mother-in-law and be rushed to our Emergency Ward. She thought she didn't want her tongue to stick out and, to tell the truth, it was an exceedingly embarrassing affair for her, but she hated that French-Canadian mother-in-law worse than pigs, and her tongue was true to her opinion, even if the rest of her wasn't. Now she didn't lay claim to any dreams. I have only the bare facts above to begin with, yet behind them I detect the bulge and promise of a dream.

So I set myself to uprooting this dream from its comfortable purchase under her tongue.

Whatever the dream I unearth, by work, taxing work, and even by a kind of prayer, I am sure to find a thumbprint in the corner, a malicious detail to the right of center, a bodiless midair Cheshire cat grin, which shows the whole work to be gotten up by the genius of

Johnny Panic, and him alone. He's sly, he's subtle, he's sudden as thunder, but he gives himself away only too often. He simply can't resist melodrama. Melodrama of the oldest, most obvious variety.

I remember one guy, a stocky fellow in a nail-studded black leather jacket, running straight in to us from a boxing match at Mechanics Hall, Johnny Panic hot at his heels. This guy, good Catholic though he was, young and upright and all, had one mean fear of death. He was actually scared blue he'd go to hell. He was a pieceworker at a fluorescent light plant. I remember this detail because I thought it funny he should work there, him being so afraid of the dark as it turned out. Johnny Panic injects a poetic element in this business you don't often find elsewhere. And for that he has my eternal gratitude.

I also remember quite clearly the scenario of the dream I had worked out for this guy: a gothic interior in some monastery cellar, going on and on as far as you could see, one of those endless perspectives between two mirrors, and the pillars and walls were made of nothing but human skulls and bones, and in every niche there was a body laid out, and it was the Hall of Time, with the bodies in the foreground still warm, discoloring and starting to rot in the middle distance, and the bones emerging, clean as a whistle, in a kind of white futuristic glow at the end of the line. As I recall, I had the whole scene lighted, for the sake of accuracy, not with candles, but with the ice-bright fluorescence that makes skin look green and all the pink and red flushes dead black-purple.

You ask, how do I know this was the dream of the guy in the black leather jacket. I don't know. I only believe this was his dream, and I work at belief with more energy and tears and entreaties than I work at re-creating the dream itself.

My office, of course, has its limitations. The lady with her tongue stuck out, the guy from Mechanics Hall—these are our wildest ones. The people who have really gone floating down toward the bottom of that boggy lake come in only once, and are then referred to a place more permanent than our office which receives the public from nine to five, five days a week only. Even those people who are barely able to walk about the streets and keep working, who aren't yet halfway down in the lake, get sent to the Out-Patient Department at another hospital specializing in severer cases. Or they may stay a month or so in our own Observation Ward in the central hospital which I've never seen.

I've seen the secretary of that ward, though. Something about her merely smoking and drinking her coffee in the cafeteria at the ten o'clock break put me off so I never went to sit next to her again. She has a funny name I don't ever quite remember correctly, something really odd, like Miss Milleravage. One of those names that seem more like a pun mixing up Milltown and Ravage than anything in the city phone directory. But not so odd a name, after all, if you've ever read through the phone directory, with its Hyman Diddlebockers and Sasparilla Greenleafs. I read through the phone book once, never mind when, and it satisfied a deep need in me to realize how many people aren't called Smith.

Anyhow, this Miss Milleravage is a large woman, not fat, but all sturdy muscle and tall on top of it. She wears a gray suit over her hard bulk that reminds me vaguely of some kind of uniform, without the details of cut having anything strikingly military about them. Her face, hefty as a bullock's, is covered with a remarkable number of tiny maculae, as if she'd been lying under water for some time and little algae had latched on to her skin, smutching it over with tobacco-browns and greens. These moles are noticeable mainly because the skin around them is so pallid. I sometimes wonder if Miss Milleravage has ever seen the wholesome light of day. I wouldn't be a bit surprised if she'd been brought up from the cradle with the sole benefit of artificial lighting.

Byrna, the secretary in Alcoholic Clinic just across the hall from us, introduced me to Miss Milleravage with the gambit that I'd "been in England too."

Miss Milleravage, it turned out, had spent the best years of her life in London hospitals.

"Had a friend," she boomed in her queer, doggish basso, not favoring me with a direct look, "a nurse at Bart's. Tried to get in touch with her after the war, but the head of the nurses had changed, everybody'd changed, nobody'd heard of her. She must've gone down with the old head nurse, rubbish and all, in the bombings." She followed this with a large grin.

Now I've seen medical students cutting up cadavers, four stiffs to a classroom, about as recognizably human as Moby Dick, and the students playing catch with the dead men's livers. I've heard guys joke about sewing a woman up wrong after a delivery at the charity ward of the Lying-In. But I wouldn't want to see what Miss Milleravage would write off as the biggest laugh of all time. No thanks and then some. You could scratch her eyes with a pin and swear you'd struck solid quartz.

My boss has a sense of humor too, only it's gentle. Generous as Santa on Christmas Eve.

I work for a middle-aged lady named Miss Taylor who is the Head Secretary of the clinic and has been since the clinic started thirty-three years ago—the year of my birth, oddly enough. Miss Taylor knows every doctor, every patient, every outmoded appointment slip, referral slip and billing procedure the hospital has ever used or thought of using. She plans to stick with the clinic until she's farmed out in the green pastures of Social Security checks. A woman more dedicated to her work I never saw. She's the same way about statistics as I am about dreams: if the building caught fire she would throw every last one of those books of statistics to the firemen below at the serious risk of her own skin.

I get along extremely well with Miss Taylor. The one thing I never let her catch me doing is reading the old record books. I have actually very little time for this. Our office is busier than the stock exchange with the staff of twenty-five doctors in and out, medical students in training, patients, patients' relatives, and visiting officials from other clinics referring patients to us, so even when I'm covering the office alone, during Miss Taylor's coffee break and lunch hour, I seldom get to dash down more than a note or two.

This kind of catch-as-catch-can is nerve-racking, to say the least. A lot of the best dreamers are in the old books, the dreamers that come in to us only once or twice for evaluation before they're sent elsewhere. For copying out these dreams I need time, a lot of time. My circumstances are hardly ideal for the unhurried pursuit of my art. There is, of course, a certain derring-do in working under such hazards, but I long for the rich leisure of the true connoisseur who indulges his nostrils above the brandy snifter for an hour before his tongue reaches out for the first taste.

I find myself all too often lately imagining what a relief it would be to bring a briefcase into work, big enough to hold one of those thick, blue, cloth-bound record books full of dreams. At Miss Taylor's lunch time, in the lull before the doctors and students crowd in to take their afternoon patients, I could simply slip one of the books, dated ten or fifteen years back, into my briefcase, and leave the briefcase under my desk till five o'clock struck. Of course, odd-looking bundles are in-spected by the doorman of the Clinics Building and the hospital has its own staff of police to check up on the multiple varieties of thievery that go on, but for heaven's sake, I'm not thinking of making off with typewriters or heroin. I'd only borrow the book overnight and slip it back on the shelf first thing the next day before anybody else came in. Still, being caught taking a book out of the hospital would probably mean losing my job and all my source material with it.

This idea of mulling over a record book in the privacy and comfort of my own apartment, even if I have to stay up night after night for this purpose, attracts me so much I become more and more impatient with my usual method of snatching minutes to look up dreams in Miss Taylor's half-hours out of the office.

The trouble is, I can never tell exactly when Miss Taylor will come back to the office. She is so conscientious about her job she'd be likely to cut her half hour at lunch short and her twenty minutes at coffee shorter, if it weren't for her lame left leg. The distinct sound of this lame leg in the corridor warns me of her approach in time for me to whip the record book I'm reading into my drawer out of sight and pretend to be putting down the final flourishes on a phone message or some such alibi. The only catch, as far as my nerves are concerned, is that Amputee Clinic is around the corner from us in the opposite direction from Nerve Clinic and I've gotten really jumpy due to a lot of false alarms where I've mistaken some pegleg's hitching step for the step of Miss Taylor herself returning early to the office.

On the blackest days, when I've scarcely time to squeeze one dream out of the old books and my copywork is nothing but weepy college sophomores who can't get a lead in *Camino Real*, I feel Johnny Panic turn his back, stony as Everest, higher than Orion, and the motto of the great Bible of Dreams, "Perfect fear casteth out all else," is ash and lemon water on my lips. I'm a wormy hermit in a country of prize pigs so corn-happy they can't see the slaughterhouse at the end of the track. I'm Jeremiah vision-bitten in the Land of Cockaigne.

What's worse: day by day I see these psyche-doctors studying to win Johnny Panic's converts from him by hook, crook, and talk, talk, talk. Those deep-eyed, bush-bearded dream collectors who preceded me in history, and their contemporary inheritors with their white jackets and knotty-pine-paneled offices and leather couches, practiced and still practice their dream-gathering for worldly ends: health and money, money and health. To be a true member of Johnny Panic's congregation one must forget the dreamer and remember the dream: the dreamer is merely a flimsy vehicle for the great Dream Maker himself. This they will not do. Johnny Panic is gold in the bowels, and they try to root him out by spiritual stomach pumps.

Take what happened to Harry Bilbo. Mr. Bilbo came into our office with the hand of Johnny Panic heavy as a lead coffin on his shoulder. He had an interesting notion about the filth in this world. I figured him for a prominent part in Johnny Panic's Bible of Dreams, Third Book of Fear, Chapter Nine on Dirt, Disease and General Decay. A friend of Harry's blew a trumpet in the Boy Scout band when they were kids. Harry Bilbo'd also blown on this friend's trumpet. Years later the friend got cancer and died. Then, one day not so long ago, a cancer doctor came into Harry's house, sat down in a chair, passed the top of the morning with Harry's mother and, on leaving, shook her hand and opened the door for himself. Suddenly Harry Bilbo wouldn't blow trumpets or sit down on chairs or shake hands if all the cardinals of Rome took to blessing him twenty-four hours around the clock for fear of catching cancer. His mother had to go turning the TV knobs and water faucets on and off and opening doors for him. Pretty soon Harry stopped going to work because of the spit and dog turds in the street. First that stuff gets on your shoes and then when you take your shoes off it gets on your hands and then at dinner it's a quick trip into your mouth and not a hundred Hail Marys can keep you from the chain reaction.

The last straw was, Harry quit weight lifting at the public gym when he saw this cripple exercising with the dumbbells. You can never tell what germs cripples carry behind their ears and under their fingernails. Day and night Harry Bilbo lived in holy worship of Johnny Panic, devout as any priest among censers and sacraments. He had a beauty all his own.

Well, these white-coated tinkerers managed, the lot of them, to talk Harry into turning on the TV himself, and the water faucets, and to opening closet doors, front doors, bar doors. Before they were through with him, he was sitting down on movie-house chairs, and benches all over the Public Garden, and weight lifting every day of the week at the gym in spite of the fact another cripple took to using the rowing machine. At the end of his treatment he came in to shake hands with the Clinic Director. In Harry Bilbo's own words, he was "a changed man." The pure Panic-light had left his face. He went out of the office doomed to the crass fate these doctors call health and happiness.

About the time of Harry Bilbo's cure a new idea starts nudging at the bottom of my brain. I find it hard to ignore as those bare feet sticking out of the lumbar puncture room. If I don't want to risk carrying a record book out of the hospital in case I get discovered and fired and have to end my research forever, I can really speed up work by staying in the Clinics Building overnight. I am nowhere near exhausting the clinic's resources and the piddling amount of cases I am able to read in Miss Taylor's brief absences during the day are nothing to what I could get through in a few nights of steady copying. I need to accelerate my work if only to counteract those doctors.

Before I know it, I am putting on my coat at five and saying good-night to Miss Taylor, who usually stays a few minutes' overtime to clear up the day's statistics, and sneaking around the corner into the ladies' room. It is empty. I slip into the patients' john, lock the door from the inside, and wait. For all I know, one of the clinic cleaning ladies may try to knock the door down, thinking some patient's passed out on the seat. My fingers are crossed. About twenty minutes later the door of the lavatory opens and someone limps over the threshold like a chicken favoring a bad leg. It is Miss Taylor, I can tell by the resigned sigh as she meets the jaundiced eye of the lavatory mirror. I hear the click-cluck of various touch-up equipment on the bowl, water sloshing, the scritch of a comb in frizzed hair, and then the door is closing with a slow-hinged wheeze behind her.

I am lucky. When I come out of the ladies' room at six o'clock the corridor lights are off and the fourth-floor hall is as empty as church on Monday. I have my own key to our office; I come in first every morning, so that's no trouble. The typewriters are folded back into the desks, the locks are on the dial phones, all's right with the world.

Outside the window the last of the winter light is fading. Yet I do not forget myself and turn on the overhead bulb. I don't want to be spotted by any hawk-eyed doctor or janitor in the hospital buildings across the little courtyard. The cabinet with the record books is in the windowless passage opening onto the doctors' cubicles, which have windows overlooking the courtyard. I make sure the doors to all the cubicles are shut. Then I switch on the passage light, a sallow twenty-five-watt affair blackening at the top. Better than an altarful of candles to me at this point, though. I didn't think to bring a sandwich. There is an apple in my desk drawer left over from lunch, so I reserve that for whatever pangs I may feel about one o'clock in the morning, and get out my pocket notebook. At home every evening it is my habit to tear out the notebook pages I've written on at the office during the day and pile them up to be copied in my manuscript. In this way I cover my tracks so no one idly picking up my notebook at the office could ever guess the type or scope of my work.

I begin systematically by opening the oldest book on the bottom shelf. The once-blue cover is no-color now, the pages are thumbed and blurry carbons, but I'm humming from foot to topknot: this dream book was spanking new the day I was born. When I really get organized I'll have hot soup in a thermos for the dead-of-winter nights, turkey pies and chocolate éclairs. I'll bring hair curlers and four changes of blouse to work in my biggest handbag on Monday mornings so no one will notice me going downhill in looks and start suspecting unhappy love affairs or pink affiliations or my working on dream books in the clinic four nights a week.

Eleven hours later. I am down to apple core and seeds and in the month of May, 1931, with a private nurse who has just opened a laundry bag in her patient's closet and found five severed heads in it, including her mother's.

A chill air touches the nape of my neck. From where I am sitting cross-legged on the floor in front of the cabinet, the record book heavy on my lap, I notice out of the corner of my eye that the door of the cubicle beside me is letting in a little crack of blue light. Not only along the floor, but up the side of the door too. This is odd since I made sure from the first that all the doors were shut tight. The crack of blue light is widening and my eyes are fastened to two motionless shoes in the doorway, toes pointing toward me.

They are brown leather shoes of a foreign make, with thick elevator soles. Above the shoes are black silk socks through which shows a pallor of flesh. I get as far as the gray pinstriped trouser cuffs.

"Tch, tch," chides an infinitely gentle voice from the cloudy regions above my head. "Such an uncomfortable position! Your legs must be asleep by now. Let me help you up. The sun will be rising shortly."

Two hands slip under my arms from behind and I am raised, wobbly as an unset custard, to my feet, which I cannot feel because my legs are, in fact, asleep. The record book slumps to the floor, pages splayed.

"Stand still a minute." The Clinic Director's voice fans the lobe of my right ear. "Then the circulation will revive."

The blood in my not-there legs starts pinging under a million sewing-machine needles and a vision of the Clinic Director acid-etches itself on my brain. I don't even need to look around: fat pot-belly buttoned into his gray pinstriped waistcoat, woodchuck teeth yellow and buck, every-color eyes behind the thick-lensed glasses quick as minnows.

I clutch my notebook. The last floating timber of the *Titanic*.

What does he know, what does he know?

Everything.

"I know where there is a nice hot bowl of chicken noodle soup." His voice rustles, dust under the bed, mice in straw. His hand welds onto my left upper arm in fatherly love. The record book of all the dreams going on in the city of my birth at my first yawp in this world's air he nudges under the bookcase with a polished toe.

We meet nobody in the dawn-dark hall. Nobody on the chill stone stair down to the basement corridors where Billy the Record Room Boy cracked his head skipping steps one night on a rush errand.

I begin to double-quickstep so he won't think it's me he's hustling. "You can't fire me," I say calmly. "I quit."

The Clinic Director's laugh wheezes up from his accordion-pleated bottom gut. "We mustn't lose you so soon." His whisper snakes off down the whitewashed basement passages, echoing among the elbow pipes, the wheelchairs and stretchers beached for the night along the steam-stained walls. "Why, we need you more than you know."

We wind and double and my legs keep time with his until we come, somewhere in those barren rat tunnels, to an all-night elevator run by a one-armed Negro. We get on, and the door grinds shut like the door on a cattle car, and we go up and up. It is a freight elevator, crude and clanky, a far cry from the plush passenger lifts I am used to in the Clinics Building.

We get off at an indeterminate floor. The Clinic Director leads me down a bare corridor lit at intervals by socketed bulbs in little wire cages on the ceiling. Locked doors set with screened windows line the hall on either hand. I plan to part company with the Clinic Director at the first red Exit sign, but on our journey there are none. I am in alien territory, coat on the hanger in the office, handbag and money in my top desk drawer, notebook in my hand, and only Johnny Panic to warm me against the ice age outside.

Ahead a light gathers, brightens. The Clinic Director, puffing slightly at the walk, brisk and long, to which he is obviously unaccustomed, propels me around a bend and into a square, brilliantly lit room.

"Here she is."

"The little witch!"

Miss Milleravage hoists her tonnage up from behind the steel desk facing the door.

The walls and the ceiling of the room are riveted metal battleship plates. There are no windows.

From small, barred cells lining the sides and back of the room I see Johnny Panic's top priests staring out at me, arms swaddled behind their backs in the white Ward nightshirts, eyes redder than coals and hungry-hot.

They welcome me with queer croaks and grunts, as if their tongues were locked in their jaws. They have no doubt heard of my work by way of Johnny Panic's grapevine and want to know how his apostles thrive in the world.

I lift my hands to reassure them, holding up my notebook, my voice loud as Johnny Panic's organ with all stops out.

"Peace! I bring to you . . ."

The Book.

"None of that old stuff, sweetie." Miss Milleravage is dancing out at me from behind her desk like a trick elephant.

The Clinic Director closes the door to the room.

The minute Miss Milleravage moves I notice what her hulk has been hiding from view behind the desk—a white cot high as a man's waist with a single sheet stretched over the mattress, spotless and drumskin tight. At the head of the cot is a table on which sits a metal box covered with dials and gauges.

The box seems to be eyeing me, copperhead-ugly, from its coil of electric wires, the latest model in Johnny-Panic-Killers.

I get ready to dodge to one side. When Miss Milleravage grabs, her fat hand comes away with a fist full of nothing. She starts for me again, her smile heavy as dogdays in August.

"None of that. None of that. I'll have that little black book."

Fast as I run around the high white cot, Miss Milleravage is so fast you'd think she wore rollerskates. She grabs and gets. Against her great bulk I beat my fists, and against her whopping milkless breasts, until her hands on my wrists are iron hoops and her breath hushabyes me with a love-stink fouler than Undertaker's Basement.

"My baby, my own baby's come back to me . . . ."

"She," says the Clinic Director, sad and stern, "has been making time with Johnny Panic again."

"Naughty naughty."

The white cot is ready. With a terrible gentleness Miss Milleravage takes the watch from my wrist, the rings from my fingers, the hairpins from my hair. She begins to undress me. When I am bare, I am anointed on the temples and robed in sheets virginal as the first snow.

Then, from the four corners of the room and from the door behind me come five false priests in white surgical gowns and masks whose one lifework is to unseat Johnny Panic from his own throne. They extend me full-length on my back on the cot. The crown of wire is placed on my head, the wafer of forgetfulness on my tongue. The masked priests move to their posts and take hold: one of my left leg, one of my right, one of my right arm, one of my left. One behind my head at the metal box where I can't see.

From their cramped niches along the wall, the votaries raise their voices in protest. They begin the devotional chant:

> The only thing to love is Fear itself.
> Love of Fear is the beginning of wisdom.
> The only thing to love is Fear itself.
> May Fear and Fear and Fear be everywhere.

There is no time for Miss Milleravage or the Clinic Director or the priests to muzzle them.

The signal is given.

The machine betrays them.

At the moment when I think I am most lost the face of Johnny Panic appears in a nimbus of arc lights on the ceiling overhead. I am shaken like a leaf in the teeth of glory. His beard is lightning. Lightning is in his eye. His Word charges and illumines the universe.

The air crackles with his blue-tongued lightning-haloed angels.

His love is the twenty-story leap, the rope at the throat, the knife at the heart.

He forgets not his own.

Above the Oxbow

Story, 1958

On all the mountain that hot August day Luke Jenness hadn't seen a thing moving. Traffic was slack on Mondays. The rickety remains of the old mountaintop hotel, half of it blown away in the '38 hurricane, seemed oddly quiet after the lines of tourist cars grinding up the steep hairpin curves in first gear all that weekend, with the children piling out in the parking lot and running around and around the four-way veranda, buying root beer and popsicles and fiddling with the telescope on the north side. The telescope opened its magnifying eye on the Oxbow, the green flats of Hadley farms across the river, and the range of hills to the north, toward Sugarloaf. You could see up to New Hampshire and Vermont, even, on clear days. But today heat hazed the view, sweat didn't dry.

Luke leaned, arms folded, on the white-painted railing, looking down at the river. The raised scar running diagonally from his right eyebrow across his nose and deep into his left cheek showed white against his tan. Pale, almost dirty, the scar tissue had a different texture from the rest of his skin; it was smoother, newer, like plastic calking a crack. At his feet, extending down to the halfway house below him, the gray, splintered timbers of the funicular railway lay bleaching in the sun in a fenced-off danger area, the warped flight of steps still intact, but ready to collapse any day now. Abraham Lincoln had stood where Luke was standing, and Jenny Lind, the famous singer. She'd called the view of the valley a view of Paradise. Visitors wanted to know things like that. What date did the hotel go up? What date did it blow down? How high was the mountain compared to Mount Tom, say, or Monadnock? Luke knew the facts: it was part of his job. Some people wanted to talk. Others paid him the fifty-cent parking fee, or the dollar on Sundays, like a tip, so he'd disappear and they could watch the view by themselves. Other people didn't seem to see him at all after they paid him; you'd think he was some kind of tree, just standing there.

Down in the clearing at the halfway house now, Luke saw two figures moving. A dark-haired boy in khaki pants and a girl in a blue jersey and white shorts were walking up the blacktop road, very slowly. From where he stood they seemed smaller than his thumb. Probably they'd parked their car somewhere a little below, in the brush at the side of the road, and walked up from there. He hadn't had a hiker for three weeks or more. People drove up, got out and looked at the view a few minutes, maybe bought a cold soda—the tap water was warm and full of air bubbles, hardly spouting high enough out of the chipped chrome fountain bowl for you to get a good gulp of it. Then they drove down. Sometimes they brought picnics for their noon meal and ate at the brown wooden tables in among the trees. Nobody walked up much anymore. It would be a good half hour before the kids got to the top. They'd just strolled out of sight to the right and would be coming up the road around the south side of the mountain. Luke sat down in a frayed wicker rocking chair and propped his feet on the veranda railing.

When he heard voices coming up the ramp onto the rocky ledge below the hotel veranda he got up and leaned on the railing again. Far down there, the speedboats were making small V-shaped wakes of white foam on the dull gray surface of the river. A queer river, for all its broad, smooth back—full of rock reefs, just under the water, and sand bars. The kids weren't coming up on the veranda. Not yet, anyway. They had spread out a khaki raincoat on the orange shale ledge just beneath Luke, and they were resting.

"I feel better," he heard the girl say. "Much better now. We'll do this every day. We'll bring up books, and a picnic."

"Maybe it'll help," the boy said. "Help you forget that place."

"It might," the girl said. "It just might."

They were quiet for a moment.

"Not a wind moving." The boy pointed down at some black birds flying over the treetops. "Look at the swifts."

Luke felt the girl glance up at him then. He shifted, and stared straight ahead, not wanting to seem an eavesdropper. If they didn't come up to the veranda the way everybody did, if they started back down, he'd have to call after them and collect the parking fee. Maybe they'd come up to the veranda and want a drink.

The voices stopped. The boy was getting up. He helped the girl to her feet, bent, picked up the raincoat, and folded it over his arm. They started to climb the veranda steps. At the top, they paused by the railing, not far from Luke.

"You sure you're all right?"

"Yes." The girl tossed her lank, shoulder-length brown hair almost impatiently. "Yes, I'm all right. Of course I'm all right." There was a little pause. "How high is it here?" she asked then, raising her voice as if she meant Luke to answer, not the boy.

Luke glanced in her direction and saw she was, in fact, looking at him and waiting. "About eight thousand feet," he said.

"What can you see from this side?"

"Three states, if the weather's clear."

They said nothing about paying him. "Is there any water?" the boy asked. The kid hadn't shaved for a day, and the stubble made a green shadow on his square chin.

Luke jutted a thumb back over his shoulder. "In there. There's cold soda, root beer, too," he added. "If you want it."

"No," the boy said. "Water's fine."

The boards sounded hollow under their feet, creaking and echoing as they went inside to the water fountain. He'd have to get the money from them sooner or later. The sign inside said people without cars paid fifteen cents each. It was a new state regulation; they hadn't charged for hikers before this year. Maybe the kids would try to get out of paying the fifty-cent parking fee when they noticed that sign and see if they could get away with the thirty cents.

"You both walk all the way up?" Luke asked when they came out again, keeping his voice casual. The girl wiped the water drops from her chin with the back of her hand, leaving a small, triangular smear of dirt. She didn't seem to be wearing any makeup, and her skin had a queer, indoor pallor. Little beads of sweat stood out on her forehead and upper lip.

"Sure we walked," she said. "It's a tough walk, too. A lot of work."

The boy didn't say anything. He had draped the raincoat over the railing and was looking through the telescope.

"Where'd you leave your car?"

"Oh, down there." The girl waved vaguely toward the foot of the mountain where the State Park road started, sloping gradually up past a hay field and a chicken farm before beginning the steep climb. "At the bottom. Right inside the gate."

"You'll have to pay for that," Luke said.

The girl looked at him. "But we walked up." She seemed to be confused about what he meant. "We walked up the whole way."

Luke tried again. "Didn't you see the sign down there?"

"At the gate? Sure we saw. It says fifty cents for parking up here. But we left the car and walked up."

"You'll have to pay anyway," Luke said. He'd have to get them to put that new bit about the fifteen cents on the old gate sign down there, too, to make things plain. "Even if you parked just inside the gate."

The boy came away from the telescope. "Well, where *can* you park the car free?" He seemed a lot easier-going than the girl. "And just walk up?"

The girl bit her lip. With a sudden, quick jerk of her head, she looked away from Luke and the boy, out over the green treetops that sloped down toward the river.

"Nowhere." Luke kept to his point. He couldn't see the girl's face. What some people wouldn't do to save twenty cents: leave their cars hidden in the brush and walk up a little way. "Nowhere in park bounds."

"What about *walk*ing, though?" The girl's voice rose in an odd way as she turned to him. "What if we just *walked* up with no car anywhere at all?"

"Look, lady," Luke said in a reasonable, even tone, "you yourself just now told me you parked your car inside the gate, and that sign in the lookout there says fifty cents for parking, regardless, and a dollar on Sundays . . ."

"But I don't *mean* parking. I mean if we *walked.*"

Luke sighed. "Walkers pay too, lady. That sign in there says fifteen cents for walkers, fifteen cents *apiece.*" He felt she was somehow getting him off the track. "Only maybe you didn't notice, maybe you want to see it?"

"You go," she said to the boy.

Doggedly, the back of his neck flushed hot, Luke led the boy into the hotel lobby. The girl stayed out on the veranda. "It really does say fifteen cents," the boy told her when he came out again. "Fifteen cents for walking, for each person."

"I don't care *what* it says." The girl hung onto the railing and kept her back to him. "It's dis*gust*ing. Making money, that's all they want. I mean, they ought to *pay* people who care enough to walk all the way up here."

Luke waited just inside the door. She sounded as though she might fly off the handle any minute; her voice was getting shriller and shriller. He'd done his job. Most of it. He'd told them what was what. Now he just had to collect the money. Slowly he walked out toward them.

"I can see the *park*ing fee." The girl whirled on him so suddenly, he wondered did she have eyes in the back of her head. "Even for parking way down there at the gate." A fleck of saliva showed at the corner of her mouth. For a second Luke thought she actually meant to spit at him. "But to pay for *walk*ing!"

Luke shrugged. "State law, lady." Squinting off into the green distance, to the far hills that melded, one into the other, in the August haze, he jingled his pouch of silver coins. What was she blaming him for? What was thirty cents, fifty cents? "Besides," he added, spacing his words carefully, the way one explains a problem to a difficult child, "you pay parking, not walking, today. So what do you want to bother yourself about the price of walking for, lady?"

"But we were going to *walk* . . ." The girl broke off. Turning from him with surprising swiftness, she rounded the corner of the hotel to the west side of the veranda, out of sight. The boy followed her.

Luke cut through the inside of the hotel and out onto the back porch, where he could see if they tried to get off down the south side of the mountain. You couldn't tell what kids like that would try to do. If they didn't want to pay, the way everybody paid, they'd probably want to get off scot-free.

The girl was standing on the top of the west staircase down to the parking lot with the boy facing her, his back to Luke. She was crying, of all things, crying and dabbing at her face with a white handkerchief. Then she glanced up and saw Luke. She bent her head; she seemed to be hunting for something she had lost through the spaced cracks of the floorboards. The boy reached out to touch her shoulder, but she dodged, in that quick way of hers, and started down the steps.

The boy let her go and came around the veranda to Luke, a battered brown leather wallet open in his hand. "How much is it, now?" He sounded tired. Whatever he thought, he must be sorry about the girl, making a scene like that. Over something nobody's fault to begin with.

"Fifty cents," Luke said, "if your car's on the park grounds."

The boy counted out a quarter, two dimes and a nickel into Luke's broad palm and went round to pick up the raincoat from the north railing where he had left it.

Dropping the coins into his money pouch, Luke followed the boy. "Thanks," he said.

The boy didn't answer, didn't apologize for the girl or anything, just took off down the stairs after her on the double-quick, the raincoat flapping out behind him like a hurt bird.

"Well," Luke said aloud, wonderingly, to nobody but himself. "Well, you'd think I was a gosh-darn *crim*inal." Down on the bland surface of the river the toy-size speedboats were zigzagging still, skirting the unseen reefs. Luke stared at them blankly for a bit, and then went round to the south side of the veranda. The two figures were dwindling on the road below him—the girl a little ahead, and the boy gaining on her; but before the boy could overtake her, they were lost to sight where the road vanished into the densely wooded mountainside. "A gosh-darn honest-to-Pete *crim*inal," Luke said.

And then he gave it up, washed his hands of the whole affair, and went inside the sun-blistered lookout to treat himself to a cold soda.

Stone Boy with Dolphin

Story, 1957/58

Because Bamber banged into her bike in Market Hill, spilling oranges, figs, and a package of pink-frosted cakes, and gave her the invitation to make up for it all, Dody Ventura decided to go to the party. Under the striped canvas awnings of the fruit stall she balanced her rust-encrusted Raleigh and let Bamber scramble for the oranges. He wore his monkish red beard barbed and scraggy. Summer sandals buckled over his cotton socks, though the February air burned blue and cold.

"You're coming, aren't you?" Albino eyes fixed hers. Pale, bony hands rolled the bright tang-skinned oranges into her wicker bike basket. "Unfortunately," Bamber restored the packet of cakes, "a bit mashed."

Dody glanced, evasive, down Great St. Mary's Passage, lined with its parked bikes, wheels upon wheels. The stone façade of King's and the pinnacles of the chapel stood elaborate, frosty, against a thin water-color-blue sky. On such hinges fate turned.

"Who'll be there?" Dody parried. She felt her fingers crisped, empty in the cold. Fallen into disuse, into desuetude, I freeze.

Bamber spread his big hands into chalk webs covering the people universe. "Everybody. All the literary boys. You know them?"

"No." But Dody read them. Mick. Leonard. Especially Leonard. She didn't know him, but she knew him by heart. With him, when he was up from London, with Larson and the boys, Adele lunched. Only two American girls at Cambridge and Adele would have to nip Leonard in the bud. Hardly bud: bloom it was, full-bloom and mid-career. Not room for the two of us, Dody had told Adele the day Adele returned the books she had borrowed, all newly underlined and noted in the margins. "But *you* underline," Adele justified sweetly, her face guileless in its cup of sheened blond hair. "I beat my own brats," Dody said, "you wipe your hand marks off." For some reason, at the game of queening, Adele won: adorably, all inno-cent surprise. Dody retreated with a taste of lemons into her green sanctum at Arden with her stone facsimile of Verrocchio's boy. To dust, to worship: vocation enough.

"I'll come," Dody suddenly said.

"With whom?"

"Send Hamish along."

Bamber sighed. "He'll be there."

Dody pedaled off toward Benet Street, red plaid scarf and black gown whipping back in the wind. Hamish: safe, slow. Like traveling by mule, minus mule kicks. Dody chose with care, with care and a curtsy to the stone figure in her garden. As long as it was someone who didn't matter, it didn't matter. Ever since the start of Lent term she had taken to brushing snow from the face of the winged, dolphin-carrying boy centered in the snow-filled college garden. Leaving the long tables of black-gowned girls chattering and clinking glasses of water over the sodden dinners of spaghetti, turnips and slick fried eggs, with purple raspberry fool for dessert, Dody would push back her chair, gliding, eyes lowered, obsequious, a false demure face on, past high table where Victorian-vintage dons dined on apples, chunks of cheese and dietetic biscuits. Out of the scrolled, white-painted hall with its gilt-framed portraits of Principals in high-necked gowns lean-ing altruistic and radiant from the walls, far from the drawn, wan blue-and-gold ferned draperies, she walked. Bare halls echoed to her heels.

In the vacant college garden, dark-needled pines made their sharp assaults of scent on her nostrils and the stone boy poised on one foot, wings of stone balancing like feathered fans on the wind, holding his waterless dolphin through the rude, clamorous weathers of an alien climate. Nightly after snows, with bare fingers, Dody scraped the caked snow from his stone-lidded eyes, and from his plump stone cherub foot. If not I, who then?

Tracking across the snow-sheeted tennis courts back to Arden, the foreign students' house with its small, elect group of South Africans, Indians and Americans, she begged, wordless, of the orange bonfire glow of the town showing faint over the bare treetops, and of the distant jewel pricks of the stars: let something happen. Let something happen. Something terrible, something bloody. Something to end this endless flaking snowdrift of airmail letters, of blank pages turning in library books. How we go waste, how we go squandering ourselves on air. Let me walk into *Phèdre* and put on that red cloak of doom. Let me leave my mark.

But the days dawned and set, neatly, nicely, toward an Honors B.A., and Mrs. Guinea came round, regular as clockwork, every Saturday night, arms laden with freshly laundered sheets and pillowcases, a testimony to the resolute and eternally renewable whiteness of the world. Mrs. Guinea, the Scottish housekeeper, for whom beer and men were ugly words. When Mr. Guinea died his memory had been folded up forever like a scrapbook newspaper, labeled and stored, and Mrs. Guinea bloomed scentless, virgin again after all these years, resurrected somehow in miraculous maidenhood.

This Friday night, waiting for Hamish, Dody wore a black jersey and a black-and-white-checked wool skirt, clipped to her waist by a wide red belt. I will bear pain, she testified to the air, painting her fingernails Applecart Red. A paper on the imagery in *Phèdre*, half done, stuck up its seventh white sheet in her typewriter. Through suffering, wisdom. In her third-floor attic room she listened, catching the pitch of last shrieks: listened: to witches on the rack, to Joan of Arc crackling at the stake, to anonymous ladies flaring like torches in the rending metal of Riviera roadsters, to Zelda enlightened, burning behind the bars of her madness. What visions were to be had came under thumbscrews, not in the mortal comfort of a hot-water-bottle-cozy cot. Unwincing, in her mind's eye, she bared her flesh. Here. Strike home.

A knock beat on the blank white door. Dody finished lacquering the nail of her left little finger, capped the bottle of blood-bright enamel, holding Hamish off. And then, waving her hand to dry the polish, gingerly she opened the door.

Bland pink face and thin lips set ready for a wise-guy smile, Hamish wore the immaculate navy blue blazer with brass buttons which made him resemble a prep school boy, or an off-duty yachtsman.

"Hello," Dody said.

"How," Hamish walked in without her asking him, "are you?"

"I've got sinus." She sniffed thickly. Her throat clotted, obliging, with an ugly frogging sound.

"Look," Hamish laved her with water-blue eyes, "I figure you and I should quit giving each other such a hard time."

"Sure." Dody handed him her red wool coat and bunched up her academic gown into a black, funereal bundle. "Sure thing." She slipped her arms into the red coat as Hamish held it flared. "Carry my gown, will you?"

She flicked off the light as they left the room and closed the cream-painted door behind them. Ahead of Hamish down the two flights of stairs, step by step, she descended. The lower hall stood empty, walled with numbered doors and dark wainscoting. No sound, except for the hollow ticking of the grandfather clock in the stairwell.

"I'll just sign out."

"No, you won't," said Hamish. "You'll be late tonight. And you've got a key."

"How do you know?"

"All the girls in this house have keys."

"But," Dody whispered protest as he swung the front door open, "Miss Minchell has such sharp ears."

"Minchell?"

"Our college secretary. She sleeps with us, she keeps us." Miss Minchell presided, tight-lipped and grim, over the Arden breakfast table. She'd stopped speaking, it was rumored, when the American girls started wearing pajamas to breakfast under their bathrobes. All British girls in the college came down fully dressed and starched for their morning hot tea, kippers and white bread. The Americans at Arden were fortunate beyond thought, Miss Minchell sniffed pointedly, in having a toaster. Ample quarter-pounds of butter were alloted each girl on Sunday morning to last through the week. Only gluttons bought extra butter at the Home and Colonial Stores and slathered it double-thick on toast while Miss Minchell dipped her dry toast with disapproval into her second cup of tea, indulging her nerves.

A black taxicab loomed in the ring of light from the porch lamp where moths beat their wings to powder on spring nights. No moths now, only the winter air like the great pinions of an arctic bird, fanning shivers up Dody's spine. The rear door of the cab, open on its black hinges, showed a bare interior, a roomy cracked-leather seat. Hamish handed her in and followed her up. He slammed the door shut, and as at a signal, the taxi spun off down the drive, gravel spurting away under the wheels.

Sodium vapor lights from the Fen Causeway wove their weird orange glare among the leafless poplars on Sheep's Green and the houses and storefronts of Newnham Village reflected the sallow glow as the cab bounced along the narrow pot-holed road, turning with a lurch up Silver Street.

Hamish hadn't said a word to the driver. Dody laughed. "You've got it all set, haven't you?"

"I always do." In the sulfur light from the street lamps Hamish's features assumed an oddly Oriental cast, his pale eyes like vacant slits above high cheekbones. Dody knew him for dead, a beer-sodden Canadian, his wax mask escorting her, for her own convenience, to the party of teatime poets and petty university D. H. Lawrences. Only Leonard's words cut through the witty rot. She didn't know him, but that she knew, that shaped her sword. Let what come, come.

"I always plan ahead," Hamish said. "Like I've planned for us to drink for an hour. And then the party. Nobody'll be there this early. Later they might even have a few dons."

"Will Mick and Leonard be there?"

"You know them?"

"No. Just read them."

"Oh, they'll be there. If anybody is. But keep away from them."

"Why? Why should I?" Worth keeping from is worth going to. Did she will such meetings, or did the stars dictate her days, Orion dragging her, shackled, at his spurred heel?

"Because they're phonies. They are also the biggest seducers in Cambridge."

"I can take care of myself." Because when I give, I never really give at all. Always some shrewd miser Dody sits back, hugging the last, the most valuable crown jewel. Always safe, nun-tending her statue. Her winged stone statue with nobody's face.

"Sure," said Hamish. "Sure."

The cab pulled up opposite the pinnacled stone façade of King's, starched lace in the lamplight, masquerading as stone. Black-gowned boys strode in twos and threes out of the gate by the porter's lodge.

"Don't worry." Hamish handed her down to the sidewalk, stopping to count his coppers into the palm of the featureless cab driver. "It's all arranged."

From the polished wooden bar of Miller's, Dody looked to the far end of the carpeted room at the couples going up and down the plush-covered stair to the dining room: hungry going up, stuffed coming down. Greasy lip prints on the goblet edge, partridge fat congealing, ruby-set with semi-precious chunks of currant jelly. The whisky was starting to burn her sinus trouble away, but her voice was going along with it, as it always did. Very low and sawdusty.

"Hamish." She tried it.

"Where have you been?" His warm hand under her elbow felt good as anybody's warm hand. People swam past, undulant, with no feet, no faces. Outside the window, bordered with green-leaved rubber plants, face shapes bloomed toward the glass from the dark outside sea and drifted away again, wan underwater planets at the fringe of vision.

"Ready?"

"Ready. Have you got my gown?" Hamish showed the black patch of cloth draped over his arm, and started to shoulder a path through the crowds around the bar toward the swinging glass door. Dody walked after him with fastidious care, focusing her eyes on his broad navy blue back, and as he opened the door, ushering her ahead of him onto the sidewalk, she took his arm. Steady as he was, she felt safe, tethered like a balloon, giddy, dangerously buoyant, but still quite safe in the boisterous air. Step on a crack, break your mother's back. With care, she square-walked.

"You'd better put your gown on," Hamish said after they'd been walking a bit. "I don't want any proctors to nab us. Especially to-night."

"Why especially?"

"They'll be looking for me tonight. Bulldogs and all."

So at Peas Hill, under the green-lit marquee of the arts theater, Hamish helped her to slip her arms into the two holes of the black gown. "It's ripped here on the shoulder."

"I know. It always makes me feel as if I'm in a straitjacket. Keeps slipping down and pinning my arms to my sides."

"They're throwing gowns away now, if they catch you in a ripped one. They just come over and ask for it and tear it up on the spot."

"I'd sew it up," Dody said. Men. Mend the torn, the tattered. Salvage the raveled sleeve. "With black embroidery thread. So it wouldn't show."

"They'd love that."

Through the cobbled open square of Market Hill they walked hand in hand. Stars showed faint above the blackened flank of Great St. Mary's Church, which had housed, last week, penitent hordes hearing Billy Graham. Past the wooden posts of the empty market stalls. Then up Petty Cury, past the wine merchant's with his windows of Chilean burgundy and South African sherry, past the shuttered butcher shops and the leaded panes of Heffer's where the books on display spoke their words over and over in a silent litany on the eyeless air. The street stretched bare to the baroque turrets of Lloyd's, deserted except for a few students hurrying to late dinners or theater parties, black gowns flapping out behind them like rooks' wings on the chill wind.

Dody gulped cold air. A last benison. In the dark, crooked alleyway of Falcon Yard, light spilled out of upper-story windows, bursts of laughter came, dovetailing with the low, syncopated strut of a piano. A doorway opened its slat of light to them. Halfway up the glaring steepness of the stair, Dody felt the building waver, rocking under the railing her hand held, her hand slimed chill with sweat. Snail tracks, fever tracks. But the fever would make everything flow right, burning its brand into her cheeks, blotting out the brown scar on her left cheek in a rose of red. Like the time she went to the circus when she was nine, with a fever, after putting ice under her tongue so the thermometer wouldn't register, and her cold had vanished when the sword-swallower sauntered into the ring and she fell for him on the spot.

Leonard would be upstairs. In the room at the top of the stairs she and Hamish were now ascending, according to the clocked stations of the stars.

"You're doing fine." Hamish, just behind her shoulder, his hand firm under her elbow, lifted her upward. Step. And then, step.

"I'm not drunk."

"Of course not."

The doorframe hung suspended in a maze of stairs, walls lowering, rising, shutting off all the other rooms, all the other exits but this one. Obedient angels in pink gauze trolleyed away on invisible wires the surplus scenery. In the middle of the doorway Dody poised. Life is a

tree with many limbs. Choosing this limb, I crawl out for my bunch
of apples. I gather unto me my Winesaps, my Coxes, my Bramleys, my
Jonathans. Such as I choose. Or do I choose?

"Dody's here."

"Where?" Larson, beaming, his open American face hearty, faintly
shiny, as always, with an unsquelchable easy pride, came up, glass in
hand. Hamish did away with Dody's coat and gown and she laid her
scarred brown leather pocketbook on the nearest windowsill. Mark
that.

"I've drunk a lot," Larson observed, amiable, shining with that
ridiculous pride, as if he had just successfully delivered quadruplets in
a nearby maternity ward. "So don't mind what I say." He, waiting for
Adele, stored niceness spilled honey-prodigal, with Adele's lily head
in mind. Dody knew him only by hellos and goodbyes, with Adele ever
in attendance. "Mick's gone already." Larson jutted his thumb into the
seethe and flux of dancers, sweat smells and the Friday night stew of
pungent warring perfumes.

Through the loose, twining rhythms of the piano, through the blue
heron-hover of smoke, Dody picked out the boy who was Mick, side-
burns dark and hair rumpled, he doing a slow wide brand of British
jive with a girl in sweater and skirt of hunter's green close-cloven as
frog skin.

"His hair's standing up like devil's horns," Dody said. They would
all be girled then, Larson, Leonard. Leonard up from London to cele-
brate the launching of the new magazine. Straight-faced, she had taken
in Adele's rumors, questioning, casual, spying from her battlement
until Leonard loomed like the one statue-breaker in her mind's eye,
knowing no statues of his own. "Is that Mick's artist girl?"

Larson beamed. "That's the ballet dancer. We're taking ballet now."
A deep knee bend, sloshing his glass, spilled half. "You know, Mick
is satanic. Like you say. You know what he did when we were kids in
Tennessee?"

"No." Dody's eyes scanned the peopled room, flicking over faces,
checking accounts for the unknown plus. "What did he do?"

There. In the far corner, by the wooden table, bare of glasses now,
the punch bowl holding only a slush of lemon peel and orange rind,
a tall one. Back to her, shoulders hunched in a thick black sweater with
a rolled-up collar, elbows of his green twill shirt stuck through the
sweater holes. His hands shot up, out, and scissored air to shape his
unheard talk. The girl. Of course, the girl. Pale, freckled, with no

mouth but a pink, dim, distant rosebud, willowed reedy, wide-eyed to the streaming of his words. It would be what's-her-name. Delores. Or Cheryl. Or Iris. Wordless and pallid companion of Dody's classical tragedy hours. She. Silent, fawn-eyed. Clever. Sending her corpse for a stand-in at supervisions. To read about the problem of Prometheus in a rustling, dust-under-the-bed voice. While shut miles away, sanctuaried safe, she knelt in her sheet before the pedestaled marble. A statue-worshiper. She, too. So.

"Who," Dody asked, sure now, "is that?"

But nobody answered.

"About wild dogs," Larson said. "And Mick was king of the wild dogs and made us fetch and carry . . ."

"Drink?" Hamish emerged at her elbow with two glasses. The music stopped. Applause spattered. Ragged scum on the surge of voices. Mick came, finning the crowd apart with his elbows.

"Dance?"

"Sure." Mick held Leonard's hours in his navy-man's hand. Dody lifted her glass and the drink rose up to meet her mouth. The ceiling wavered and walls buckled. Windows melted, belling inward.

"Oh, Dody," Larson grinned. "You've spilled."

Wet drops watered the back of Dody's hand, a dark stain extended, spreading on her skirt. Marked already. "I want to meet some of these writers."

Larson craned his thick neck. "Here's Brian. The editor himself. Will he do?"

"Hello." Dody looked down at Brian, who looked up at her, dark-haired, impeccable, a dandy little package of a man. Her limbs began to mammoth, arm up the chimney, leg through the window. All because of those revolting little cakes. So she grew, crowding the room. "You wrote that one about the jewels. The emerald's lettuce-light. The diamond's eye. I thought it was . . ."

Beside the polished black hearse of the piano Milton Chubb lifted his saxophone, his great body sweating dark crescents under the arms. Dilys, shy, fuzzy chick of a thing that she was, nestled under his arm, blinking her lashless lids. He would crush her. He must be four times her size. Already, at college, a private fund had been raised among the girls to send Dilys to London to rid herself and her small rounding belly of Milton's burgeoning and unwanted heir. A whine. A thump-thump.

Mick's fingers gripped for Dody's. His hand, lean, rope-hard, palm callused, swung her off the hook of her thought and she kept going out, out of gravity's clutch. Planets sparked in the far reaches of her head. M. Vem. Jaysun Pa. Mercury. Venus. Earth. Mars. I'll get there. Jupiter. Saturn. Turning strange. Uranus? Neptune, tridented, green-haired. Far. Mongoloid-lidded Pluto, then. And asteroids innumerable, a buzz of gilded bees. Out, out. Bumping against someone, rebounding gently, and moving back to Mick again. To the here, to the now.

"I can't dance at all."

But Mick turned a deaf ear, whorls waxed against siren calls. Grinning at her from far, from farther away, he receded. Over the river and into the woods. His Cheshire-cat grin hung luminous. Couldn't hear a word in his canary-feathered heaven.

"You wrote those poems," Dody shouted over the roar of the music which swelled loud, louder, like the continuous roar of airplanes taking off from the runway across Boston Harbor. She taxied in for a close-up, the room blinking one, seen through the wrong end of a telescope. A red-haired boy bent over the piano, fingers cake-walking, invisible. Chubb, sweating and flushed, lifted the horn and wailed, and Bamber, there too, flicked his bony chalk hand over and over the guitar.

"Those words. You made them." But Mick, wrinkled and gone in his baggy checked pants, swung her out, and back, and caught her up again, with Leonard nowhere. Nowhere at all. All the hours wasting. She, squandering hours like salt-shaker grains on the salt sea in her hunt. That one hunt.

Hamish's face kindled before her like a sudden candle from the ring of faces that spun away, features blurred and smeared as warming wax. Hamish, watchful, guardian-angeling, waited in attendance, coming no nearer. But the man in the black sweater had come near. His shoulders, hunching, closed out the room piece by piece by piece. Pink, luminous and ineffectual, the face of Hamish winked out behind the blackness of the worn, torn sweater.

"Hello." His square chin was green and rough. "I'm out at the elbows." It was a beard of moss on his chin. Room and voices hushed in the first faint twirl of a rising wind. Air sallowed, the storm to come. Air sultry now. Leaves turning up white-bellied sides in the queer sulfur light. Flags of havoc. His poem said.

"Patch the havoc." But the four winds rose, unbuckled, from the stone cave of the revolving world. Come thou, North. Come thou, South. East. West. And blow.

"Not all their ceremony can patch the havoc."

"You like that?"

Wind smacked and bellowed in the steel girders of the world's house. Perilous scaffold. If she walked very carefully. Knees gone jelly-weak. The room of the party hung in her eye like a death's-door camera shot: Mick beginning again to dance with the girl in green, Larson's smile widening great as the grin on Humpty's head. Knitting up the sleeve of circumstance. She moved. And moved into the small new room.

A door banged shut. People's coats slumped in piles on the tables, cast-off sheaths and shells. Ghosts gone gallivanting. I chose this limb, this room.

"Leonard."

"Brandy?" Leonard plucked a fogged glass from the yellowing sink. Raw reddish liquid sloshed out of the bottle into the glass. Dody reached. Her hands came away drenched. Full of nothing.

"Try again."

Again. The glass rose and flew, executing first a perfect arc, an exquisite death leap, onto the flat umber-ugly wall. A flower of wink-ing sparks made sudden music, unpetaling then in a crystalline glis-sade. Leonard pushed back the wall with his left arm and set her in the space between his left arm and his face. Dody pitched her voice above the rising of the winds, but they rose higher in her ears. Then, bridging the gap, she stamped. Shut those four winds up in their goatskin bags. Stamp. The floor resounded.

"You're all there," Leonard said. "Aren't you?"

"Listen. I've got this statue." Stone-lidded eyes crinkled above a smile. The smile millstoned around her neck. "I've got this statue to break."

"So?"

"So there's this stone angel. Only I'm not sure it's an angel. This stone gargoyle maybe. A nasty thing with its tongue stuck out." Under floorboards tornadoes rumbled and muttered. "I'm crazy maybe." They stopped their circus to listen. "Can you do it?"

For answer, Leonard stamped. Stamped out the floor. Stamp, the walls went. Stamp, the ceiling flew to kingdom come. Stripping her red hairband off, he put it in his pocket. Green shadow, moss shadow, raked her mouth. And in the center of the maze, in the sanctum of the garden, a stone boy cracked, splintered, million-pieced.

"When can I see you again?" Fever-cured, she stood, foot set victorious on a dimpled stone arm. Mark that, my fallen gargoyle, my prince of pebbles.

"I work in London."

"When?"

"I've got obligations." The walls closed in, wood grains, glass grains, all in place. "In the next room." The four winds sounded retreat, defeat, hooing off down their tunnel in the world's sea-girdled girth. Oh, hollow, hollow. Hollow in the chambered stone.

Leonard bent to his last supper. She waited. Waited, sighting the whiteness of his cheek with its verdigris stain, moving by her mouth.

Teeth gouged. And held. Salt, warm salt, laving the tastebuds of her tongue. Teeth dug to meet. An ache started far off at their bone root. Mark that, mark that. But he shook. Shook her bang against the solid-grained substance of the wall. Teeth shut on thin air. No word, but a black back turned, diminished, diminishing, through a sudden sprung-up doorway. Grains of wood molding, level floorboard grains, righted the world. The wrong world. Air flowed, filling the hollow his shape left. But nothing at all filled the hollow in her eye.

The half-open door thronged with snickers, with whispers. On the smoke-burdened air of the party that fissured through the crack Hamish came, intent, behind a glistening pink rubber mask.

"Are you all right?"

"Of course I'm all right."

"I'll get your coat. We're going now." Hamish went away again. A small boy wearing glasses and a drab mustard-colored suit scuttled from a hole in the wall on his way to the lavatory. He ogled her, propped against the wall as she was, and she felt her hand, held to her mouth, jerking sudden like a spastic's.

"Can I get you anything?" A queer light flickered in his eye, the light people have when the blood of a street accident gathers, puddling prodigal on the pavement. How they came to stare. Curious arenas of eyes.

"My pocketbook," Dody steadily said. "I left it behind the curtain on the first windowsill."

The boy went out. Hamish appeared with her red coat, black gown dangling its rag of crepe. She shoved her arms in, obedient. But her face burned, unskinned, undone.

"Is there a mirror?"

Hamish pointed. A blurred, cracked oblong of glass hung over the once-white sink that was yellowed with a hundred years of vomit and liquor stains. She leaned to the mirror and a worn, known face with vacant brown eyes and a seamed brown scar on the left cheek came swimming at her through the mist. There was no mouth on the face: the mouth place was the same sallow color as the rest of the skin, defining its shape as a badly botched piece of sculpture defines its shape, by shadows under the raised and swollen parts.

The boy stood beside her holding up a pocketbook of scratched brown leather. Dody took it. With a cartridge of red lipstick she followed the mouth shape and made the color come back. Thank you, she smiled at the boy with her bright new red mouth.

"Take care of me now," she told Hamish. "I have been rather lousy."

"You're all right." But that was not what the others would say.

Hamish pushed the door open. Out into the room. No one stared: a ring of turned backs, averted faces. The piano notes still sauntered underneath the talk. The people were laughing very much now. Beside the piano Leonard hunched, holding a white handkerchief to his left cheek. Tall, pale, Delores-Cheryl-Iris with the tiger-lily freckles willowed up to help him blot the blood. I did that, Dody informed the deaf air. But the obligation got in the way, smirking. Obligations. Soap and water would not wash off that ring of holes for a good week. Dody Ventura. Mark me, mark that.

Because of Hamish, protecting, not angry at all, she got to the doorway of the room with no stone thrown, not wanting to go, but going. Starting down the narrow-angled stair, with Adele's face, cupped by the shining blond hair, coming up at her, open and frank and inviolable as a water lily, that white-blondness, all pure, all folding purely within itself. Multi-manned, yet virginal, her mere appearance shaped a reprimand like the hushed presence of a nun. Oswald backed her up, and behind him marched the tall, gawky and depressive Atherton. Oswald, his receding Neanderthal head brushed straight across with slicked hair to hide the shiny retreating slope, peered at Dody through his tortoiseshell glasses.

"Tell us something about bone structure, Dody." She saw, clear in

the yet unbreached light of minutes to come, the three of them, together, walking into the room brimming with her act, with versions
and variations on the theme of her act which would mark her by
tomorrow like the browned scar on her cheek among all the colleges
and all the town. Mothers would stop in Market Hill, pointing to their
children: "There's the girl who bit the boy. He died a day after." Hark,
hark, the dogs do bark.

"That was last week." Dody's voice rasped hollow, as from the
bottom of a weed-grown well. Adele kept smiling her sublime, altruistic smile. Because she knew already what she would find in the room:
no grab bag of star-sent circumstance, but her chosen friends, and
Larson, her special friend. Who would tell her everything, and keep
the story on the tongues, changing, switching its colors, like a chame-
leon over smeared and lurid territory.

Back to the wall, Dody let Adele, Oswald and Atherton move past
her up the stair to the room she was leaving and to the red circle of
teeth marks and Leonard's obligation. Cold air struck, scything her
shins. But no faces came to recognize Dody, nor fingers, censorious,
to point her out. Blind storefronts and eyeless alley walls said: comfort
ye, comfort ye. Black sky spaces spoke of the hugeness, the indifference
of the universe. Greening pricks of stars told her how little they cared.

Every time Dody wanted to say Leonard to a lamppost she would
say Hamish, because Hamish was taking the lead, leading her away,
safely, though damaged and with interior lesions, but safe now,
through the nameless streets. Somewhere, from the dark sanctuarial
belly of Great St. Mary's, or from deep, deeper within the town, a
clock bonged out. Bong.

Black streets, except for the thin string of lights at the main corners.
Townfolks all abed. A game began, a game of hide-and-go-seek with
nobody. Nobody. Hamish stationed her behind a car, advancing,
alone, peering around corners, then returning to lead her after him.
Then, before the next corner, Dody ducking again behind a car, feeling the metal fender like dry ice, magnet-gripping her skin. Hamish
leaving her again, walking off to look again, and then coming back and
saying it was safe so far.

"The proctors," he said, "will be out after me."

A damp mist rose and spired about their knees, blurring patches of
the buildings and the bare trees, a mist blued to phosphor by the high,
clear moon, dropping over a maple tree, a garden shed, here, there, its

theatrical scrim of furred blue haze. After back alleys, after crossing
the corner of Trumpington Street under the blackened scabrous walls
of Pembroke College, a graveyard on the right, askew with stones,
snow drifted white in patches, and patches of dark where ground
showed, they came to Silver Street. Boldly now they walked past the
woodwork frame of the butcher shop with its surgical white venetian
blind drawn on all the hanging heel-hooked pigs and the counters full
of freckled pork sausages and red-purple kidneys. At the gate of
Queens', locked for the night, five boys in black gowns were milling
under the moon. One began to sing:

A-las, my love, you do me wrong

"Wait." Hamish placed Dody in a corner outside the spiked gates.
"Wait, and I'll find a good place to get you over."

To cast me off discourteously.

The five boys surrounded Dody. They had no features at all, only
pale, translucent moons for face shapes, so she would never know them
again. And her face, too, felt to be a featureless moon. They could
never recognize her in the light of day.
"What are you doing here?"
"Are you all right?"
The voices whispered, batlike, about her face, her hands.
"My, you smell nice."
"That perfume."
"May we kiss you."
Their voices, gentle and light as paper streamers, fell, gentle, touch-
ing her, like leaves, like wings. Voices web-winged.
"What are you doing here?"
Backed up against the barbed fence, staring at the white snow field
beyond the crescent of dark Queens' buildings and at the blued fen fog
floating waist-high over the snow, Dody stood her ground. And the
boys dropped back, because Hamish had come up. The boys began to
climb, one by one, over the spiked fence. Dody counted. Three. Four.
Five. Sheep-counting sleepward. Holding onto the metal railing, they
went swinging themselves over the pointed black spikes into the
grounds of Queens', eft and drunken, reeling pussyfooted on the
crusted snow.
"Who are they?"

"Just some late guys going into the court." The boys were all over now, and they went away across the arched wooden bridge over the narrow green river, the bridge that Newton had once put together without bolts.

"We're going over the wall," Hamish said. "They've found a good place. Only you mustn't talk until we're in."

"I can't go over. Not with this tight skirt. I'll get spikes through my hands."

"I'll help you."

"But I'll fall." Still, Dody pulled her tweed skirt up to her thighs, to the top of her nylon stockings, and put one foot up on the wall. Game, oh, game. She lifted her left leg over the spikes where they were lowest, but the black tips caught and pierced through her skirt. Hamish was helping, but she stuck there, one leg over the spikes, teetering. Would it hurt? Would she bleed at all? Because the spikes were going through her hands, and her hands were so cold she couldn't feel them. And then Hamish was all at once on the inside of the fence, cupping his hands into a stirrup for her to step in, and without arguing it out or thinking, she simply stepped, pivoting herself over with her hands, and the spikes looked to be going right through them.

"My hands," she began, "they'll bleed . . ."

"Shh!" Hamish put his hand over her mouth. He was looking around the inside of the crescent toward a dark doorway. The night stood still and the moon, far off and cold in its coat of borrowed light, made a round O mouth at her, Dody Ventura, coming into Queens' court at three in the morning because there was nowhere else to go, because it was a station on the way. A place to get warm in, for she felt very cold. Wasted, wasting, her blood gone to redden the circle of teeth marks on Leonard's cheek, and she, a bloodless husk, left drifting in limbo. Here with Hamish.

Dody followed Hamish down the side of the building, tracing her fingers along the rough-textured brick until they were at the doorway, with Hamish being furtive and quiet for no reason, because there was no sound, only the great snow silence and the silence of the moon and the hundreds of Queens' men breathing silent in their deep early morning sleep before the dawn. The first stair on the landing creaked, even though they had taken their shoes off. The next was quiet. And so the next.

A room all by itself. Hamish shut the ponderous oaken door behind them, and then the thin inner door, and lit a match. The big room jumped into Dody's view, with its dark, shiny cracked-leather couch and thick rugs and a wallful of books.

"Made it. I'm in a good entry."

From behind the paneled wainscoting, a bed creaked. There sounded a stifled sigh.

"What's that? Rats?"

"No rats. My roommate. He's all right . . ." Hamish vanished, and the room with him. Another match scritched, and the room came back. Hamish, squatting, turned on the gas jet for the fire. The hissing sound lighted with a soft whoosh, a blue flare, and the gas flames in their neat row behind the white asbestos lattice started shadows flickering behind the great couch and the heavy chairs.

"I'm so cold." Dody sat on the rug before the fire, which made Hamish's face yellowish, instead of pink, and his pale eyes dark. She rubbed her feet, putting her red shoes, which looked black, into the grate before the fire. The shoes were all wet inside, she could feel the dampness with her finger, but she could not feel the cold, only the numb hurt of her toes as she rubbed them, rubbing the blood back into them.

Then Hamish pushed her back on the rug, so her hair fell away from her face and wound among the tufts of the rug, for it was a deep rug, thick-piled, with the smell of shoe leather about it, and ancient tobacco. What I do, I do not do. In limbo one does not really burn. Hamish began kissing her mouth, and she felt him kiss her. Nothing stirred. Inert, she lay staring toward the high ceiling crossed by the dark wood beams, hearing the worms of the ages moving in them, riddling them with countless passages and little worm-size labyrinths, and Hamish let his weight down on top of her, so it was warm. Fallen into disuse, into desuetude, I shall not be. (It is simple, if not heroic, to endure.)

And then at last Hamish just lay there with his face in her neck, and she could feel his breathing quiet.

"Please scold me." Dody heard her voice, strange and constricted in her chest, from lying on her back on the floor, from the sinus, from the whisky. I am sick of labeled statues. In a gray world no fires burn. Faces wear no names. No Leonards can be, for no Leonards live: Leonard is no name.

"What for?" Hamish's mouth moved against her neck, and she felt now again how unnaturally long her neck was, so that her head nodded far from her body, on a long stem, like the picture of Alice after eating the mushroom, with her head on its serpent neck above the leaves of the treetops. A pigeon flew up, scolding, Serpents, serpents. How to keep the eggs safe?

"I am a bitch," Dody heard her voice announce from out of the doll-box in her chest, and she listened to it, wondering what absurd thing it would say next. "I am a slut," it said with no conviction.

"No, you're not." Hamish made a kiss shape with his mouth on her neck. "But you should have learned your lesson. I told you about them, and you should have learned your lesson."

"I've learned it," the small voice lied. But Dody hadn't learned her lesson, unless it was the lesson of this limbo where no one got hurt because no one took a name to tie the hurt to like a battered can. Nameless I rise. Nameless and undefiled.

One more lap of her journey loomed ahead: the safe getting in the door at Arden, and then up to her room with no stairs creaking. With no simmering Miss Minchell bursting out of her room on the landing between the first and second stair, raging in her red flannel bathrobe, her hair undone for the night from the bun and hanging in a straight black braid down her back, with the gray strands braided into it, down to her buttocks, and no one to see. No one to know that Miss Minchell's hair, when undone, reached her buttocks. Someday, some year hence, it would be a braid of battleship gray, probably, by that time, reaching down to her knees. And by the time it grew to touch the floor, it would be turned pure white. White, and wasting its whiteness on the blank air.

"I am going now."

Hamish heaved himself up, and Dody lay indifferent, feeling the warm place where he had been, and the warm sweat drying and cooling on the cool air through her sweater. "You do just what I tell you," Hamish said. "Or we'll never get out."

Dody put on her ribboned shoes, grown so hot from the fire that they seared her soles.

"Do you want to climb over the spikes again? Or try the brook?"

"The brook?" Dody looked up at Hamish, standing over her, solid and warm, like a horse, breathing hay in its stable. "Is it deep?" It might have been Larson, or Oswald, or even Atherton standing there, standing in with the pleasant warmth common to horses. Immortal horses, for one replaced another. And so all was well in an eternity of horses.

"Deep? It's frozen over. I'd test it first, anyway."

"The brook, then."

Hamish stationed Dody by the doorway. First he opened the inside door, and then, after peering out the crack, the outside door. "You wait here." He wedged her against the doorjamb. "When I signal, come."

Stairs chirked faintly under his weight, and then, after a pause, a match flared, lighting the entrance, showing the grain of wood, worn to a satin patina by the hands of ghosts. Dody began to descend. How we pass and repass ourselves, never fusing, never solidifying into the perfect stances of our dreams. Tiptoeing down, her right hand sliding along the rail, Dody felt all Queens' crescent list and recover, and list again, a ship rolling on heavy seas. Then a splinter entered her index finger, but she kept her hand sliding down along the rail, right on into it. Unwincing. Here. Strike home. The splinter broke off, embedded in her finger with a small nagging twinge. Hamish stationed her in the dark niche of the entry, a dressmaker's dummy.

"Wait," he whispered, and the whisper ran up the stairs, twining around the banisters, and there might be someone on the next landing, wary, listening, with flashlights and an official badge. "I'll beckon if it's all clear, and you run like hell. Even if anyone starts coming after, you run, and we'll get over the brook and across the road before they can catch us up."

"What if they arrest you?"

"They won't do any more than send me down." Hamish dropped the match to the ground. He crushed it under his foot. The small yellow world went out and the courtyard flowered, large, luminous, blue in the light of the moon. Hamish stepped out into the courtyard, his dark shape cut itself clear against the snow, a pasteboard silhouette, moving, diminishing, blending into the darkness of the bushes bordering the brook.

Dody watched, hearing her own breathing, a cardboard stranger's, until a dark figure detached itself from the shrubbery. It made a motion. She ran out. Her shoes crunched loud, breaking through the crust of the snow, each step crackling, as if someone were crumpling up newspapers, one after the other. Her heart beat, and the blood beat up in her face, and still the snow crusts broke and broke under her feet. She could feel the soft snow dropping like powder into her shoes, in the space between the arch of her foot and the instep of the shoe, dry, and then melting cold. No sudden searchlight, no shouts.

Hamish reached for her as she stumbled up and they stood for a moment by the hedge. Then Hamish began shouldering through the rough-thicketed bush, making a path for her, and she followed him, setting her feet down, tramping the lower branches, scratching and scraping her legs on the brittle twigs. They were through, at the bank of the brook, and the hedge closed behind them its gate of briers, dark, unbroken.

Hamish slid down the bank, ankle-deep in snow, and held out his hand, so Dody would not fall coming down. Snow-covered ice bore them up, but before they had reached the other shore, the ice began to boom and crack in its depths. They jumped clear onto the opposite bank and started to crawl up the steep, slippery side, losing their footing, reaching for the top of the bank with their hands, their hands full of snow, their fingers stinging.

Crossing the snow field toward the bare expanse of Queen's Road, stilled now, muted and relieved of the daily thunder of lorries and market vans, they walked hand in hand, not saying a word. A clock struck clear out of the dead quiet. Bong. Bong. And bong. Newnham Village slumbered behind glazed windows, a toy town constructed of pale orange taffy. They met no one.

Porch light and all the house lights out, Arden stood dark in the weak blue wash of the setting moon. Wordless, Dody put her key in the lock, turned it, and pressed the door handle down. The door clicked open on the black hall, thick with the ticking of the coffin-shaped clock and hushed with the unheard breathing of sleeping girls. Hamish leaned and put his mouth to her mouth. A kiss that savored of stale hay through the imperfect clothwork of their faces.

The door shut him away. A mule that didn't kick. She went to the pantry closet just outside Mrs. Guinea's quarters and opened the door. The smell of bread and cold bacon rose to meet her nostrils, but she was not hungry. She reached down until her hand met the cool glass shape of a milk bottle. Taking off her shoes again, and her black gown and her coat, she started up the back stairs with the milk bottle, weary, yet preparing, from a great distance, the lies that would say, if necessary, how she had been in Adele's room, talking with Adele until late, and had just come up. But she remembered with lucid calm that she had not looked in the signing-out book to see if Adele had checked herself back yet. Probably Adele had not signed out either, so there was no knowing, unless she tried Adele's door, whether Adele really was back. But Adele's room was on the first floor, and it was too late now. And then she remembered why she did not want to see Adele at all anyway.

When Dody flicked on the light switch, her room leapt to greet her, bright, welcoming, with its grass-green carpet and the two great bookcases full of books she had bought on her book allowance and might never read, not until she had a year of nothing to do but sit, with a locked door, and food hoisted up by pulleys, and then she might read through them. Nothing, the room affirmed, has happened at all. I, Dody Ventura, am the same coming in as I was going out. Dody dropped her coat on the floor, and her torn gown. The gown lay in a black patch, like a hole, a black doorway into nowhere.

Carefully Dody put her shoes on the armchair so she would not wake Miss Minchell, who slept directly below, coiled up for the night in her braid of hair. The gas ring on the hearth, black and greasy, was stuck with combings of hair, speckled with face powder fallen from past makeup jobs in front of the mirror on the mantel over the fireplace. Taking a Kleenex, she wiped the gas ring clean and threw the stained tissue into the wicker wastepaper basket. The room always got musty over the weekend and only really cleared on Tuesdays when Mrs. Guinea came in with the vacuum cleaner and her bouquet of rushes and feather dusters.

Dody took one match from the box with the swan on it which she kept on the floor by the gray gas meter with all its myriad round dial faces and numbers stenciled black on white. She lit the gas fire and then the gas ring, its circle of flames flaring up blue to her retreating hand, leaping to scorch. For a minute she squatted there, absorbed, to remove the splinter from her right hand where it had dug itself into a little pocket of flesh, showing dark under the transparent covering of skin. With thumb and forefinger of her left hand she pinched the skin together and the head of the splinter came out, black, and she took the thin sliver between her fingernails, slowly drawing it out until it came clear. Then she put the small, battered aluminum pot on the gas ring, poured the pint of milk into it, and sat on the floor, cross-legged. But her stockings cut tight into her thighs, so she got up and ripped down her girdle like the peel of a fruit, and pulled the stockings off, still gartered to it, because they were shredded past saving from the twigs of the bushes outside Queens'. And she sat down again in her slip, rocking back and forth gently, her mind blank and still, her arms around her knees and her knees hugged against her breasts, until the milk began to show bubbles around the brim of the pan. She sat then in the green-covered chair, sipping the milk from the Dutch pottery cup she had picked up in New Compton Street that first week in London.

The milk seared her tongue, but she drank it down. And knew that tomorrow the milk would not pass, all of it, out of her system, extricable as a splinter, but that it would stay to become part of herself, inextricable, Dody. Dody Ventura. And then, slowly, upon this thought, all the linked causes and consequences of her words and acts began to gather in her mind, slowly, like slow-running sores. The circle of teeth marks hung out its ring of bloodied roses for Dody Ventura to claim. And the invariable minutes with Hamish would not be spat out like thistles, but clung, clung fast. No limbo's nameless lamb, she. But stained, deep-grained with all the words and acts of all the Dodys from birth cry on. Dody Ventura. She saw. Who to tell it to? Dody Ventura I am.

The top floor of Arden did not respond, but remained dead still in the black dawn. Nothing outside hurt enough to equal the inside mark, a Siamese-twin circle of teeth marks, fit emblem of loss. I lived: that once. And must shoulder the bundle, the burden of my dead selves until I, again, live.

Barefoot, Dody stripped off her white nylon slip, and her bra and pants. Electricity crackled as the warmed silk tore clear of her skin. She flicked out the light and moved from the wall of flame, and from the ring of flame, toward the black oblong of the window. Rubbing a clear round porthole in the misted pane, she peered out at the morning, caught now in a queer no-man's-land light between moonset and sunrise. Noplace. Noplace yet. But someplace, someplace in Falcon Yard, the panes of the diamond-paned windows were falling in jagged shards to the street below, catching the light from the single lamp as they fell. Crash. Bang. Jing-jangle. Booted feet kicked the venerable panes through before dawning.

Dody undid the catch on the window and flung it open. The frame screaked on its hinges, banging back to thud against the gable. Kneeling naked on the two-seated couch in the window niche, she leaned out far over the dead dried garden. Over the marrowless stems marking iris roots, bulbs of narcissus and daffodil. Over the bud-nubbed branches of the cherry tree and the intricate arbor of laburnum boughs. Over the great waste of earth and under the greater waste of sky. Orion stood above the peaked roof of Arden, his gold imperishable joints polished in the cold air, speaking, the way he always spoke, his bright-minted words out of the vast wastage of space: space where, he testified, space where the Miss Minchells, the Hamishes, all the extra Athertons and the unwanted Oswalds of the world went round and round, like rockets, squandering the smoky fuse of their lives in the limbo of unlove. Patching the great gap in the cosmos with four o'clock teas and crumpets and a sticky-sweet paste of lemon curd and marzipan.

The cold took her body like a death. No fist through glass, no torn hair, strewn ash and bloody fingers. Only the lone, lame gesture for the unbreakable stone boy in the garden, ironic, with Leonard's look, poised on that sculpted foot, holding fast to his dolphin, stone-lidded eyes fixed on a world beyond the clipped privet hedge, beyond the box borders and the raked gravel of the cramped and formal garden paths. A world of no waste, but of savings and cherishings: a world love-kindled, love-championed. As Orion went treading riveted on his track toward the rim of that unseen country, his glitter paling in the blue undersea light, the first cock crowed.

Stars doused their burning wicks against the coming of the sun.

Dody slept the sleep of the drowned.

Nor saw yet, or fathomed how now, downstairs in the back kitchen, Mrs. Guinea began another day. Saver, cherisher. No waster, she. Splitting the bony kippers into the black iron frying pan, crisping the fat-soaked toast in the oven, she creakily hummed. Grease jumped and spat. Sun bloomed virginal in the steel-rimmed rounds of her eyeglasses and clear light fountained from her widowed bosom, giving back the day its purity.

To her potted hyacinths, budding on the windowsill in their rare ethereal soil of mother-of-pearl shells, Mrs. Guinea affirmed, and would forever affirm, winter aside, what a fine, lovely day it was after all.

All the Dead Dears

Story, 1957/58

'I don't care what Herbert says," declared Mrs. Nellie Meehan, dumping two spoonfuls of sugar in her tea, "I saw an angel once. It was my sister Minnie, the night Lucas died."

The four of them were sitting late around the red coal fire that November evening in the Meehans' new-bought house: Nellie Meehan and her husband Clifford, Nellie's Cousin Herbert, lodger with the Meehans since his red-headed wife left him at haymaking time some twenty-seven years before, and Dora Sutcliffe, who had dropped over for a pot of tea on the way back home up Caxton Slack after visiting her friend Ellen, just out of hospital, recovering from a cataract operation.

The dying fire still glowed warm, the battered aluminum tea kettle steamed on the hearth, and Nellie Meehan had gotten out her hand-embroidered linen tablecloth, all wreathed with violets and crimson poppies, in honor of Dora's coming. A snowdrift of currant cakes and buttered scones banked the blue-willow platter and a little cut-glass bowl held generous dollops of Nellie Meehan's homemade gooseberry

jam. Outside, in the clear, windy night, the moon shone high and full;
a blue, luminous mist was rising from the bottom of the valley where
the mountain stream flowed black and deep over those foaming falls
in which Dora's brother-in-law had chosen to drown himself a week
ago come Monday. The Meehans' house (bought early that autumn
from spinster Katherine Edwards after her mother Maisie died at the
doughty age of eighty-six) clung halfway up the steep hill of red-
berried ash and bracken, which flattened out at the top, stretching
away into wild and barren moorland, twigged with heather and
prowled by the black-faced moor sheep, with their curling horns and
mad, staring yellow eyes.

Already, during the long evening, they had discussed the days of the
Great War, and the various ends of those who thrived and those who
died, Clifford Meehan creaking to his feet at the appropriate point in
the course of conversation, as was his habit, and taking out of the
bottom drawer in the polished mahogany china cabinet the cardboard
box of souvenirs—medals, ribbons, and the shattered paybook provi-
dentially in his breast pocket when the bullet struck (bits of shrapnel
still lodged in its faded pages)—to show Dora Sutcliffe the blurred
ocher daguerreotype snapped in the hospital the Christmas before
Armistice, with the faces of five young men smiling out, lit by the wan
winter sun that rose and set some forty years back. "That's me,"
Clifford had said, and, as if naming the fates of characters in some
well-known play, jutted his thumb at the other faces, one by one. "He's
got his leg off. He was killed. He's dead, and he's dead."

And so they gossiped gently on, calling up the names of the quick
and the dead, reliving each past event as if it had no beginning and no
end, but existed, vivid and irrevocable, from the beginning of time, and
would continue to exist long after their own voices were stilled.

"What," Dora Sutcliffe asked Nellie Meehan now in hushed, church-
going tones, "was Minnie wearing?"

Nellie Meehan's eyes grew dreamy. "A white Empire smock," she
said. "All gathered about the waist, it was, with hundreds and hundreds of little pleats. I remember just as clear. And wings, great feath-
ery white wings coming down over the bare tips of her toes. Clifford
and I didn't get word about Lucas till the next morning, but that was
the night I had the pain and heard the knocking. The night Minnie
came. Wasn't it, Clifford?"

Clifford Meehan puffed meditatively on his pipe, his hair silvery in the firelight, his trousers and sweater bayberry gray; except for his vivid, purple-veined nose, he seemed on the verge of becoming translucent, as if the chimney mantel, hung with its gleaming horse brasses, might at any moment begin to show faintly through his thin, grayed frame. "Aye," he said finally. "That was the night." His wife's undeniable flashes of second sight had always awed and somewhat chastened him.

Cousin Herbert sat dour and skeptical, his huge, awkward hands, cracked with wrinkles, hanging loose at his sides. Herbert's mind had long ago riveted itself on that distant sunny day, the first fair weather after a week's downpour, when his wife Rhoda's folks, up visiting to help with the haymaking, jaunted off to Manchester with Rhoda, leaving Herbert alone with the hay. On returning at dusk, they'd found their luggage packed, hurled into the far corner of the cow field; Rhoda had left him then, indignant, with her parents. Stubborn and proud, Herbert had never asked her back; and, stubborn and proud as he, she had never come.

"I woke up . . ." Nellie Meehan's eyes blurred, as if in some visionary trance, and her voice grew rhythmic. Outside, the wind blasted away at the house, which creaked and shuddered to its foundations under those powerful assaults of air. "I woke up that night with a terrible pain in my left shoulder, hearing this loud knocking all around, and there was Minnie, standing at the foot of the bed, right pale and sweet-faced—I was about seven, the winter she took pneumonia; we slept in the same bed then. Well, as I looked, she kept fading and fading, until she went fading clear away into nothing. I got up real careful so as not to wake Clifford, and went downstairs to make myself a pot of tea. My shoulder was hurting something terrible, and all the time I heard this knock knock knock . . ."

"What *was* it?" Dora Sutcliffe begged, her watery blue eyes wide. She had heard the story of Lucas' hanging countless times, at second and third hand, but with every fresh telling the previous tales blurred, merging into one, and each time, at this juncture, she asked, eager, curious, as if part of some perpetually inquiring chorus: "What was knocking?"

"First I thought it was the carpenter next door," Nellie Meehan said, "because he was often up till all hours hammering away in his workshop in the garage, but when I looked out the kitchen window it was pitch dark. And still I kept hearing this knock knock knock, and all the time the pain throbbing so in my shoulder. I sat up in the living room, then, trying to read, and I must have fallen asleep, because that's where Clifford found me when he came down to go to work in the morning. When I woke up it was dead quiet. The pain in my shoulder was gone, and the mailman came with the letter about Lucas, all bordered in black."

"It wasn't a letter," Clifford Meehan contradicted. Without fail, at some point in her story, Nellie was carried away by inaccuracy of this sort, improvising whatever details eluded her memory at the moment. "It was a telegram. They couldn't have had a letter in the post and you getting it the same morning."

"A telegram, then," Nellie Meehan acquiesced. "Saying: Come, Lucas dead."

"It must be one of your uncles, I told her," Clifford Meehan put in. "I said it couldn't be Lucas, him so young, a real fine master joiner he was."

"But it was Lucas," Nellie Meehan said. "He'd hung himself that night. His daughter Daphne found him in the attic. Imagine."

"Just imagine," Dora Sutcliffe breathed. Her hand, as if independent of her motionless, attentive body, reached for a buttered scone.

"It was the war," Cousin Herbert announced suddenly in sepulchral tones, his very voice gone rusty from disuse. "No lumber to be had for love nor money."

"Well, however it might be, there was Lucas." Clifford Meehan knocked his pipe against the grate and took out his tobacco pouch. "Just made partner of his joining firm. Only a few days before he went and hung himself, he'd stood out where the new apartments were going up and said to his old boss, Dick Greenwood: 'I wonder, will these apartments ever get built.' Folks spoke to him the night he did it, and noticed nothing wrong."

"It was his wife, Agnes," Nellie Meehan maintained, shaking her head sadly as she recalled the fate of her departed brother, her brown eyes gentle as a cow's. "Agnes killed him sure as if she'd poisoned him; never a kind word had Agnes. She just let him worry, worry, worry to his death. Sold his clothes at an auction, too, straight off, and bought a sweet shop with the money she took in, that and what he'd left her."

"Fancy!" Dora Sutcliffe sniffed. "I always said there was something mean about Agnes. She kept handkerchiefs over her scales, and everything in her shop was just that many coppers dearer than anywhere else. I bought a Christmas cake off Agnes only two years back and priced one exactly like it in Halifax the next week. Half a crown more, Agnes' cake was."

Clifford Meehan tamped the fresh tobacco down in his pipe. "Lucas went driving about the pubs with his daughter Daphne on the very night," he said slowly. He, too, had told his part of the story so many times, and each time it seemed to him as though he were pausing here, expectant, waiting for some clear light to spring out of his own words, to illumine and explain the bleak, threadbare facts of the going of Lucas. "Lucas went upstairs after dinner, and when Daphne called him down to drive out, it was a couple of minutes before he came—his face was puffed funny, Daphne said afterwards, and his lips kind of purple. Well, they stopped for a few bitters at the Black Bull, as was Lucas' habit of a Thursday night, and when he came back home, after sitting about downstairs with Daphne and Agnes a bit, he put his hands down on the arms of his chair and heaved himself up—I remember him getting up like that a hundred times—and said, 'I guess I'll go get ready.' Daphne went up a little later and called to Agnes, 'Pa's not upstairs.' Then Daphne started up the attic steps; it was the only other place he could have been. And there she found him, hanging from the rafter, stone dead."

"There was a hole bored in the middle rafter," Nellie Meehan said. "Lucas had fixed a swing up there for Daphne when she was just a young thing, and he strung the rope he hung himself with through that very hole."

"They found scuff marks on the floor," Clifford Meehan reported, coldly factual as the account in the yellowed newspaper dated nine years back preserved in Nellie's family album, "where Lucas tried to hang himself the first time, just before he went out, only the rope was too long. But when he came back he cut it short enough."

"I wonder Lucas could do it," Dora Sutcliffe sighed. "Like I wonder about my brother-in-law Gerald."

"Aye, Gerald was a fine man," Nellie Meehan sympathized. "Stout and red-faced, husky as you could wish. What'll Myra do with the farm, now he's gone?"

"Ee, Lord knows," Dora Sutcliffe said. "It was in and out of hospital with Gerald this past winter. On account of his kidneys. Myra said the doctor'd just told him he'd have to go back again, they still weren't right. And Myra all alone now. Her daughter Beatrice married the one who's experimenting with cows down in South Africa."

"I wonder your brother Jake's kept on so chipper, like he has these thirty years, Nellie," Clifford Meehan mused, taking up that fugue of family phantoms, his voice melancholy as a man's might be whose two stalwart sons had left him in his old age, the one for Australia and the sheep farms, the other for Canada and a flighty secretary named Janeen. "With that witch of a wife Esther and his one surviving daughter Cora twenty-eight and numb as a tree. I remember Jake coming to our place, before he married Esther . . ."

"Those days absolutely shone with bright and funny conversation," Nellie Meehan interrupted, her own smile pale and wistful, as if already frozen in some dated family photograph.

". . . coming to our place and throwing himself down on the sofa and saying: 'Don't know as I ought to marry Esther; she's in weak health, always talking about ailments and hospital.' Sure enough, one week after they were married, Esther's in hospital having an operation that cost Jake a hundred pound; she'd been saving it up till he'd married her and would have to pay for the whole do."

"Slaved all his life for his woolen mill, my brother Jake did." Nellie Meehan stirred the cold dregs of her tea. "And now he's a fortune and ready to see the world, and Esther won't stir a step out of the house; just sits and nags at that poor silly Cora; wouldn't even let her be put in a home where she'd be among her own kind. Always taking herbs and potions, Esther is. When Gabriel was on the way, the only good one of the lot, right in his senses, after that queer Albert was born with his tongue in wrong, Jake came right out and told Esther: 'If you ruin this one, I'll kill you.' And then pneumonia took the two boys, good and bad, not seven years after."

Nellie Meehan turned her tender eyes on the red embers in the grate as if the hearts of all those dead glowed there. "But they're waiting." Her voice dropped, low and reassuring as a lullaby. "They come back." Clifford Meehan puffed slowly on his pipe. Cousin Herbert sat stonestill; the fading fire carved his brooding features in stark light and shadow, as if out of rock. "I know," Nellie Meehan whispered, almost to herself. "I've seen them."

"You mean," Dora Sutcliffe shivered in the thin, chill draft sifting through the window frame at her back, "you've seen *ghosts*, Nellie?" Dora Sutcliffe's question was rhetorical; she never tired of Nellie Meehan's accounts of her spasmodic commerce with the spirit world.

"Not ghosts, exactly, Dora," Nellie Meehan said quietly, modest and reserved as always about her strange gift, "but *presences*. I've come into a room and I've felt somebody standing there, big as life. And it's often I've said to myself: 'If you could just see that bit *harder*, Nellie Meehan, you'd see them plain as day.' "

"Dreams!" Cousin Herbert's voice rasped harsh. "Stuff!"

As if Cousin Herbert were not in the room, as if his words met deaf ears, the three others spoke and gestured. Dora Sutcliffe rose to leave. "Clifford'll walk you up Slack way," Nellie Meehan said.

Cousin Herbert got up, without another word, his shoulders hunched, as if laboring under some great, private, unspeakable pain. He turned his back on the group about the fire and stalked to bed, his footsteps hollow and heavy on the stairs.

Nellie Meehan saw her husband and Dora Sutcliffe to the door and waved them off into the gusts of wind and drifting moon-haze. For a minute she stood in the doorway, gazing after those two figures vanished in the dark, feeling a cold more deadly than any knife strike to the marrow of her bones. Then she closed the door and went back toward the parlor to clear away the tea things. As she entered the parlor, she stopped, stunned. There, in front of the flowered upholstered sofa, hung, a few inches above the floor, a column of dazzle—not so much a light bodied on the air, but a blur superimposed upon the familiar background, a misting across the sofa, and the mahogany china cabinet behind it, and the sprigged rose and forget-me-not wallpaper. As Nellie Meehan watched, the blur began to shape itself into a vaguely familiar form, its features pale, solidifying like ice on the vaporous air until it bulked real as Nellie Meehan herself. Nellie Meehan stood, unblinking, and with her steady eyes fixed the bright apparition. "I know you, Maisie Edwards," she said in soft, placating tones. "You're looking for your Katherine. Well, you won't find her here any more. She's living away now, away down in Todmorden."

And then, almost apologetically, Nellie Meehan turned her back on the glimmering form, which still hung in the air, to stack and wash the tea service before Clifford returned. It was with a queer new lightness in her head that she noticed the plump, tiny little woman propped stiff, mouth open, eyes staring, stock-still in the rocking chair next to the tea table. As Nellie Meehan gaped, she felt the encroaching cold take the last sanctum of her heart; with a sigh that was a slow, released breath, she saw the delicate blue-willow pattern of the saucer showing clear through the translucence of her own hand and heard, as if echoing down a vaulted corridor sibilant with expectant, gossiping shadows, the voice at her back greeting her like a glad hostess who has waited long for a tardy guest: "Well," said Maisie Edwards, "it's about time, Nellie."

The Wishing Box

Story, 1956

Agnes Higgins realized only too well the cause of her husband Harold's beatific, absent-minded expression over his morning orange juice and scrambled eggs.

"Well," Agnes sniffed, smearing beach-plum jelly on her toast with vindictive strokes of the butter knife, "what did you dream *last* night?"

"I was just remembering," Harold said, still staring with a blissful, blurred look right through the very attractive and tangible form of his wife (pink-cheeked and fluffily blond as always that early September morning, in her rose-sprigged peignoir), "those manuscripts I was discussing with William Blake."

"But," Agnes objected, trying with difficulty to conceal her irritation, "how did you *know* it was William Blake?"

Harold seemed surprised. "Why, from his pictures, of course."

And what could Agnes say to that? She smoldered in silence over her coffee, wrestling with the strange jealousy which had been growing on her like some dark, malignant cancer ever since their wedding night only three months before when she had discovered about Harold's dreams. On that first night of their honeymoon, in the small hours of the morning, Harold startled Agnes out of a sound, dreamless sleep by a violent, convulsive twitch of his whole right arm. Momentarily frightened, Agnes had shaken Harold awake to ask in tender, maternal tones what the matter was; she thought he might be struggling in the throes of a nightmare. Not Harold.

"I was just beginning to play the Emperor Concerto," he explained sleepily. "I must have been lifting my arm for the first chord when you woke me up."

Now at the outset of their marriage, Harold's vivid dreams amused Agnes. Every morning she asked Harold what he had dreamed during the night, and he told her in as rich detail as if he were describing some significant, actual event.

"I was being introduced to a gathering of American poets in the Library of Congress," he would report with relish. "William Carlos Williams was there in a great, rough coat, and that one who writes about Nantucket, and Robinson Jeffers looking like an American Indian, the way he does in the anthology photograph; and then Robert Frost came driving up in a saloon car and said something witty that made me laugh." Or, "I saw a beautiful desert, all reds and purples, with each grain of sand like a ruby or sapphire shooting light. A white leopard with gold spots was standing over this bright blue stream, its hind legs on one bank, its forelegs on the other, and a little trail of red ants was crossing the stream over the leopard, up its tail, along its back, between its eyes, and down on the other side."

Harold's dreams were nothing if not meticulous works of art. Undeniably, for a certified accountant with pronounced literary leanings (he read E. T. A. Hoffman, Kafka, and the astrological monthlies instead of the daily paper on the commuters' special), Harold possessed an astonishingly quick, colorful imagination. But, gradually, Harold's peculiar habit of accepting his dreams as if they were really an integral part of his waking experience began to infuriate Agnes. She felt left out. It was as if Harold were spending one third of his life among celebrities and fabulous legendary creatures in an exhilarating world from which Agnes found herself perpetually exiled, except by hearsay.

As the weeks passed, Agnes began to brood. Although she refused to mention it to Harold, her own dreams, when she had them (and that, alas, was infrequently enough), appalled her: dark, glowering landscapes peopled with ominous unrecognizable figures. She never could remember these nightmares in detail, but lost their shapes even as she struggled to awaken, retaining only the keen sense of their stifling, storm-charged atmosphere which, oppressive, would haunt her throughout the following day. Agnes felt ashamed to mention these fragmentary scenes of horror to Harold for fear they reflected too unflatteringly upon her own powers of imagination. Her dreams—few and far between as they were—sounded so prosaic, so tedious, in comparison with the royal baroque splendor of Harold's. How could she tell him simply, for example: "I was falling," or "Mother died and I was so sad," or "Something was chasing me and I couldn't run"? The plain truth was, Agnes realized, with a pang of envy, that her dream life would cause the most assiduous psychoanalyst to repress a yawn.

Where, Agnes mused wistfully, were those fertile childhood days when she believed in fairies? Then, at least, her sleep had never been dreamless nor her dreams dull and ugly. She had in her seventh year, she recalled wistfully, dreamed of a wishing-box land above the clouds where wishing boxes grew on trees, looking very much like coffee grinders; you picked a box, turned the handle around nine times while whispering your wish in this little hole in the side, and the wish came true. Another time, she had dreamed of finding three magic grass blades growing by the mailbox at the end of her street: the grass blades shone like tinsel Christmas ribbon, one red, one blue, and one silver. In yet another dream, she and her young brother Michael stood in front of Dody Nelson's white-shingled house in snowsuits; knotty maple tree roots snaked across the hard, brown ground; she was wearing red-and-white-striped wool mittens; and, all at once, as she held out one cupped hand, it began to snow turquoise-blue sulfa gum. But that was just about the extent of the dreams Agnes remembered from her infinitely more creative childhood days. At what age had those benevolent painted dream worlds ousted her? And for what cause?

Meanwhile, indefatigably, Harold continued to recount his dreams over breakfast. Once, at a depressing and badly aspected time of Harold's life before he met Agnes, Harold dreamed that a red fox ran through his kitchen, grievously burnt, its fur charred black, bleeding from several wounds. Later, Harold confided, at a more auspicious time shortly after his marriage to Agnes, the red fox had appeared again, miraculously healed, with flourishing fur, to present Harold with a bottle of permanent black Quink. Harold was particularly fond of his fox dreams; they recurred often. So, notably, did his dream of the giant pike. "There was this pond," Harold informed Agnes one sultry August morning, "where my cousin Albert and I used to fish; it was chock-full of pike. Well, last night I was fishing there, and I caught the most enormous pike you could imagine—it must have been the great-great-grandfather of all the rest; I pulled and pulled and pulled, and still he kept coming out of that pond."

"Once," Agnes countered, morosely stirring sugar into her black coffee, "when I was little, I had a dream about Superman, all in technicolor. He was dressed in blue, with a red cape and black hair, handsome as a prince, and I went flying right along with him through the air—I could feel the wind whistling, and the tears blowing out of my eyes. We flew over Alabama; I could tell it was Alabama because the land looked like a map, with 'Alabama' lettered in script across these big green mountains."

Harold was visibly impressed. "What," he asked Agnes then, "did you dream last night?" Harold's tone was almost contrite: to tell the truth, his own dream life preoccupied him so much that he'd honestly never thought of playing listener and investigating his wife's. He looked at her pretty, troubled countenance with new interest: Agnes was, Harold paused to observe for perhaps the first time since their early married days, an extraordinarily attractive sight across the breakfast table.

For the moment, Agnes was confounded by Harold's well-meant question; she had long ago passed the stage where she seriously considered hiding a copy of Freud's writings on dreams in her closet and fortifying herself with a vicarious dream tale by which to hold Harold's interest each morning. Now, throwing reticence to the wind, she decided in desperation to confess her problem.

"I don't dream anything," Agnes admitted in low, tragic tones. "Not anymore."

Harold was obviously concerned. "Perhaps," he consoled her, "you just don't use your powers of imagination enough. You should practice. Try shutting your eyes."

Agnes shut her eyes.

"Now," Harold asked hopefully, "what do you see?"

Agnes panicked. She saw nothing. "Nothing," she quavered. "Nothing except a sort of blur."

"Well," said Harold briskly, adopting the manner of a doctor dealing with a malady that was, although distressing, not necessarily fatal, "imagine a goblet."

"What *kind* of goblet?" Agnes pleaded.

"That's up to you," Harold said. *"You* describe it to *me."*

Eyes still shut, Agnes dragged wildly into the depths of her head. She managed with great effort to conjure up a vague, shimmery silver goblet that hovered somewhere in the nebulous regions of the back of her mind, flickering as if at any moment it might black out like a candle.

"It's silver," she said, almost defiantly. "And it's got two handles."

"Fine. Now imagine a scene engraved on it."

Agnes forced a reindeer on the goblet, scrolled about by grape leaves, scratched in bare outlines on the silver. "It's a reindeer in a wreath of grape leaves."

"What color is the scene?" Harold was, Agnes thought, merciless.

"Green," Agnes lied, as she hastily enameled the grape leaves. "The grape leaves are green. And the sky is black"—she was almost proud of this original stroke. "And the reindeer's russet flecked with white."

"All right. Now polish the goblet all over into a high gloss."

Agnes polished the imaginary goblet, feeling like a fraud. "But it's in the *back* of my head," she said dubiously, opening her eyes. "I see everything way in the back of my head. Is that where you see *your* dreams?"

"Why, no," Harold said, puzzled. "I see my dreams on the front of my eyelids, like on a movie screen. They just come; I don't have anything to do with them. Like right now," he closed his eyes, "I can see these shiny crowns coming and going, hung in this big willow tree."

Agnes fell grimly silent.

"You'll be all right," Harold tried, jocosely, to buck her up. "Every day, just practice imagining different things like I've taught you."

Agnes let the subject drop. While Harold was away at work, she began, suddenly, to read a great deal; reading kept her mind full of pictures. Seized by a kind of ravenous hysteria, she raced through novels, women's magazines, newspapers, and even the anecdotes in her *Joy of Cooking;* she read travel brochures, home appliance circulars, the Sears Roebuck catalog, the instructions on soap-flake boxes, the blurbs on the back of record jackets—anything to keep from facing the gaping void in her own head of which Harold had made her so painfully conscious. But as soon as she lifted her eyes from the printed matter at hand, it was as if a protecting world had been extinguished.

The utterly self-sufficient, unchanging reality of the *things* surrounding her began to depress Agnes. With a jealous awe, her frightened, almost paralyzed stare took in the Oriental rug, the Williamsburg-blue wallpaper, the gilded dragons on the Chinese vase on the mantel, the blue-and-gold medallion design of the upholstered sofa on which she was sitting. She felt choked, smothered by these objects whose bulky pragmatic existence somehow threatened the deepest, most secret roots of her own ephemeral being. Harold, she knew only too well, would tolerate no such vainglorious nonsense from tables and chairs; if he didn't like the scene at hand, if it bored him, he would change it to suit his fancy. If, Agnes mourned, in some sweet hallucination an octopus came slithering towards her across the floor, paisley-patterned in purple and orange, she would bless it. Anything to prove that her shaping imaginative powers were not irretrievably lost; that her eye was not merely an open camera lens which recorded surrounding phenomena and left it at that. "A rose," she found herself repeating hollowly, like a funeral dirge, "is a rose is a rose . . ."

One morning when Agnes was reading a novel, she suddenly realized to her terror that her eyes had scanned five pages without taking in the meaning of a single word. She tried again, but the letters separated, writhing like malevolent little black snakes across the page in a kind of hissing, untranslatable jargon. It was then that Agnes began attending the movies around the corner regularly each afternoon. It did not matter if she had seen the feature several times previously; the fluid kaleidoscope of forms before her eyes lulled her into a rhythmic trance; the voices, speaking some soothing, unintelligible code, exorcised the dead silence in her head. Eventually, by dint of much cajolery, Agnes persuaded Harold to buy a television set on the installment plan. That was much better than the movies; she could drink sherry while watching TV during the long afternoons. These latter days, when Agnes greeted Harold on his return home each evening, she found, with a certain malicious satisfaction, that his face blurred before her gaze, so she could change his features at will. Sometimes she gave him a pea-green complexion, sometimes lavender; sometimes a Grecian nose, sometimes an eagle beak.

"But I *like* sherry," Agnes told Harold stubbornly when, her afternoons of private drinking becoming apparent even to his indulgent eyes, he begged her to cut down. "It relaxes me."

The sherry, however, didn't relax Agnes enough to put her to sleep. Cruelly sober, the visionary sherry-haze worn off, she would lie stiff, twisting her fingers like nervous talons in the sheets, long after Harold was breathing peacefully, evenly, in the midst of some rare, wonderful adventure. With an icy, increasing panic, Agnes lay stark awake night after night. Worse, she didn't get tired any more. Finally, a bleak, clear awareness of what was happening broke upon her: the curtains of sleep, of refreshing, forgetful darkness dividing each day from the day before it, and the day after it, were lifted for Agnes eternally, irrevocably. She saw an intolerable prospect of wakeful, visionless days and nights stretching unbroken ahead of her, her mind condemned to perfect vacancy, without a single image of its own to ward off the crushing assault of smug, autonomous tables and chairs. She might, Agnes reflected sickly, live to be a hundred: the women in her family were all long-lived.

Dr. Marcus, the Higgins' family physician, attempted, in his jovial way, to reassure Agnes about her complaints of insomnia: "Just a bit of nervous strain, that's all. Take one of these capsules at night for a while and see how you sleep."

Agnes did not ask Dr. Marcus if the pills would give her dreams; she put the box of fifty pills in her handbag and took the bus home.

Two days later, on the last Friday of September, when Harold returned from work (he had shut his eyes all during the hour's train trip home, counterfeiting sleep but in reality voyaging on a cerise-sailed dhow up a luminous river where white elephants bulked and rambled across the crystal surface of the water in the shadow of Moorish turrets fabricated completely of multicolored glass), he found Agnes lying on the sofa in the living room, dressed in her favorite princess-style emerald taffeta evening gown, pale and lovely as a blown lily, eyes shut, an empty pillbox and an overturned water tumbler on the rug at her side. Her tranquil features were set in a slight, secret smile of triumph, as if, in some far country unattainable to mortal men, she were, at last, waltzing with the dark, red-caped prince of her early dreams.

The Day Mr. Prescott Died

Story, 1956

It was a bright day, a hot day, the day old Mr. Prescott died. Mama and I sat on the side seat of the rickety green bus from the subway station to Devonshire Terrace and jogged and jogged. The sweat was trickling down my back, I could feel it, and my black linen was stuck solid against the seat. Everytime I moved it would come loose with a tearing sound, and I gave Mama an angry "so there" look, just like it was her fault, which it wasn't. But she only sat with her hands folded in her lap, jouncing up and down, and didn't say anything. Just looked resigned to fate is all.

"I say, Mama," I'd told her after Mrs. Mayfair called that morning, "I can see going to the funeral even though I don't believe in funerals, only what do you mean we have to sit up and watch with them?"

"It is what you do when somebody close dies," Mama said, very reasonable. "You go over and sit with them. It is a bad time."

"So it is a bad time," I argued. "So what can I do, not seeing Liz and Ben Prescott since I was a kid except once a year at Christmastime for giving presents at Mrs. Mayfair's. I am supposed to sit around hold handkerchiefs, maybe?"

With that remark, Mama up and slapped me across the mouth, the way she hadn't done since I was a little kid and very fresh. "You are coming with me," she said in her dignified tone that means definitely no more fooling.

So that is how I happened to be sitting in this bus on the hottest day of the year. I wasn't sure how you dressed for waiting up with people, but I figured as long as it was black it was all right. So I had on this real smart black linen suit and a little veil hat, like I wear to the office when I go out to dinner nights, and I felt ready for anything.

Well, the bus chugged along and we went through the real bad parts of East Boston I hadn't seen since I was a kid. Ever since we moved to the country with Aunt Myra, I hadn't come back to my home town. The only thing I really missed after we moved was the ocean. Even today on this bus I caught myself waiting for that first stretch of blue.

"Look, Mama, there's the old beach," I said, pointing.

Mama looked and smiled. "Yes." Then she turned around to me and her thin face got very serious. "I want you to make me proud of you today. When you talk, talk. But talk nice. None of this fancy business about burning people up like roast pigs. It isn't decent."

"Oh, Mama," I said, very tired. I was always explaining. "Don't you know I've got better sense. Just because old Mr. Prescott had it coming. Just because nobody's sorry, don't think I won't be nice and proper."

I knew that would get Mama. "What do you mean nobody's sorry?" she hissed at me, first making sure people weren't near enough to listen. "What do you mean, talking so nasty?"

"Now, Mama," I said, "you know Mr. Prescott was twenty years older than Mrs. Prescott and she was just waiting for him to die so she could have some fun. Just waiting. He was a grumpy old man even as far back as I remember. A cross word for everybody, and he kept getting that skin disease on his hands."

"That was a pity the poor man couldn't help," Mama said piously. "He had a right to be crotchety over his hands itching all the time, rubbing them the way he did."

"Remember the time he came to Christmas Eve supper last year?" I went on stubbornly. "He sat at the table and kept rubbing his hands so loud you couldn't hear anything else, only the skin like sandpaper flaking off in little pieces. How would you like to live with *that* every day?"

I had her there. No doubt about it, Mr. Prescott's going was no sorrow for anybody. It was the best thing that could have happened all around.

"Well," Mama breathed, "we can at least be glad he went so quick and easy. I only hope I go like that when my time comes."

Then the streets were crowding up together all of a sudden, and there we were by old Devonshire Terrace and Mama was pulling the buzzer. The bus dived to a stop, and I grabbed hold of the chipped chromium pole behind the driver just before I would have shot out the front window. "Thanks, mister," I said in my best icy tone, and minced down from the bus.

"Remember," Mama said as we walked down the sidewalk, going single file where there was a hydrant, it was so narrow, "remember, we stay as long as they need us. And no complaining. Just wash dishes, or talk to Liz, or whatever."

"But, Mama," I complained, "how can I say I'm sorry about Mr. Prescott when I'm really not sorry at all? When I really think it's a good thing?"

"You can say it is the mercy of the Lord he went so peaceful," Mama said sternly. "Then you will be telling the honest truth."

I got nervous only when we turned up the little gravel drive by the old yellow house the Prescotts owned on Devonshire Terrace. I didn't feel even the least bit sad. The orange-and-green awning was out over the porch, just like I remembered, and after ten years it didn't look any different, only smaller. And the two poplar trees on each side of the door had shrunk, but that was all.

As I helped Mama up the stone steps onto the porch, I could hear a creaking and sure enough, there was Ben Prescott sitting and swinging on the porch hammock like it was any other day in the world but the one his Pop died. He just sat there, lanky and tall as life. What really surprised me was he had his favorite guitar in the hammock beside him. Like he'd just finished playing "The Big Rock Candy Mountain," or something.

"Hello Ben," Mama said mournfully. "I'm so sorry."

Ben looked embarrassed. "Heck, that's all right," he said. "The folks are all in the living room."

I followed Mama in through the screen door, giving Ben a little smile. I didn't know whether it was all right to smile because Ben was a nice guy, or whether I shouldn't, out of respect for his Pop.

Inside the house, it was like I remembered too, very dark so you could hardly see, and the green window blinds didn't help. They were all pulled down. Because of the heat or the funeral, I couldn't tell. Mama felt her way to the living room and drew back the portieres. "Lydia?" she called.

"Agnes?" There was this little stir in the dark of the living room and Mrs. Prescott came out to meet us. I had never seen her looking so well, even though the powder on her face was all streaked from crying.

I only stood there while the two of them hugged and kissed and made sympathetic little noises to each other. Then Mrs. Prescott turned to me and gave me her cheek to kiss. I tried to look sad again but it just wouldn't come, so I said, "You don't know how surprised we were to hear about Mr. Prescott." Really, though, nobody was at all surprised, because the old man only needed one more heart attack and that would be that. But it was the right thing to say.

"Ah, yes," Mrs. Prescott sighed. "I hadn't thought to see this day for many a long year yet." And she led us into the living room.

After I got used to the dim light, I could make out the people sitting around. There was Mrs. Mayfair, who was Mrs. Prescott's sister-in-law and the most enormous woman I've ever seen. She was in the corner by the piano. Then there was Liz, who barely said hello to me. She was in shorts and an old shirt, smoking one drag after the other. For a girl who had seen her father die that morning, she was real casual, only a little pale is all.

Well, when we were all settled, no one said anything for a minute, as if waiting for a cue, like before a show begins. Only Mrs. Mayfair, sitting there in her layers of fat, was wiping away her eyes with a handkerchief, and I was reasonably sure it was sweat running down and not tears by a long shot.

"It's a shame," Mama began then, very low. "It's a shame, Lydia, that it had to happen like this. I was so quick in coming I didn't hear tell who found him even."

Mama pronounced "him" like it should have a capital H, but I guessed it was safe now that old Mr. Prescott wouldn't be bothering anybody again, with that mean temper and those raspy hands. Anyhow, it was just the lead that Mrs. Prescott was waiting for.

"Oh, Agnes," she began, with a peculiar shining light to her face,

"I wasn't even here. It was Liz found him, poor child."

"Poor child," sniffed Mrs. Mayfair into her handkerchief. Her huge red face wrinkled up like a cracked watermelon. "He dropped dead right in her arms, he did."

Liz didn't say anything, but just ground out one cigarette only half smoked and lit another. Her hands weren't even shaking. And believe me, I looked real carefully.

"I was at the rabbi's," Mrs. Prescott took up. She is a great one for these new religions. All the time it is some new minister or preacher having dinner at her house. So now it's a rabbi, yet. "I was at the rabbi's, and Liz was home getting dinner when Pop came home from swimming. You know the way he always loved to swim, Agnes."

Mama said yes, she knew the way Mr. Prescott always loved to swim.

"Well," Mrs. Prescott went on, calm as this guy on the *Dragnet* program, "it wasn't more than eleven-thirty. Pop always liked a morning dip, even when the water was like ice, and he came up and was in the yard drying off, talking to our next-door neighbor over the holly-hock fence."

"He just put up that very fence a year ago," Mrs. Mayfair interrupted, like it was an important clue.

"And Mr. Gove, this nice man next door, thought Pop looked funny, blue, he said, and Pop all at once didn't answer him but just stood there staring with a silly smile on his face."

Liz was looking out of the front window, where there was still the sound of the hammock creaking on the front porch. She was blowing smoke rings. Not a word the whole time. Smoke rings only.

"So Mr. Gove yells to Liz and she comes running out, and Pop falls like a tree right to the ground, and Mr. Gove runs to get some brandy in the house while Liz holds Pop in her arms . . ."

"What happened then?" I couldn't help asking, just the way I used to when I was a kid and Mama was telling burglar stories.

"Then," Mrs. Prescott told us, "Pop just . . . passed away, right there in Liz's arms. Before he could even finish the brandy."

"Oh, Lydia," Mama cried. "What you have been through!"

Mrs. Prescott didn't look as if she had been through much of anything. Mrs. Mayfair began sobbing in her handkerchief and invoking the name of the Lord. She must have had it in for the old guy, because she kept praying, "Oh, forgive us our sins," like she had up and killed him herself.

"We will go on," Mrs. Prescott said, smiling bravely. "Pop would have wanted us to go on."

"That is all the best of us can do," Mama sighed.

"I only hope I go as peacefully," Mrs. Prescott said.

"Forgive us our sins," Mrs. Mayfair sobbed to no one in particular.

At this point, the creaking of the hammock stopped outside and Ben Prescott stood in the doorway, blinking his eyes behind the thick glasses and trying to see where we all were in the dark. "I'm hungry," he said.

"I think we should all eat now." Mrs. Prescott smiled on us. "The neighbors have brought over enough to last a week."

"Turkey and ham, soup and salad," Liz remarked in a bored tone, like she was a waitress reading off a menu. "I just didn't know where to put it all."

"Oh, Lydia," Mama exclaimed, "let *us* get it ready. Let *us* help. I hope it isn't too much trouble . . ."

"Trouble, no." Mrs. Prescott smiled her new radiant smile. "We'll let the young folks get it."

Mama turned to me with one of her purposeful nods and I jumped up like I had an electric shock. "Show me where the things are, Liz," I said, "and we'll get this set up in no time."

Ben tailed us out to the kitchen, where the black old gas stove was, and the sink, full of dirty dishes. First thing I did was pick up a big heavy glass soaking in the sink and run myself a long drink of water.

"My, I'm thirsty," I said and gulped it down. Liz and Ben were staring at me like they were hypnotized. Then I noticed the water had a funny taste, as if I hadn't washed out the glass well enough and there were drops of some strong drink left in the bottom to mix with the water.

"That," said Liz after a drag on her cigarette, "is the last glass Pop drank out of. But never mind."

"Oh, Lordy, I'm sorry," I said, putting it down fast. All at once I felt very much like being sick because I had a picture of old Mr. Prescott drinking his last from the glass and turning blue. "I really am sorry."

Ben grinned. "Somebody's got to drink out of it someday." I liked Ben. He was always a practical guy when he wanted to be.

Liz went upstairs to change then, after showing me what to get ready for supper.

"Mind if I bring in my guitar?" Ben asked, while I was starting to fix up the potato salad.

"Sure, it's okay by me," I said. "Only won't folks talk? Guitars being mostly for parties and all?"

"So let them talk. I've got a yen to strum."

I made tracks around the kitchen and Ben didn't say much, only sat and played these hillbilly songs very soft, that made you want to laugh and sometimes cry.

"You know, Ben," I said, cutting up a plate of cold turkey, "I wonder, are you really sorry."

Ben grinned, that way he has. "Not really sorry, now, but I could have been nicer. Could have been nicer, that's all."

I thought of Mama, and suddenly all the sad part I hadn't been able to find during the day came up in my throat. "We'll go on better than before," I said. And then I quoted Mama like I never thought I would: "It's all the best of us can do." And I went to take the hot pea soup off the stove.

"Queer, isn't it," Ben said. "How you think something is dead and you're free, and then you find it sitting in your own guts laughing at you. Like I don't feel Pop has really died. He's down there somewhere inside of me, looking at what's going on. And grinning away."

"That can be the good part," I said, suddenly knowing that it really could. "The part you don't have to run from. You know you take it with you, and then when you go anyplace, it's not running away. It's just growing up."

Ben smiled at me, and I went to call the folks in. Supper was kind of a quiet meal, with lots of good cold ham and turkey. We talked about my job at the insurance office, and I even made Mrs. Mayfair laugh, telling about my boss Mr. Murray and his trick cigars. Liz was almost engaged, Mrs. Prescott said, and she wasn't half herself unless Barry was around. Not a mention of old Mr. Prescott.

Mrs. Mayfair gorged herself on three desserts and kept saying, "Just a sliver, that's all. Just a sliver!" when the chocolate cake went round.

"Poor Henrietta," Mrs. Prescott said, watching her enormous sister-in-law spooning down ice cream. "It's that psychosomatic hunger they're always talking about. Makes her eat so."

After coffee, which Liz made on the grinder so you could smell how good it was, there was an awkward little silence. Mama kept picking up her cup and sipping from it, although I could tell she was really all through. Liz was smoking again, so there was a small cloud of haze around her. Ben was making an airplane glider out of his paper napkin.

"Well," Mrs. Prescott cleared her throat, "I guess I'll go over to the parlor now with Henrietta. Understand, Agnes, I'm not old-fashioned about this. It said definitely no flowers and no one needs to come. It's only a few of Pop's business associates kind of expect it."

"I'll come," said Mama staunchly.

"The children aren't going," Mrs. Prescott said. "They've had enough already."

"Barry's coming over later," Liz said. "I have to wash up."

"I will do the dishes," I volunteered, not looking at Mama. "Ben will help me."

"Well, that takes care of everybody, I guess." Mrs. Prescott helped Mrs. Mayfair to her feet, and Mama took her other arm. The last I saw of them, they were holding Mrs. Mayfair while she backed down the front steps, huffing and puffing. It was the only way she could go down safe, without falling, she said.

Widow Mangada

From Notebooks, Summer 1956

Widow Mangada's house: pale, peach-brown stucco on the main Avenida running along shore, facing the beach of reddish yellow sand with all the gaily painted cabanas making a maze of bright blue wooden stilts and small square patches of shadow. The continuous poise and splash of incoming waves mark a ragged white line of surf beyond which the morning sea blazes in the early sun, already high and hot at ten-thirty; the ocean is cerulean toward the horizon, vivid azure nearer shore, blue and sheened as peacock feathers. Out in the middle of the bay juts a rock island, slanting up from the horizon line to form a sloped triangle of orange rock which takes the full glare of sun on its crags in the morning and falls to purple shadow toward late afternoon.

Sun falls in flickering lines and patches on the second-story terrace through waving fans of palm leaves and the slats of the bamboo awning. Below is the widow's garden, with dry, dusty soil from which sprout bright red geraniums, white daisies, and roses; spined cacti in reddish earthenware pots line the flagstone paths. Two blue-painted chairs and a blue table are set under the fig tree in the backyard in the shade; behind the house rises the rugged purplish range of mountainous hills, dry, sandy earth covered with scrub clumps of grass.

Early in the morning, when the sun is still cool and the breeze is wet and salt-fresh from the sea, the native women, dressed in black, with black stockings, go to the open market in the center of town with their wicker baskets to bargain and buy fresh fruit and vegetables at the stalls: yellow plums, green peppers, large ripe tomatoes, wreaths of garlic, bunches of yellow and green bananas, potatoes, green beans, squashes and melons. Gaudy striped beach towels, aprons and rope sneakers are hung up for sale against the white adobe pueblos. Within the dark caverns of the stores are great jugs of wine, oil and vinegar in woven straw casings. All night the lights of the sardine boats bob and duck out in the bay, and early in the morning the fish market is piled high with fresh fish: silvered sardines cost only eight pesetas the kilo, and are heaped on the table, strewn with a few odd crabs, starfish and squid.

Doors consist of a swaying curtain of long beaded strips which rattle apart with the entry of each customer and let in the breeze, but not the sun. In the bread shop, there is always the smell of fresh loaves as, in the dark, windowless inner room, men stripped to the waist tend the glowing ovens. The milk boy delivers milk early in the morning, pouring his liter measure from the large can he carries on his bicycle into each housewife's pan, which she leaves on her doorstep. Mingling with motor scooters, bicycles and the large, shiny grand tourist cars are the native donkey carts, loaded with vegetables, straw or jugs of wine. Workers wear sombreros, take siesta from two to four in the afternoon in the shade of a wall, or tree, or their own carts.

The widow's house has only cold water and no refrigerator; the dark, cool cupboard is full of ants. A shining array of aluminum pots, pans and cooking utensils hang on the wall; one washes dishes and vegetables in large marble basins, scrubbing them with little snarled bunches of straw. All cooking—fresh sardines fried in oil, potato-and-onion tortillas, *café con lèche*—is done on the blue flame of an antique petrol burner.

BENIDORM: JULY 15

We met Widow Mangada one Wednesday morning on the hot, crowded bus jolting over the desert-dusty roads from Alicante to Benidorm. She heard us exclaiming about the blue bay and turned from her seat in front of us to ask whether we spoke French. A little, we said, whereupon she broke explosively into description of her wonderful house by the sea, with garden and balcony terrace and kitchen rights. She was a small, dark woman of middle age, stylishly dressed in white knitted lace over a black slip, white heeled sandals, terrifically *comme il faut;* her coal-black hair was done in many waves and curls, her saucer-black eyes were emphasized by blue eye shadow and two startling black eyebrows penciled straight slanting upward from the bridge of her nose to her temples.

She bustled about getting native boys to put her baggage on their hand-drawn carts and hustled us to the main road, trotting slightly ahead and babbling in her peculiar French about her house, and how she was lonely and wanted to let out apartments, and she knew right away that we were *"gentil."* When we said we were writers and wanted a quiet place by the sea to work, she jumped to agree that she knew how it was exactly: "I too am a writer; of love stories and poems."

Her house, facing the cool blue blaze of the bay, was more than we had dreamed; we fell in love immediately with the smallest room, its French window-doors opening onto a balcony terrace, perfect for writing: vines wove green leaves in the railing; a palm and a pine tree grew alongside, shading one side, and a slatted bamboo awning could be drawn out to form a little roof as shelter from the direct noon sun. We knocked her down from the first price to one hundred pesetas a night, figuring we could save immensely by doing our own marketing and cooking. From her rapid babble of French, mangled by a strong Spanish accent, we gathered that she would trade Spanish lessons for English lessons, that she had been a teacher, and lived in France for three years.

As soon as we moved in, it became clear that Madame was not used to running a *maison* for boarders. There were three other empty rooms on the second floor which she evidently hoped to let out, for she spoke continually of how we must manage for *"les autres,"* when they arrived. She had amassed a great quantity of white china plates, cups and saucers in the formal dining room, and an equally large amount of aluminum pots and pans hung on hooks lining the kitchen walls, but there was absolutely no silver tableware. Señora seemed shocked that we did not carry knives, forks and spoons about with us, but brought out, finally, three elaborate place settings of her best silver, which she laid out, saying that this was only for the three of us, and she would soon go to Alicante to buy some simple kitchen silver for us and put her best silver away. Also, the problem of a small bathroom, fine for the two of us, but hardly fitted for eight, and the trouble of arranging cooking and dinner schedules on one petrol burner, seemed not to have occurred to her either.

We held our breath and wished fervently that she would have no customers when she put up the sign APARTMENTS FOR RENT on our balcony terrace. We had, at least, made sure that she would not use our balcony, which adjoined another, larger room, as a selling point, by explaining that it was the only place we could write in peace, since our room was too small for a table, and the beach and garden were fine for vacationers, but not for writers' workrooms. Occasionally, from our balcony (where we soon took to eating meals: steaming mugs of *café con lèche* in the morning, a cold picnic of bread, cheese, tomatoes and onions, fruit and milk at noon, and a cooked dinner of meat or fish with vegetables, and wine, at twilight under the moon and stars) we could hear Señora conducting people around the house, speaking in her rapid staccato French. But during the first week, although she had conducted several potential roomers about, no one had come. We had fun hazarding on the objections they might make: no hot water, one small bathroom, only an antique petrol burner. With such modern hotels in town, probably her price was too high: what wealthy people would be willing to market and cook? who but poor students & writers like us? Perhaps the roomers might decide to eat out in the expensive restaurants; that was a possibility. We had found out, too, that although she had made wild, extravagant gestures when showing us about the house—pointing to an empty, iceless icebox, motioning out an imaginary electrical machine for making the freezing shower water warm—that none of these comforts were forthcoming. We found the water from the taps was unpalatable and strange to the taste; when the Señora miraculously produced a glass pitcher full of delicious sparkling water for our first dinner, we asked incredulous if it came from the taps. She burbled on evasively about the health-giving qualities of the water, and it was a full day before I caught her drawing up a pail of it from a cistern sunk deep in the kitchen, covered by a blue board. The tap water, it turned out, was *non potable*.

The Señora was a fanatic about the house being *propre* for her prospective lodgers: we were to wash all dishes after meals, put them away, keep the bathroom tidy. She gave us two dishtowels to be hung behind the door, and hung up several decoy clean towels on the wall for *les autres*. We were also to have a small petrol burner of our own, for which we should buy petrol and matches, another dent in our desperate food budget of forty pesetas a day for the two of us. In spite of her concern for the *propre* condition of the house, Señora washed her greasy dishes in standing cold water, often dirtier than the dishes themselves, scrubbing them with frayed tangles of straw.

Our first morning was a nightmare. I woke early, still exhausted from our continuous traveling, uneasy in the strange bed, to find no water in the taps. I tiptoed down the stone stairs to turn on the peculiar machine with odd blue-painted spigots and wires jutting out which the Señora had said "made water," turning the switch the day before, upon which there was a convincing rumble as some complicated machinery started up. I turned the switch; there was a blue flash and acrid smoke began pouring from the box. Quickly I shut off the switch and went to knock on the Señora's door. No answer. I went upstairs and woke Ted, who was burned scarlet from the day before in the sun.

Sleepily, Ted came down in his bathing trunks to turn the switch. There was another blue flash; no sound. He tried the light switch. No electricity. We pounded on the Señora's door. No answer. "She's either gone out or dead," I said, wishing for water to make some coffee; the milk had not yet come.

"No, she'd have turned on the water if she'd gone out. She's probably lying in there refusing to get up." At last, grumpily, we went back upstairs to bed. About nine o'clock we heard the front door open. "Probably she's sneaked around from the back to come in as if she'd been out all morning." I padded barefoot downstairs, where the Señora, crisp in her white knitted dress, freshly made-up black eyebrows, greeted me cheerily. "You slept well, Madame?"

I was still smoldering. "There is no water," I said without preamble. "No water to wash or make coffee." She laughed a queer deep laugh which she used whenever anything went wrong, as if either I, or the water supply, were very childish and silly, but she would make it all right. She tried the light switch. "No light," she exclaimed triumphantly, as if all were solved. "It is so in all the village." "This is usual in the morning?" I asked coldly. "*Pas de tout, de tout, de tout,*" she rattled off from under raised eyebrows, apparently just noticing my cool irony. "You must not take it so hard, Madame." She bustled into the kitchen, lifted the blue-painted lid by the sink, dropped a bucket on a string and drew up a sloshing pailful of clear water. "Plenty of water," she gurgled, "all the time." So that was where she kept her store of health-giving water; I nodded grimly and began to make coffee, while she ran next door to investigate the state of affairs. I was pretty sure that with my native inability to manage machines, I had "fused" something and blasted the whole water and electric supply in the town. Evidently it was just local, for the Señora fiddled with the machine, crowed that water was coming everywhere, and said never never to touch the machine but to call her immediately when we were worried about the water. She would fix everything.

We also had trouble with the petrol stove. For our first dinner I planned one of Ted's favorite suppers: a platter of stringbeans and fried fresh sardines, which we had bought early at the fish market for eight pesetas the kilo and kept cool in a homemade water container of several pans covered with a wet cloth and a plate. I put the beans on to cook, but after twenty minutes they were still as hard as they had been at first and I noticed the water wasn't even boiling; Ted doubted if there was any heat and said maybe the petrol was used up; he turned the heat higher and the flame burned a thin, smoking green. "Señora," we called. She came rushing in clucking from the living room, whipped off bean pot, cooking ring and burner to reveal the damning sight of over an inch of frayed, burned wick. We'd turned it up too high and the wick itself had been burning for lack of petrol. After filling the tank with petrol, messing about with the wick, raising the fresh part left, Señora started the burner again, tested the beans. She was not at all satisfied; running out of the room, she came back and tossed in a handful of powder, which fizzed and foamed. I asked her what it was, but she just chuckled and said she had been cooking a lot longer than I and knew some "*petites choses.*" Magic powder, I thought. Poison. "Bicarbonate of soda," Ted reassured.

Señora, we began to realize, had been accustomed to a far grander scale of living than her present circumstances. Each evening she set out to town to see about a *bonne* for cleaning house; the little girl who had been scrubbing floors the day we arrived had not showed up since. "It is the hotels," the Señora told us. "All the maids go to the hotels, they pay so much. If you have a maid, you must be very nice and careful of her feelings nowadays; she breaks your best china bowl, and you must smile and say: do not trouble yourself over it, mademoiselle." The second morning I came down to make coffee, I found the Señora in a soiled towel bathrobe, her eyebrows not yet drawn on, cleaning the stone floors with a wet mop. "I am not used to this," she explained. "I am used to three maids: a cook, a cleaner ... three maids. I do not work when the front door is open, for the public to see. But when it is shut," she shrugged her shoulders, gestured comprehensively with her hands, "I do everything, everything."

In the milk shop one day, we were trying to explain where we wanted our two liters a day delivered. The houses on the Avenida were not numbered, and it was impossible to make the delivery boy understand our elementary Spanish; finally a French-speaking neighbor was called in. "Oh," she smiled, "you live with Widow Mangada. Everybody here knows her. She dresses very stylish, with much make-up." The woman grinned as if Widow Mangada were a town character. "Does she do the cooking for you," she asked curiously. A kind of instinctive loyalty toward the Señora and her straitened circumstances sprang up in me. "Oh, of course not," I exclaimed. "We do all our own cooking." The woman nodded and smiled like a cream-fed cat.

That Widow Mangada

Story, Autumn 1956

It was a blazing hot Spanish morning when they met her. The bus from Alicante to Villaviento, packed with jabbering Spaniards, jolted along the narrow road raising a cloud of red dust. Sitting beside her husband Mark, Sally tried to keep the heavy green watermelon from bouncing off her lap. Mark's rucksack and their antique black-cased portable typewriter jounced in the rack above their heads. They were house-hunting again.

"Now that's the sort of place." Mark pointed through the window at a square white pueblo set on the barren hillside. "Quiet. Simple. Nobody rolling oil cans down the street and ringing bells all night the way they did in Alicante."

"Not so fast," Sally countered. Experience was beginning to make even Sally cautious. "It's so far out there's probably no electricity. Or drinking water. Besides, how would I ever get to a market?"

The bus lumbered on through arid reddish hills terraced with groves of olive trees, their dark leaves blanched by dust. They'd been on the road for almost an hour when, caroming around a curve, the bus began plummeting down toward a small village bordering a pea-cock-blue bay. Its white pueblos shone like salt crystals in the sun.

Sally was leaning over the seat in front of her, exclaiming at the brilliance of the sea, when all at once the little black-haired woman in the seat ahead turned around. She was heavily made-up and wore a pair of dark sunglasses.

"You understand Spanish?" she asked Sally. Slightly taken aback, Sally answered, "A little." She could understand Spanish well enough, but spoke haltingly as yet. Mark's Spanish was fluent; he was translating some modern Spanish poetry that summer for an anthology.

"It is very beautiful here, isn't it?" The woman quickly picked up the drift of Sally's last sentences. She tossed a nod toward the bay. "I myself have a house in Villaviento," she ran on. "A lovely house, with a garden and a kitchen. Right on the sea . . ."

"How nice," Sally said. Vaguely she wondered if this were at last a fairy godmother in disguise, about to offer her palatial villa to them for the summer. Sally had never quite gotten over her childhood con-viction that there were still whimsical, magic agents operating in the workaday world.

"I rent rooms in the summer," the woman pursued, waving her expensively manicured hand on which several rings winked and shone. "Beautiful. Comfortable. Kitchen rights. Garden rights. Bal-cony rights . . ."

Sally relinquished her dream of free castles in Spain. "Is it really near the ocean?" she asked eagerly. Already weary of the dry Spanish landscape, she could not conquer her nostalgia for the great honest blue sea pounding along Nauset Beach at home.

"Of course! I'll show you everything. Everything!" the dark little woman promised. Carried along by the momentum of her own rapid speech, she seemed unable to stop, but went rattling on in staccato phrases, dotted with abrupt, dramatic gestures. "I'm Señora Mangada. They know me here. Just ask anybody: who's Widow Mangada? They'll tell you Of course," she shrugged eloquently, as if Mark and Sally might not, after all, be wise enough to appreciate the privilege she was offering them, "of course, you can decide for yourselves. It's up to you."

The bus was pulling up in the center of Villaviento. One large dusty palm tree sprouted in the middle of the little square, surrounded by simple white shop fronts and private houses, their slatted wooden shutters tightly drawn.

"Villaviento!" Widow Mangada proclaimed, with a proprietary flaunt of her red-nailed hand. She bustled out from her seat then and preceded them down the aisle, short and lumpy as a plum pudding. Her stylish white lace dress revealed a black slip underneath; her blue-black hair was elegantly marceled in a broth of little waves and curls.

Mark's eyes followed her meditatively as she flounced down the steps into the street with an important air.

"You might think," he mused, "that a row of photographers was lying in wait for her."

A motley crew of tanned native boys battled among themselves to carry the Widow's luggage. She scurried about, at last electing a young boy with a cart to load on her bulging canvas suitcase and an immense knobbly burlap bag.

Then she was back, with the boy and laden cart in tow, chattering and gesticulating as if she'd never left off. Mark hoisted the rucksack on his shoulder and Sally balanced typewriter and watermelon.

"This way," the Widow said, sliding her hand under Sally's arm in an intimate, friendly fashion and trotting along beside them in her stumpy openwork pumps.

Modern hotels lined the main Avenida, with bright red, yellow and green balconies, as gaudy as if colored at random from a child's paint-box.

"Hotels!" The Widow clucked disapprovingly and hurried them on. "Terrible! Expensive! A hundred pesetas a night, for one person only. And then all the little extra charges. Cigarettes. Telephone." She shook her frizzed black curls.

Mark slanted Sally a warning look over Widow Mangada's head. The Widow was already launched on an enthusiastic sales talk.

"Look!" She threw out her arm triumphantly as they turned the corner to walk along the ocean boulevard. The bay lay before them, vivid, blue, rimmed by a crest of orange hills. "And here we are." Widow Mangada was unlocking the gate of a creamy beige stucco villa.

Sally stood, mouth open. "Talk about dreams," she said to Mark. The house, with a vine-grown second-floor terrace, was set deep in a grove of palm trees. Beds of red geraniums and white daisies blazed like bonfires in the garden; spined cacti bordered the flagstone path.

Chattering on about natural beauty, the Widow led them around to the back to point out her grape arbor, her fig tree thick with green fruit, and the splendid view of purple hills in the background, suspended in a scrim of mist.

Within, the stone-tiled house was cool and dark as a well. The Widow flew about, throwing open shutters and indicating the shining rows of aluminum pans in the kitchen with its blackened one-ring petrol stove, the stacks of plates and wineglasses amassed in the dining room. She yanked out drawers, rummaged in cupboards. Sally, already delighted with the housekeeping possibilities, was won completely by the tiny room upstairs. It opened, together with one of the larger rooms, onto the balcony terrace and a view of the blue Mediterranean framed in palm fronds.

"Oh, Mark," Sally pleaded. "Let's stay."

The Widow's black beady eyes darted from one to the other. "Nothing like it. Perfect." Her words rippled over themselves, smooth as oil. "I'll show you the town. The market. Everything. We'll be friends. Not impersonal as they are in the hotels . . ."

"How much," Mark asked matter-of-factly, "does it cost?"

The Widow paused, hesitating, as if he had brought up something just a touch indelicate. "One hundred pesetas a night," she said at last. She hurried on then: "For both of you. Plus the service. You'll have all the comfort . . ."

"Service?" Mark stopped her. "How much does that make it?"

"A hundred and ten."

Mark exchanged a look with Sally. "That's more than we can spend for two months," he said simply.

Wistfully, Sally recalled the wire whisks and soup ladles lining the kitchen. "But I'll cook," she volunteered, although as yet rather dismayed by the stubborn look of the unfamiliar petrol stove. "We'll go to the peasant market, and that will bring the cost of living way down."

"We're writers." Mark turned to the Widow. All we want is a quiet place where we can write for the summer. We can't afford one hundred and ten pesetas a night."

"Ah! You are writers!" Widow Mangada grew effusive. "I, too, am a writer. Stories. Poems. Many poems." The Widow subsided then, dropping her blue-shadowed lids. "For you," she said, stressing her words, "I will not charge service. But you understand," she glanced up quickly, "you must not tell anyone. The Others will pay service. The government demands it. But you and I, we will be friends." She gave them a blinding smile, displaying a row of large, protruding yellow teeth. "I will treat you like my own son and daughter."

Mark shifted uneasily from one foot to the other, glancing at Sally's eager face. He sighed. "All right, then," he said at last. "We'll take it."

Shortly after three o'clock that afternoon, Mark and Sally were lying on the deserted beach in front of the Widow's house, drying off after a swim in the mild green surf. They had spent the rest of the morning at the outdoor peasant market shopping for food supplies.

Sally glanced up at the balcony across the street and giggled. "The Widow's mincing around in our room now, putting those embroidered sheets and valuable bedspreads on the beds. 'Especially for us.'"

Mark grunted skeptically from where he lay stretched face down on their beach towel. "I still think there's something queer about her being a landlady after all the talk of noble birth and university degrees and her brilliant dead doctor husband she gave us over lunch."

"I wonder what her poems are like," Sally mused, gazing out at the barren island in the middle of the bay. An elaborate white schooner was slowly crossing along the horizon line, like the fabulous relic of an old legend. "She told me she's written an exquisite description of moonlight on the water at Villaviento. 'A luster of pearls,' she called it."

"Don't let that fancy tinsel fool you," Mark cautioned. "She probably writes torrid Spanish love stories for the pulp magazines."

That evening, Sally struggled to light the smoking petrol stove while Mark lay upstairs, burned raw from the afternoon sun, radiating heat like a Sunday roast. She was just warming up the frying pan of olive oil when Widow Mangada materialized in the doorway. In a flash, the Widow was at the range, turning down the wick of the petrol stove.

"Not so high," she chided Sally. "Or it wastes the wick. What are you making?" She peered curiously at the heap of sliced potatoes and onions Sally was planning to fry.

"Ah!" the Widow exclaimed. "I'll show you how we do things!"

Sally lounged patiently against the big black range while the Widow got the pan of oil steaming and tossed in the potatoes and onions, prattling rapidly all the while about how Sally must order milk to be delivered daily, go early to market for fresh fish, and take care to watch the scales and not get cheated; those tricky peasants weren't above using rocks instead of proper weights and measures.

When the potatoes and onions were browning, the Widow whipped up two eggs in a cup and poured them into the pan. "Somebody came to look at the front room while you and your husband were at the beach this afternoon," she said gaily, poking at the pan, as if thinking of nothing but the welfare of the onions and potatoes. "They asked about the balcony going off the big front room and I told them, of course: the balcony is for the use of everybody."

Sally felt a queer catch in her stomach, as if knifed unexpectedly from behind. She thought fast. The only windows to their tiny bedroom, which wasn't even big enough for a writing table, were in the French doors opening onto the balcony. If other people sat out there, she and Mark would have absolutely no privacy.

"Why," Sally covered her incredulity with a calm, reasonable tone, "that would really be impossible." The Widow seemed deeply absorbed in sliding the tortilla onto a plate. As Sally spoke, she flipped the plate expertly upside down, dropping the tortilla back in the pan to brown on the other side.

"The other tourists can sun on the beach or in the garden," Sally went on, "but we can't write in public. We can only write where it's quiet, on our balcony. Being a writer, as you are"—Sally picked up the Widow's words, amazed at her own sudden turn for flattery—"I am sure you understand that absolute peace is essential for work."

The Widow flashed Sally a grin, which sheathed an intent side glance. Then, almost immediately, she broke into a rich, deep chuckle, as if laughing at a joke on both of them. "But of course. Of course I understand," she said soothingly. "To the next person who asks about the balcony, I'll say: why, I've rented that to two American writers. It is just for them."

In triumph, Sally bore the savory tortilla upstairs together with a bottle of wine. She felt she had somehow outfinessed the Widow at a game yet new to her.

As she shut the bedroom door behind her, Mark groaned, "Listen!"

"What's the matter?" Sally asked, concerned. She went out on the balcony to set the tray on the table. It was already twilight, and a bright white moon was rising out of the sea. From below their balcony, along the ocean boulevard, came a loud murmur as of gathering multitudes before some large mob scene.

Sally stared. Crowds of lavishly dressed summer tourists were strolling below, glancing up in curiosity at the balcony. Along the low wall bordering the beach, white-uniformed Spanish maids sat tending squalling children. A donkey was pulling a hand organ past. Vendors pushed by carts of coconuts and ice cream.

"It's the town's evening sport," Mark lamented. "The idle rich. Gabbing and gawping. They siesta all afternoon. No wonder the beach was so magnificently empty today."

"Well, if it's just in the evening," Sally consoled, "we'll get up and start work at dawn." But she, too, felt a bit self-conscious pouring wine, trying to avoid the inquisitive eyes below. The Widow had put up a ROOMS FOR RENT sign on the balcony that afternoon.

"I feel like a living illustrated ad of Balcony Dwellers in Villaviento," Mark grumbled.

"Oh, it's only for an hour or so," Sally said, watching Mark take his first bite of the tortilla. He murmured approval. "Wait till you hear about the coup d'état I've just managed," she went on proudly, and told him that the balcony was now exclusively theirs.

"I was beginning to worry about the balcony," Mark said. "She's a subtle lady, that one."

Sally woke early the next morning to hear the seethe and rush of waves on the beach. Slipping carefully out of bed so as not to wake Mark, still sleeping, shrimp-red, in a tangle of sheets, she crossed the hall to the bathroom to wash up. No water came from the single cold-water tap. Dimly she remembered that yesterday, in the flurry of instructions and useful information, the Widow had switched on the lever of a strange, blue-painted box in the kitchen, claiming that the motor made water.

Sally tiptoed downstairs in the still house. The kitchen was darkly shuttered. Opening the shutters, Sally regarded the blue box mistrustfully, with its odd blue spigots and frayed wires. She had a blind respect for electricity. Bracing herself, she pulled the lever. A flash of blue sparks shot from the box, and a thin column of acrid smoke began twisting out from the heart of the machine.

Guiltily, Sally switched back the lever. The smoke stopped. She knocked on the Widow's door, next to the kitchen. There was no answer. She called, softly, then louder. Still no answer. This is ridiculous, Sally thought, shifting from one cold bare foot to the other: no water, no Widow. No coffee, either, she added to the list of grievances. For a moment she had the absurd conviction that the Widow had sneaked away overnight, leaving them with an unmanageable elephant of a house. She went upstairs to wake Mark.

"There's no water," Sally announced in tragic tones. Mark squinted up at her from swollen pink eyelids. "And the Widow has disappeared."

Sleepily, Mark pulled on his bathing trunks and accompanied Sally downstairs to the kitchen. He turned the lever of the water-making machine. No response. He tried the light switch. No electricity. "Something's fused," he said. "The whole house is probably a web of defective wiring."

"*You* knock on the Widow's door and call her," Sally said. "Your voice is louder. If she's renting us the house, the least she can do is keep the water running."

Mark knocked on the door. He called the Widow. The house was deathly still except for the grandfather clock in the hall, ticking like a coffined heart.

"Maybe she's dead in there," Sally said. "I have the strangest feeling there's nobody breathing behind that door."

"Maybe she went out early." Mark yawned. "I miss my coffee."

At last they decided to go back to bed and wait for the Widow. Just as Sally was closing her eyes, she heard the screak of the front-gate hinges, and brisk staccato footsteps tripping up the walk. Jumping into her bathrobe, she padded downstairs to meet the Widow, fresh and lacy as a daisy in her white dress, coming in the door with a bundle of parcels.

"Ah," the Widow crowed merrily on seeing Sally. "Have you slept well?" Sally, looking at the Widow with a more jaundiced eye than on the previous day, wondered if there wasn't an ironic note veiled in her honey tones.

"There's no water," Sally stated bleakly. "No water for washing. Or coffee."

The Widow laughed brightly, as if Sally were a charming but rather maladroit child. "Why, of course there's water," she said, dropping her parcels on a chair and making a little rush into the kitchen. "So simple!"

Following her, Sally felt grimly positive that the machine was primed so it would work only for the Widow. With a certain satisfaction, she watched the Widow turn on the lever. There were no results.

"I tried that, too," Sally told her, lounging casually against the doorjamb. "And nothing happened."

The Widow tried the light switch. "No light!" she exclaimed triumphantly and gave another one of her deep, confidential laughs with a long, shrewd look at Sally hidden in the middle of it.

"It is so in all the village," the Widow said then. "No light, no machine."

"Then this is usual in the morning?" Sally queried coolly.

The Widow appeared, for the first time, to realize that Sally was annoyed. "Ah, you mustn't take things so serious." She shook her dark head reprovingly. "There is always water here. Plenty of water."

Sally waited, with what she trusted was a skeptical, challenging expression.

With the lofty air of a woman far above mere worldly emergencies, the Widow glided over to the sink, lifted from the counter a wooden lid which Sally had used as a chopping board the night before, and revealed a bottomless black hole. Whisking a pail and long rope from one of her myriad cupboards, the Widow dropped the pail down the hole. There was an echoing splash. The Widow gave the rope a series of short, energetic tugs and hauled up a sloshing bucketful of sparkling water.

"You see," she moralized to Sally. "Plenty of water. All the time." She began filling three pitchers of various sizes. "Marvelous water. Beneficial for the stomach." She motioned at the cold-water tap in the sink, wrinkling her nose up in a grimace of disgust and shaking her head. "That water's bad," she told Sally. *"Non potable."*

Sally gasped. Fortunately she and Mark had drunk wine the previous evening. The tap water was no doubt slow poison. Had the Widow forgotten to mention it before? Or hadn't she wanted to bring up any disadvantages until they were well settled in her house? Sally wondered, then, with increasing unease, whether the Widow *ever* would have told them about her secret store of drinkable, health-giving water if the machine hadn't broken down that morning.

With a new reserve, Sally took a pitcher of water from the cheerfully voluble Widow and went upstairs to wash. In a few minutes, the Widow trilled up that the lights were on and water was coming everywhere.

"She's probably been prancing around the yard with a divining rod," Mark said grumpily. He went down to heat a kettle of water on the petrol stove for shaving.

As they sat on the balcony, shaded by a slatted bamboo awning, sipping their steaming mugs of coffee, Sally rambled on about the quirks of Spanish housekeeping. "Imagine," she told Mark, "the Widow doesn't have any soap and washes her dishes in cold water with little tangles of straw. She was sermonizing at me just now about how neat I'll have to be when the Others come. Well, you should see her own cupboard—all higgledy-piggledy, with scraps of cold beans and dead fish and a pack of ants carrying away her sugar grain by grain. It'll be gone by tomorrow."

Mark broke into a laugh. "I'd give anything to know what the townspeople of Villaviento think about her. We've probably got in with the village witch."

Sally typed some letters home on the balcony that morning, while Mark propped himself up on pillows in the bedroom, nursing his burn and writing an animal fable. From the street below came the cry of the bread woman, strolling by with a basket of fried rolls over her arm; the milk boy biked past with a gallon can in his basket. As Sally lazed, her fingers lagging over the keys, the sound of voices drifted up to her.

Widow Mangada was showing a young Spanish couple about the garden, gesturing grandiloquently at the geraniums, the view of the sea. Sally peered down at them through the vine leaves. She half hoped the Widow would have no other customers, it was so quiet and pleasant in the dark house with just Mark and herself.

Preparing lunch that noon, Sally put a pan of string beans on to boil and began cutting up some cold sausage. After ten minutes, she checked the beans. They were as hard as ever, and the water wasn't even warm. Sally turned the wick higher, hoping to make more heat come out of the stove. An unhealthy flame flared up, thin, smoking green.

At that moment, as if beckoned by some occult signal, Widow Mangada appeared in the doorway, took one look at the smoke funneling out of the stove, and rushed bleating in horror to the range. Whipping off the pan of beans and the chimney of the petrol stove, she revealed, with a flourish, the criminal evidence of over an inch of frayed, charred wick.

"No petrol!" she announced with all the drama of a doctor diagnosing cancer. She scuttled over to her cupboard, pulled out a bottle of transparent liquid, and poured it into the tank of the stove. Then she fussed about with the wick, snipping off the charred ends with her fingers, raising the wick higher on the shaft. She lit the wick again and replaced the beans. Not satisfied with this, she tasted a bean and shook her head sadly at Sally.

"You wait a minute," she said, and went running out of the room. She returned with a handful of powder which she tossed into the beans, just now beginning to boil. The water fizzed and foamed.

"What's that?" Sally asked, suspicious.

The Widow gave her a coy little look and shook her finger as at a naughty child. "It's just something." She smiled evasively. "I've been cooking a lot longer than you and know a few small tricks."

Then, as if in chance afterthought, the Widow went on: "Oh, by the way, a doctor has rented the room upstairs for a few days." She hung poised in the doorway like a white gull ready for flight. "He's coming in about an hour."

"Oh, just *one* man," Sally remarked in prosaic tones. She was beginning to enjoy playing dense and making the Widow detail her maneuvers at a slower rate.

"No," the Widow said, obviously a bit nettled. "He has a wife. And two friends." She hesitated. "And the other couple has a baby."

"Oh," Sally said eloquently, bending over the steaming beans.

The Widow, about to retreat, thought better of it and advanced again to the stove. "You understand," her playful tone with Sally changed, barbed now with an odd emotional intensity, "I do not care how many people are in the house as long as it is always full. You must learn to share. The cupboards, the stove, they are not just for you. They are also for the Others." She put on her glittering yellow-toothed smile then, as if to outshine her bluntness.

"Why, of course!" Sally said to the Widow in bland astonishment.

But something else was evidently bothering the Widow's conscience, too. "The Spaniards, Señora," she told Sally gravely, "are very different from you Americans." Her tone made no secret of which side her sympathies were on. "They sing all the time. They turn radios loud. They leave things here and there." Carried away by her own speech, the Widow began to sway her plump little body to and fro dramatically, acting it all out in a sort of pantomime. "They come in late at night. And their children cry. It is very natural."

Sally couldn't restrain a smile as she envisioned a bevy of Spaniards bellowing arias in the cold shower and executing flamenco dances around the petrol stove. "I understand perfectly," she assured the Widow.

"Perhaps," the Widow brightened, as if struck by a new and marvelously advantageous scheme for Sally, "you would like to move your cooking things out of the cupboard, over here. Then the cupboard would not bother you, helter-skelter with Spanish dishes." Sally's look followed the Widow's cavalier gesture. She was pointing to an open shelf over the garbage can.

So that was it. Sally's intuitions were quickening; she felt stripped for action. "Why, I am perfectly delighted where I am," she told the Widow in demure but firm tones. "I wouldn't dream of being bothered."

The Widow disappeared from the kitchen with a dazzling false grin, which Sally felt lingering on as she finished preparing the meal, disquieting as the smile of the Cheshire cat.

While Mark and Sally were eating lunch on the balcony, a car drew up in front of the house. The Spanish couple Sally had seen that morning got out, with another couple and a little girl, frilled as a peony in her starched petticoats.

The Widow ran out to greet them, swinging the gate wide as if it were crusted with gold and costly gems, almost curtsying as the four Spaniards walked in, carrying the child.

At three, Mark and Sally left their room to go for a swim. Mark disliked the crowds of fat, swarthy women and oiled dandies thronging the beach at midday, and during siesta time, from three to five, they had the beach completely to themselves. In the upstairs hall, all the window shutters were closed and the other rooms were hushed and darkened as in a hospital. Sally shut the door behind them. The sound echoed sepulchrally.

"*Ssst!*" With a venomous hiss, Widow Mangada was at the foot of the stairs. In a tirade of exaggerated wavings and whispers, she announced that the Spaniards were all sleeping and ordered Mark and Sally to be more considerate.

"Whew!" Mark exclaimed as they were safe on the beach. "What a change of tone."

It developed that the Spaniards were going to eat at one of the town hotels. Sally stood over the petrol stove that night, stirring tuna in a thick cream sauce and listening warily for the light, almost inaudible tread of the Widow. She had grown to dread those footsteps. Outside their bedroom, now, she felt vulnerable as a sniper's target in enemy territory.

After she had turned off the petrol stove, she heard the fire still burning in the chimney. Leaning down, she blew to extinguish it. With a loud pouf, a long leaping tongue of flame forked up at her. Startled, Sally jumped back. Aiming for my eyes, she thought uneasily as she rubbed away the tears from the stinging smoke.

While she was letting the water run freely over her cooking dishes, the Widow darted in, crossed to the sink, and put the cork in to stop the drain. "You mustn't waste water here," she lectured Sally. "It is very precious."

Sally waited until the Widow was out of the kitchen, removed the plug, and turned the water on full force with a rich sense of illicit extravagance.

The next morning, Sally woke to hear the Widow's voice in the hall. From her unusually flustered, apologetic tones, Sally gathered something was wrong. Curious, she tiptoed to the door. As if developing symptoms of the Widow's tactics like a contagious disease, she stooped to peer out from the keyhole. Giggling, then, she poked Mark awake.

"Guess what," she informed him. "The five of them are all queued up around the bathroom and the Widow's in her bathrobe, lugging up great pitchers of water. The doctor's in there shaving now."

The water machine had broken down completely. "From over-work," Mark hazarded. "Her whole fancy house is probably tottering over a pit of quicksand."

When Sally went downstairs to draw water from the well for their coffee, she found the Widow in the hall, swathed in a soiled yellow satin wrapper, wet-mopping the stone tiles. In the frank morning light, her face appeared haggard and slightly green; her eyebrows were not yet penciled on, and her mouth hung loose and froggish without lipstick.

"Ah!" the Widow sputtered, leaning on her mop and speaking in hoarse, fretful tones. "This morning I go to town to look for a maid. I am not used to this. At home in Alicante I had three maids . . ."

Sally murmured sympathetically. With dignity, the Widow stretched to her full height, her chin not reaching far above the mop handle. "When I go out to town," her look blurred beyond Sally, lost in some luminous far vision, "I am a *grande dame*. I do not work when the front door is open, for the people to see. You understand? But . . ." the Widow fixed Sally with a stern, proud glare. ". . . when the door is shut"—she shrugged her shoulders and spread her hands comprehensively—"I do everything. Everything."

The Widow sailed home from town that morning with a black-clad maid in her wake. She supervised imperiously for an hour, while the maid swept, scrubbed, and dusted. Then the maid returned to town.

"It is very difficult," the Widow confided to Sally, with the air of a born duchess fallen upon hard times, "to find a maid in Villaviento. They are so expensive in the summer. They get paid too much by the hotels. If you have a maid nowadays, you must be very careful of her feelings."

The Widow rallied enough to mimic the tender treatment a maid must have. She nodded, minced about, grinned sugarily. "If she breaks your priceless crystal vase, you must laugh and say: 'Ah, do not trouble yourself over it, mademoiselle.' "

Sally smiled. The Widow was always complaining about expense; how much of her moaning was an act, Sally couldn't truly tell.

That morning, from the balcony, Sally and Mark watched Widow Mangada fussing about with repairmen, a gardener, and three native workers with a donkey cart who began to remove all the stones and rubble choking her unused driveway.

"I suppose it's a sign of aristocracy here," Mark said, "having a team of men constantly slaving for you. And a donkey or two."

"She's so desperate about keeping up her royal front in Villaviento," Sally said.

"Royal front," Mark snorted. "It's rank humbug. She may have taught Spanish to the governor's wife in Gibraltar but I haven't been able to corner her for one of her promised lessons yet."

"Wait till she gets the house settled down," Sally soothed. "She still hasn't found anyone to rent the front room, and it's probably bothering her."

"I'm sure she can't rent it because of the balcony being shut off. No doubt she's furious with herself for letting us win her best selling point."

"She knows she would have lost us if she didn't give in," Sally reminded.

Mark shook his head. "She'll try to fox us yet."

"I don't see how," Sally said. "If we just keep to ourselves."

As Sally was dreamily peeling the potatoes for lunch, Widow Mangada entered the kitchen. She pounced on the potato in Sally's hand and took up the knife. "Now *this* is the way you should peel a potato!" She instructed Sally patronizingly, making the brown skin fly off in one continuous corkscrew strip. Sally sighed. More and more she resented the Widow's little meddling forays into the kitchen. The Widow even rearranged her cupboard on the sly, mixing the onions in the egg dish to free another bowl for her own sodden dabs of cold, fishy pottage which she left lying about on her shelves for days.

As the Widow plucked up another potato, Sally realized she was using even more flowery oratory than usual. "Every other summer, of course," the Widow was saying, "I've rented the house out to one family. Complete. For twenty, thirty thousand pesetas. But," the knife flew, stripping the potato bare, "this summer for the first time I stay here to rent rooms. Only it proves impossible."

Sally felt a chill of foreboding. She waited. "The government . . ." Widow Mangada smiled up ingratiatingly with a helpless shrug at Sally, all the while continuing to skin the potato by some deft sleight-of-hand. "The government forces us to fill every room. And today the Alcalde, the Mayor of Villaviento, tells me I must rent the house entire since I cannot fill all the rooms."

Sally caught her breath and took her first clear look at the Widow. The ornate painted mask cracked in a wolfish grin. Eyes exposed a black, bottomless pool into which a stone had vanished, ring after surface ring rippling outward.

Leaving the Widow holding the scraped white potato, open-mouthed, in the middle of a sentence, Sally turned and ran. Her breath caught tight in her chest, she burst in on Mark.

"Oh, stop her," she cried, throwing herself on the bed. There was the sound of quick, tapping footsteps following her up the stairs. "Stop that woman," Sally begged, almost hysterical now. "She's going to evict us."

"Señora," the Widow was calling in dulcet tones outside the door. Sally heard the cockroach rustle in the cupboard, the spider knitting hexes across the well.

Mark opened the door a crack and looked down at Widow Mangada. "Well?" he said.

Widow Mangada practiced her charms. With beseeching eyes, she gazed up at Mark, crooning: "Ah, Señor. The Señora is so excitable. She does not even listen to what I am going to say. Men are . . ." she fumbled prettily, ". . . so much more practical than young girls about such things."

Mark beckoned to Sally, who was eyeing them broodingly from the bed. "Come on back to the kitchen and finish getting lunch," he said. "We'll talk about it there."

In the kitchen, the Widow spoke beguilingly to Mark while Sally tended the fried potatoes, still shaken, ashamed of letting her defenses down in front of the Widow.

"Now of course," the Widow was assuring Mark in mellifluous tones, "I do not want you and the Señora to go. I do not look for anybody to rent the whole house. But," she shrugged with wheedling philosophy, "if the Alcalde sends someone, what am I to do?"

"Ask her how much notice she'll give us," Sally said to Mark sulkily in English. She refused to speak Spanish to the Widow now, retreating as if for protection to the language the Widow did not understand and putting Mark between them as interpreter.

"How much notice?" Mark asked the Widow. She looked surprised at Mark for bringing up such apparently trifling concerns. "Ah, two days, three days . . ." she drawled finally, as if conceding a great favor.

Sally was aghast. "And where do we go then?" she stormed at Mark. "Into the streets?" She felt sick at the thought of packing up and moving again, furious at the Widow's sly weathercock shifts.

"We'll talk about it later." Mark closed the subject. Silenced for the time being, the Widow retreated.

"If she thinks," Sally raged over lunch, "that we're going to live here at her convenience, paying her until she finds someone else, so she won't lose a peseta . . . And using the government as an excuse for her own sweet whims . . ."

"Take it easy," Mark placated. "She's crooked as a crab, that's all. Face up to it."

They decided to go house-hunting around Villaviento early that evening without telling the Widow until they were actually moving out.

That night, over supper on the balcony, Sally exulted: "We've bought a house. A whole house. I'll have my own kitchen. And my own snarls of straw for the dishes."

"Oh, our new landlady's probably having a fiesta right now at the way we let her jump the rent." Mark was characteristically reserved, but even he couldn't hide his pleasure. They were paying almost a thousand pesetas less for a quiet house in the native quarter than they were spending for Widow Mangada's cramped, noisy room. And they were moving in the next morning.

Mark and Sally lingered over the wine, toasting their success, relaxing easily and fully for the first time since they had arrived at Widow Mangada's.

Sally laughed happily as they finished the bottle of wine. "It's like being freed from a jinx," she said.

While Mark was helping Sally wash up the dishes, the Widow tripped blithely into the kitchen. "Ah," she chirruped with a bright new-minted smile, "and did you have a nice walk? I do hope," she raced on, "you won't trouble yourselves over what the Alcalde said." She gave them a cajoling look. "We'll have such a nice summer. Probably no one will even ask about the house. Now, if you were Spanish . . ." she tossed Mark an arch glance, "you wouldn't dream of being so serious about such a little thing . . ."

"I think we should tell you," Mark said without preamble, overriding Sally's motions to silence, "that we've found a new place. With a summer contract. And we're moving out tomorrow."

Sally forgave Mark for springing the surprise a day early. Widow Mangada's jaw dropped. Her face flushed an ugly purple.

"What?" her voice shrilled up a scale, incredulous. She began trembling, as if shaken in the teeth of a high wind. "After all I've done for you! After I gave you the balcony . . ." Her voice frayed to a coarse squawk.

"Our room's too small to live in without the balcony, and you know it," Sally inserted truthfully.

Widow Mangada flew at her like a maddened wasp, brandishing a furious finger in Sally's face. "It's you, you!" she accused spitefully, shedding all pretense of decorum. "Always complaining. The room's too small! This and that! Your husband never complains . . ." The Widow veered in a last desperate bid to flatter Mark.

"I ask my wife to manage household affairs," he cut the Widow off firmly. "I'm ready to stand behind everything she's said."

"Well!" the Widow fumed, outraged. "After all my consideration, my generosity, my frankness . . ." She paused, breathless.

Then, her flair for rhetoric returning, she began to gather up the ragged shreds of ceremony. "As you wish," she managed at last with a wobbly smile; the yellow teeth gleamed. "You say you leave tomorrow?" she asked, the metallic light of the adding machine already back in her eye. She turned on her heel. The front door slammed behind her.

Late that night, the front gate screaked open. Mark and Sally could hear the Widow muttering from the lower hall. She began to mount the stairs, grumbling loudly and incoherently all the while. Sally drew the sheet up over her head, fully believing some immediate judgment was at hand. Savagely, the Widow stamped across the upstairs hall, through the vast, empty front room and onto the balcony, spitting out curses and unintelligible snarls. Sally could see her squat, lumpish shape silhouetted in the moonlight, busy about the balcony railing.

"She's ripping down the rental sign," Mark whispered.

Bearing the sign as if it were a severed human head, the Widow stormed downstairs.

The next morning, as Sally boiled mounds of potatoes and eggs for a picnic lunch to take to their new home, pleasantly conscious she was using up much of the Widow's petrol, Widow Mangada appeared in the kitchen. Her mood of the night before had altered completely. She was bland as butter.

"I met the woman who owns the place you're moving to last night," she informed Sally. "She told me exactly what you're paying for the summer." The Widow pronounced the sum with something akin to reverence. "Is that correct?"

"Yes," Sally said a bit shortly. She resented Widow Mangada's finding out such details. Yet she was aware that the Widow could not accuse them of being cheated: she herself was charging them more for so much less.

"It's a beautiful big house," Sally could not resist adding. She lifted the hard-boiled eggs from the steaming kettle.

The Widow made a wry face. "I wouldn't know. I never walk up to that part of town. So far from the beach and all." The house was a mere ten minutes from the sea.

"Mark and I love to walk," Sally replied sweetly.

"I told the woman," the Widow went on, fiddling with the lace collar of her dress, "that you and your husband were very nice. I said of course you would have stayed on with me for the summer if I hadn't been forced suddenly by the Alcalde to rent the house as a whole to one family."

Sally was silent, letting the fib hang fire in empty air.

"We will still be good friends," the Widow proclaimed then, with a magnanimous smile. "Anything you need, you just come over and ask me. Haven't I taught you all about Spanish cooking?" She teetered on tiptoe and peered almost pleadingly into Sally's face.

Before they left, the Widow had enthusiastically made an appointment for an English lesson from Mark at her home the following afternoon.

"I want to know everything. Everything!" she repeated, accompanying them to the door, her black saucer-eyes brimming with a thirst for scholarship.

Mark and Sally woke the next morning in their spacious new house to hear a thin jangle of bells as a herd of black goats went stepping delicately up the street on their way to pasture. A strong, freakish wind was blowing out of the low hills. At market, the old banana vendor claimed Villaviento hadn't seen a wind like that for eighty years.

The day grew bleak, curded over with clouds. Sally tried to read in the unhealthy yellow light, waiting for Mark to return from his afternoon English lesson with Widow Mangada.

The wind howled about the house, raising eddies of dust and rattling the window frames. Scraps of paper and torn grape leaves swatted against the panes. Some storm was brewing.

Mark was back twenty minutes after he'd left. "She's vanished," he said, tramping in and brushing the dust off his jacket. "There's a German family living there now. She must have skipped back to Alicante the minute we left yesterday morning."

Rain began to splatter down in large drops on the dusty pavement outside.

"Do you suppose she honestly had all those university degrees?" Sally asked. "And a brilliant doctor husband?"

"Maybe," Mark said. "Or maybe she's just a clever quack."

"Or a weird sister."

"Who's to tell?"

The wind screeched around the corners of the house, whirling this way and that, blinding the windowpanes with rain out of the labyrinth of those dark, malignant hills.

Cambridge Notes

From Notebooks, February 1956

February 19, Sunday night

To whom it may concern: Every now and then there comes a time when the neutral and impersonal forces of the world turn and come together in a thundercrack of judgment. There is no reason for the sudden terror, the feeling of condemnation, except that circumstances all mirror the inner doubt, the inner fear. Yesterday, walking quite peacefully over the Mill Lane bridge, after leaving my bike to be repaired (feeling lost, pedestrian, impotent), smiling that smile which puts a benevolent lacquer on the shuddering fear of strangers' gazes, I was suddenly turned upon by little boys making snowballs on the dam. They began to throw them at me, openly, honestly, trying to hit. They missed every time, and with that wary judgment that comes with experience, I watched the dirty snowballs coming at me, behind and in front, and, sick with wonder, kept walking slowly, determinedly, ready to parry a good hit before it struck. But none struck, and with a tolerant smile that was a superior lie, I walked on.

Today my thesaurus, which I would rather live with on a desert isle than a bible, as I have so often boasted cleverly, lay open after I'd written the rough draft of a bad, sick poem, at 545: Deception; 546: Untruth; 547: Dupe; 548: Deceiver. The clever reviewer and writer who is an ally of the generous creative opposing forces, cries with deadly precision: "Fraud, fraud." Which has been cried solidly for six months during that dark year of hell.

Yesterday night: coming into the party at Emmanuel (ah, yes) they were hypnotizing someone named Morris in the dark, crowded room, lit with conscious bohemianism by candles in old wine bottles. The fat, yet strong, ugly boy was saying with commanding mastery and power: "When you try to go through the door there will be glass in the way. You cannot go through the door, there will be glass. When I say 'gramophone' you will fall asleep again." Then he brought Morris out of the trance, and Morris tried to go through the door, but stopped. He could not go through the door, there was glass in the way. The fat boy said "gramophone," and two laughing, nervous boys caught Morris as he fell. Then they made Morris become stiff as a steel bar; he seemed to know just how stiff that was, and went rigid on the floor.

And I talked and talked with Win: pink-faced, blue-eyed, blond, confident, on the beginnings of love with a girl he met skiing who is engaged and going home to see about breaking it off and coming back and maybe living and traveling with him. And I learned that I was not wrong about L, and that we both love N and I talked of R. Such games. I talked of R as if he were dead. With a deadly nobility. And tall, good-looking John put his warm hand on my shoulder and I asked him intently about hypnotism, while Chris's eager, shiny, red-cheeked baby face and curly hair floated on the edge, and out of misplaced kindness I refused to go into the raw room oozing dance music with John, and went to talk chastely with Win and drink and tell Rafe who was the host with a shining face and a bowl perpetually full of fruit and liquor of a different color each time he came: "You are a wonderful host."

Then, Chris left, and in the back of talk, knelt to hug the little black-clad miniature Sally Bowles with minute black slacks and jersey and cropped blond Joan of Arc hair and a long wicked cigarette holder (matching exactly her very small man Roger who was all in black like a pale ballet dancer and very little, with a review he had just written on Yeats in print in a magazine called Khayyam, after Omar). Chris then sat a red-dressed girl on his lap, and then they went to dance. Meanwhile, Win and I talk very wisely and the appalling easiness of this strikes me down: I could throw everything away and make a play for John, who is now making a play for the nearest and easiest. But everybody has exactly the same smiling frightened face, with the look that says: "I'm important. If you only get to know me, you will see how important I am. Look into my eyes. Kiss me, and you will see how important I am."

I too want to be important. By being different. And these girls are all the same. Far off, I go to my coat with Win; he brings me my scarf as I wait on the stair, and Chris is being red-cheeked and dramatic and breathless and penitent. He wants to be scolded, and punished. That is too easy. That is what we all want.

I am rather high, and distant, and it is convenient to be led home across the snow fields. It is very cold, and all the way back I am thinking: Richard, you live in this moment. You live now. You are in my guts and I am acting because you are alive. And meanwhile you are probably sleeping exhausted and happy in the arms of some brilliant whore, or maybe even the Swiss girl who wants to marry you. I cry out to you. I want to write you, of my love, that absurd faith which keeps me chaste, so chaste, that all I have ever touched or said to others becomes only the rehearsal for you, and preserved only for this. These others now pass the time, and even so little a way over the boundary, to kisses, and touches, I cry mercy and back away, frozen. I am in black, dressed more and more often in black now. I lost one of my red gloves at a cocktail party. I only have black ones left, and they are cold and comfortless.

"Richard," I say, and tell Nat, and tell Win, and tell Chris, as I have told Mallory, and Iko, and Brian, and Martin, and David: There is This Boy in France. And today I told John, who is an excellent listener and who is willing to sit and hear me say how I have once been happy, and once been the highest in me, and grown to the woman I am now, all because of this boy named Richard. And John says: "I could love you violently, if I let myself." But he has not let himself. Why? Because I haven't touched him, I haven't looked into his eyes with the image he wants to see there. And I could. But I am too tired, too noble, in a perverse way. It sickens me. I wouldn't want him, even as he became a victim. So I tell him casually that I won't let it happen, playfully, because it is a stillborn child. I have given birth to so many of these.

And then, bitterly, I say: do I love Richard? Or do I use him as an excuse for a noble, lonely, unloving posture, under the perverse label of faith? Using him so, would I want him on the scene, thin, nervous, little, moody, sickly? Or would I rather cherish the strong mind and soul and blazing potency alone, refined from the marring details of the real world? Coward.

And coming into the dining room unexpectedly at breakfast, the three bright ones turn with a queer look and go on talking the way they do when Mrs. Milne comes in, in apparent continuity, veiling the subject of their words: "So strange, just staring into the fire." And they have condemned you for being mad. Just like that. Because the fear is already there, and has been for so long. The fear that all the edges and shapes and colors of the real world that have been built up again so painfully with such a real love can dwindle in a moment of doubt, and "suddenly go out" the way the moon would in the Blake poem.

A morbid fear: that protests too much. To the doctor. I am going to the psychiatrist this week, just to meet him, to know he's there. And, ironically, I feel I need him. I need a father. I need a mother. I need some older, wiser being to cry to. I talk to God, but the sky is empty, and Orion walks by and doesn't speak. I feel like Lazarus: that story has such a fascination. Being dead, I rose up again, and even resort to the mere sensation value of being suicidal, of getting so close, of coming out of the grave with the scars and the marring mark on my cheek which (is it my imagination) grows more prominent: paling like a death spot in the red, wind-blown skin, browning darkly in photographs, against my grave winter pallor. And I identify too closely with my reading, with my writing. I *am* Nina in *Strange Interlude;* I *do* want to have husband, lover, father and son, all at once. And I depend too desperately on getting my poems, my little glib poems, so neat, so small, accepted by *The New Yorker.* To revenge myself on the blond one, as if the mere paper dikes of print can keep out the creative flood which annihilates all envy, all mere niggling fearful jealousy. Be generous.

Yes. That is what Stephen Spender misses in Cambridge criticism. And what I miss in the miserly back-biting which jokes and picks at grotesqueries. What of ourselves: Jane, gesturing clumsily with knives, knocking over toasters and table silver, breaking Gordon's necklace with awkward clutching mirth, taking supper from Richard, sleep and a room and a key from me, and never caring, utterly casual. How symbolic can we get? Resentment eats, killing the food it eats. Can she resent? She is on the side of the big, conquering boys, the creative ones. We have the impetuous puppies. Could we find those others? We have our Chris, our Nat. But do we?

Generous. Yes, today, I forgave Chris. For deserting me, and hurting me a little, even as the two faceless girls he has known hurt me, only because, a woman, I fight all women for my men. My men. I am a woman, and there is no loyalty, even between mother and daughter. Both fight for the father, for the son, for the bed of mind and body. I also forgave John, for having a rotten tooth, and a lousy pallor, because he was human, and I felt "I need human kind." Even John, as he sat there, distanced by those wise words of ours, even he could be a father. And I cry so to be held by a man; some man, who is a father.

So, now I shall talk every night. To myself. To the moon. I shall walk, as I did tonight, jealous of my loneliness, in the blue-silver of the cold moon, shining brilliantly on the drifts of fresh-fallen snow, with the myriad sparkles. I talk to myself and look at the dark trees, blessedly neutral. So much easier than facing people, than having to look happy, invulnerable, clever. With masks down, I walk, talking to the moon, to the neutral impersonal force that does not hear, but merely accepts my being. And does not smite me down. I went to the bronze boy whom I love, partly because no one really cares for him, and brushed a clot of snow from his delicate smiling face. He stood there in the moonlight, dark, with snow etching his limbs in white, in the semicircle of the privet hedge, bearing his undulant dolphin, smiling still, balancing on one dimpled foot.

And he becomes the child in *When We Dead Awaken*. And Richard will give me no child. And it is his child I could want. To bear, to having growing. The only one whom I could stand to have a child with. Yet. I have a fear, too, of bearing a deformed child, a cretin, growing dark and ugly in my belly, like that old corruption I always feared would break out from behind the bubbles of my eyes. I imagine Richard here, being with me, and my growing big with his child. I ask for less and less. I would face him, and say simply: I am sad that you are not strong, and do not swim and sail and ski, but you have a strong soul, and I will believe in you and make you invincible on this earth. Yes, I have that power. Most women do, to one degree or another. Yet the vampire is there, too. The old, primal hate. That desire to go around castrating the arrogant ones who become such children at the moment of passion.

How the circling steps in the spiral tower bring us back to where we were! I long for Mother, even for Gordon, though his weaknesses . . . sicken me. And he will be financially comfortable. And he is handsome and strong. He skis, swims, yet all the attributes of God could not console me for his weak mind and his physical weakness. God, I would almost have him just to prove he were weak, although my doubt would not let him have the chance to be strong. Unless I were very careful. I would like him to be strong, too. Only there is so little hope, it is so late.

The only perfect love I have is for my brother. Because I cannot love him physically, I shall always love him. And be jealous of his wife, too, a little. Strange, that having lived in such passion, such striking and tears, such fierce joy, I could turn so cold, so disgusted, at all the superfluous playings with others, those flash attractions that seem my doom, now, because each one brings me so much closer to Richard. And still I hope there will be some man in Europe whom I will meet and love and who will free me from this strong idol. Whom I accept even in the heart of his weakness, whom I can make strong, because he gives me a soul and mind to work with.

And now it grows late, late. And I have the old beginning-of-the-week panic, because I cannot read and think enough to meet my little academic obligations, and I have not written at all since the Vence story (which will be rejected with *The New Yorker* rejection of my poems, and even as I bravely say so, I hope I am lying, because my love for Richard is in the story, and my wit, a little bit, and I want to have it frozen in print, and not rejected: see, how dangerous, I again identify with rejections too much!). But how can I go on being quiet, without a soul to talk to wholly here, who is not somehow drastically involved, or near enough to at least be glad that I am unhappy. I want to cry to Richard, to all my friends at home, to come and rescue me. From my insecurity which I must fight through myself. Finishing the next year here, enjoying the pressure of reading, thinking, while at my back is always the mocking tick: A Life is Passing. My Life.

So it is. And I waste my youth and days of radiance on barren ground. How I cried that night I wanted to go to bed, and there was no one, only my dreams of Christmas, and the last year with Richard, whom I have so loved. And I drank the last of the bad sherry, and cracked a few nuts, which were all sour and withered to nothing inside, and the material, inert world mocked me. Tomorrow what? Always patching masks, making excuses for having read a bare half of what I purposed. Yet a life is passing!

I long to permeate the matter of this world: to become anchored to life by laundry and lilacs, daily bread and fried eggs, and a man, the dark-eyed stranger, who eats my food and my body and my love and goes around the world all day and comes back to find solace with me at night. Who will give me a child, that will bring me again to be a member of that race which throws snowballs at me, sensing perhaps the rot at which they strike?

Well: Elly is coming this summer (and Mother and Mrs. Prouty) and Sue next fall. I love both girls, and for once, with them can be wholly woman, and we can talk and talk. I am lucky. That is not long to wait. Yet now, how much do I give? Nothing. I am selfish, scared, crying too much to save myself for my phantom writing. But at any rate it is better than last term, when I was going mad night after night being a screaming whore in a yellow dress. A mad poet. How clever of Dick Gilling; but he is very intuitive. I had not the heart, not the flexible heart, not the guts. But I refused to go on, knowing I could not be big, refusing to be small. I retreated, to work. And it *has* been better: fifteen plays a week instead of two. Number? Not only that, but a real feeling of mastery, of occasional insight. And that is what we wait for.

Will Richard ever need me again? Part of my bargain is that I will be silent until he does. Why is it that the man must so often take the lead? Women can do so much, but apart like this, I can do nothing, shut off from writing him as I am by a kind of honor and pride (I refuse to babble any more about how I love him) and I must wait until he needs me. If ever, in the next five years. And look, with love and faith, not turning sour and cold and bitter, to help others. That is salvation. To give of love inside. To keep love of life, no matter what, and give to others. Generously.

FEBRUARY 20, MONDAY

Dear Doctor: I am feeling very sick. I have a heart in my stomach which throbs and mocks. Suddenly the simple rituals of the day balk like a stubborn horse. It gets impossible to look people in the eye:

corruption may break out again? Who knows. Small talk becomes desperate.

Hostility grows, too. That dangerous, deadly venom which comes from a sick heart. Sick mind, too. The image of identity we must daily fight to impress on the neutral, or hostile, world collapses inward; we feel crushed. Standing in line in the hall, waiting for a lousy dinner of hard-boiled egg in cheese-cream sauce, mashed potatoes and sallow parsnips, we overheard one girl say to another: "Betsy is depressed today." It seems almost an incredible relief to know that there is someone outside oneself who is not happy all the time. We must be at low ebb when we are this far into the black: that everyone else, merely because they are "other," is invulnerable. That is a damn lie.

But I am foundering in relativity again. Unsure. And it is damn uncomfortable: with men (Richard gone, no one here to love), with writing (too nervous about rejections, too desperate and scared about bad poems; but do have ideas for stories; just try soon), with girls (house bristles with suspicion and frigidity; how much is paranoia transference? the damnable thing is that they can sense insecurity and meanness like animals smell blood), with academic life (have deserted French and feel temporarily very wicked and shirking, must atone; also, feel stupid in discussion; what the hell is tragedy? I am).

So there. With bike at repair shop, gulped down coffee-with-milk, bacon and cabbage mixed with potato, and toast, read two letters from Mother which cheered me quite a bit: she is so courageous, managing Grammy and the house, and building up a new life, hoping for Europe. I want to make happy days for her here. She also was encouraging about teaching. Once I started *doing* it I wouldn't feel so sick. That frozen inertia is my worst enemy; I get positively sick with doubt. I must break through limit after limit: learn to ski (with Gordon & Sue next year?) and perhaps teach at an army base this summer. It would do me a hell of a lot of good. If I went to Africa or Istanbul, I could do articles about the place on the side. Enough romance. Get to work.

Thank God the *Christian Science Monitor* bought the Cambridge article and drawing. They should write a letter, too, about my request to write more. *New Yorker* rejection of poems may smack me in the stomach any morning. God, it is pretty poor when a life depends on such ridiculous sitting ducks as those poems, ready for editors' grape-shot.

Tonight must *think* about O'Neill's plays; sometimes, in panic, mind goes blank, world whooshes away in void, and I feel I have to run, or walk on into the night for miles till I drop exhausted. Trying to escape? Or be alone enough to unriddle the secret of the sphinx. Men forget. Said Laughing Lazarus. And I forget the moments of radiance. I must get them down in print. Make them up in print. Be honest.

Anyway, after breakfast, leaped into clothes and started off at a dogtrot to Redpath class at Grove Lodge through snow. Gray day, moment of joy as snow tangled with blowing hair and felt red-cheeked and healthy. Wished I'd started earlier so I could linger. Noticed rooks squatting black in snow-white fen, gray skies, black trees, mallard-green water. Impressed.

Great crowd of cars and trucks at corner by Royal Hotel. Hurried to Grove Lodge, noticed gray pleasantness of stone; liked building. Went in, took off coat, and sat down among boys, none of whom spoke. Felt sick of staring industriously down at the desk like a female yogi. Blond boy rushes in to announce Redpath has flu. And we stayed up till two last night virtuously reading *Macbeth*. Which was fine. Went awestruck over old speeches: "tale of sound and fury," especially. So ironic: I pick up poetic identities of characters who commit suicide, adultery, or get murdered, and I believe completely in them for a while. What they say is True.

Well, then, a walk to town, staring as ever at the towers of King's chapel, feeling happy at Market Hill, but all stores closed, except Sayle's, where I bought an identical pair of red gloves to make up for the one I lost. Can't be completely in mourning. Is it possible to love the neutral, objective world and be scared of people? Dangerous for long, but possible. I love people I don't know. I smiled at a woman coming back over the fen path, and she said, with ironic understanding, "Wonderful weather." I loved her. I didn't read madness or superficiality in the image reflected in her eyes. For once.

It is the strangers that are easiest to love at this hard time. Because they do not demand and watch, always watch. I am sick of Mallory, Iko, John, even Chris. There is nothing there for me. I am dead to them, even though I once flowered. That is the latent terror, a symptom: it is suddenly either all or nothing; either you break the surface shell into the whistling void or you don't. I want to get back to my more normal intermediate path where the *substance* of the world is permeated by my being: eating food, reading, writing, talking, shopping: so all is good in itself, and not just a hectic activity to cover up the fear that must face itself and duel itself to death, saying: A Life is Passing!

The horror is the sudden folding up and away of the phenomenal world, leaving nothing. Just rags. Human rooks which say: Fraud. Thank God I get tired and can sleep; if that is so, all is possible. And I like to eat. And I like to walk and love the countryside here. Only these eternal questions keep knocking at the gate of my daily reality, which I cling to like a mad lover, questions which bring the dark perilous world where all is the same, there are no distinctions, no discriminations, no space and no time: the whistling breath of eternity, not of God, but of the denying devil. So we will turn to a few thoughts on O'Neill, steel ourselves to meet accusations about French, a *New Yorker* rejection, and the hostility or, even worse, utter indifference, of the people we break bread with.

Wrote one Good Poem: "Winter Landscape with Rooks": it moves, and is athletic: a psychic landscape. Began another big one, more abstract, written from the bathtub: take care it doesn't get too general. Goodnight, sweet princess. You are still on your own; be stoic; don't panic; get through this hell to the generous sweet overflowing *giving* love of spring.

PS. Winning or losing an argument, receiving an acceptance or rejection, is no proof of the validity or value of personal identity. One may be wrong, mistaken, a poor craftsman, or just ignorant—but this is no indication of the true worth of one's total human identity: past, present and future!

Crash! I am psychic, only not quite drastically enough. My baby "The Matisse Chapel," which I have been spending the imaginary money from and discussing with modest egoism, was rejected by *The New Yorker* this morning with not so much as a pencil scratch on the black-and-white doom of the printed rejection. I hid it under a pile of papers like a stillborn illegitimate baby. I shuddered at the bathos in it. Especially after I read Pete de Vries' recent scintillant *Afternoon of a Faun.* There are ways and ways to have a love affair. Above all, one must not be serious about it.

Still, the accommodating mind imagines that the poems, sent a week before, must be undergoing detailed scrutiny. I shall no doubt get them back tomorrow. Maybe even with a note.

FEBRUARY 25, SATURDAY

So we are scrubbed, hair washed fresh, feeling gutted and shaky; a crisis is passed. We reassemble forces, marshal a stiff squadron of optimism, and trek. On and on. Earlier in the week I started thinking about how stupid I was to have to make all those final declarations to all those boys last term. This is ridiculous; it should not be. Not that I can't choose the people I want to spend my time with, but there must have been some reason for getting into a situation where there was nothing to do but be final and obvious.

Probably it was because I was too intense with one boy after another. That same horror came with them which comes when the paraphernalia of existence whooshes away and there is just light and dark, night and day, without all the little physical quirks and warts and knobby knuckles that make the fabric of existence: either they were all or nothing. No man is all, so, ipso facto, they were nothing. That should not be.

They were also very conspicuously not Richard; I eventually came to telling them this as if they had a fatal disease and I was oh, so sorry. Fool: be didactic, now; take boys named Iko and Hamish for what they are, which may be coffee or rum and *Troilus and Cressida* or a sandwich on the millrace. These small particular things are good in themselves. I do not have to do them with the Only Soul in the world in the Only Body that is mine, my true one. There is a certain need of practical Machiavellian living: a casualness that must be cultivated. I was too serious for Peter, but that was mainly because he did not participate in the seriousness deeply enough to find out the gaiety beyond. Richard knows that joy, that tragic joy. And he is gone, and I should probably be glad. It would somehow be more embarrassing to have him want to marry me now. I would, I think, probably say no. Why? Because both of us are moving toward security and somehow, accepting him, he might be drowned, squashed, by the simple bourgeois life I come from with its ideals for big men, conventional men: he is someone I could never live home with. Maybe someday he will want a home, but he is so damn far from it now. Our life would be so private: he would perhaps miss the blood background and social strata I don't come from; I would miss the healthy physical bigness. How important is all this? I don't know: it changes, like looking in different ends of a telescope.

Anyway, I am tired, and it is Saturday afternoon and I have all the academic reading and papers to do which I should have done two days ago, but for my misery. A lousy sinus cold that blunted up all my senses, bunged up nose, couldn't smell taste see through rheumy eyes, or even hear, which was worst, almost. And atop of this, through the hellish sleepless night of feverish sniffling and tossing, the macabre cramps of my period (curse, yes) and the wet, messy spurt of blood.

Dawn came, black and white graying into a frozen hell. I couldn't relax, nap, or anything. This was Friday, the worst, the very worst. Couldn't even read, full of drugs which battled and banged in my veins. Everywhere I heard bells, telephones not for me, doorbells with roses for all the other girls in the world. Utter despair. Ugly, red nose, no force. When I was psychically saddest, crash, the sky falls in and my body betrays.

Now, despite the twitch of a drying cold, I am cleansed, and once again, stoic, humorous. Made a few criticisms of action and had a chance to prove points this week. Ran through lists of men I knew here, and was appalled: granted, the ones I'd told to take off were not worth seeing (well, it's true), but how few I knew were! And how few I knew. So, again, I decided, again, it is time to accept the party, the tea. And Derek asked me to a wine party Wednesday. I froze, like usual, but said probably and went. It was, after the first scare (I always feel I turn into a gargoyle when too long alone, and that people will point), it was good. There was a fire, five guitar players, nice guys, pretty girls, one Norwegian blonde named Gretta, who sang "On Top of Old Smoky" in Norwegian, and a divine hot wine and gin punch with lemon and nutmeg which was good to savor and relieved the tremors I'd been having prior to the breaking of the cold. Then, too, a boy named Hamish (who is probably another Ira) asked me out next week, and, quite by chance, said he'd take me to the St. Botolph's party (tonight).

This was enough. I had acted, and this Good Thing happened. I am a victim of prestige, too. I mean, prestige-consciousness. And the superficiality of what I have written, the glib, smug littleness, is evident. But it is not me. Not wholly. And I twinge when I see such magnificent stuff. Not because I believe I'm jealous, but because of the blonde one being In. Fear is the worst enemy. And does she fear? Assuming humanity, yes. But, like Hunter, the bone structure and coloring can take it. And hide it. If there is any.

And I have learned something from E. Lucas Myers, although he does not know me and will never know I've learned it. His poetry is great, big, moving through technique and discipline to master it and bend it supple to his will. There is a brilliant joy, there, too, almost of an athlete, running, using all the divine flexions of his muscles in the act. Luke writes alone, much. He is serious about it; he does not talk much about it. This is the way. A way, and I believe in not being Roget's trollop, parading words and tossing off bravado for an audience.

Now, friend C. writes too, and a certain social and public view has been learned from him. But, as I remarked that frozen winter night to himself, his ego is like an unbroken puppy: scampering about spurting effusively over everything, especially if Everything is admiring. He flies socially, from girl to girl and party to party and tea to tea; God knows when he has time to write, but it is too accessible. Although, justly, some of his poems are quite fine; he misses the athletic force of Luke, though, except in one or two poems, and can't sustain discipline in his less good ones, falling apart into facilities of speech which show up like a sagging hemline on a really good dress. Luke is all tight and packed and supple and blazing. He will be great, greater than anyone of my generation whom I've read yet.

So I am, however, not worth the really good boys; or is it me? If poems were really good, there might be some chance; but, until I make something tight and riding over the limits of sweet sestinas and sonnets, away from the reflection of myself in Richard's eyes and the inevitable narrow bed, too small for a smashing act of love, until then, they can ignore me and make up pretty jokes. The only cure for jealousy that I can see is the continual, firm, positive forging of an identity and set of personal values which I believe in; in other words, if I believe it is right to go to France, it is absurd to feel pangs because Someone Else has gone to Italy. There is no compare.

The fear that my sensibility is dull, inferior, is probably justified; but I am not stupid, if I am ignorant in many ways. I will tighten up my program here, knowing as I do that it is important for me to do a small number of things well, rather than a wide number sketchily. That much of the perfectionist is still with me. In this daily game of choice and sacrifice, one needs a sure eye for the superfluous. It changes every day, too. Some days the moon is superfluous, some days, most emphatically not.

Last night, blunted as I was by agony, revolted at food and the distant bumbling noise of talk and laughter, I ran out of the dining room and walked alone back to the house. What word blue could get that dazzling drench of blue moonlight on the flat, luminous field of white snow, with the black trees against the sky, each with its particular configuration of branches? I felt shut in, imprisoned, aware that it was fine and shudderingly beautiful, but too gone with pain and aching to respond and become part of it.

The dialogue between my Writing and my Life is always in danger of becoming a slithering shifting of responsibility, of evasive rationalizing; in other words: I justified the mess I made of life by saying I'd give it order, form, beauty, writing about it; I justified my writing by saying it would be published, give me life (and prestige to life). Now, you have to begin somewhere, and it might as well be with life; a belief in me, with my limitations, and a strong punchy determination to fight to overcome one by one: like languages, to learn French, ignore Italian (a sloppy knowledge of three languages is dilettantism) and revive German again, to build each solid. To build all solid.

Went to psychiatrist this morning and like him: attractive, calm and considered, with that pleasant feeling of age and experience in a reservoir; felt: Father, why not? Wanted to burst out in tears and say Father, Father, comfort me. I told him about my breakup and found myself complaining mainly about not knowing mature people here: that's it, too! There is not one person I know here whom I admire who is older than I! In a place like Cambridge, that is scandalous. It means that there are many fine people I have not met; probably many young dons and men are mature. I don't know (and, I always ask, would they want to know me?). But at Newnham, there isn't one don I admire *personally*. The men are probably better, but there is no chance of getting them for supervisors, and they are too brilliant to indulge in that friendly commerce which Mr. Fisher, Mr. Kazin and Mr. Gibian were so dear about.

Well, I shall look up Beuscher's friend, and plan to see the Clarabuts at Easter. I can give them youth, enthusiasm and love to make up for the ignorances. Sometimes I feel so very stupid; yet, if I were, would I not be happy with some of the men I've met? Or is it because I'm stupid that I'm not; hardly. I long so for someone to blast over Richard; I deserve that, don't I, some sort of blazing love that I can live with. My God, I'd love to cook and make a house, and surge force into a man's dreams, and write, if he could talk and walk and work and passionately want to do his career. I can't bear to think of this potential for loving and giving going brown and sere in me. Yet the choice is so important, it frightens me a little. A lot.

Today I bought rum and marketed for cloves, lemons, and nuts and got the recipe for buttered rum, which I should have had to take me through the beginning of my cold; but I will make it soon. Hamish is so bored, he drinks. How horrible. And I drink sherry and wine by myself because I like it and I get the sensuous feeling of indulgence I do when I eat salted nuts or cheese: luxury, bliss, erotic-tinged. I suppose if I gave myself the chance I could be an alcoholic.

What I fear most, I think, is the death of the imagination. When the sky outside is merely pink, and the rooftops merely black: that photographic mind which paradoxically tells the truth, but the worthless truth, about the world. It is that synthesizing spirit, that "shaping" force, which prolifically sprouts and makes up its own worlds with more inventiveness than God which I desire. If I sit still and don't do anything, the world goes on beating like a slack drum, without meaning. We must be moving, working, making dreams to run toward; the poverty of life without dreams is too horrible to imagine: it is that kind of madness which is worst: the kind with fancies and hallucinations would be a Bosch-ish relief. I listen always for footsteps coming up the stairs and hate them if they are not for me. Why, why, can I not be an ascetic for a while, instead of always teetering on the edge of wanting complete solitude for work and reading, and, so much, so much, the gestures of hands and words of other human beings. Well, after this Racine paper, this Ronsard purgatory, this Sophocles, I shall write: letters and prose and poetry, toward the end of the week; I must be stoic till then.

Tongues of Stone

Story, 1955

The simple morning sun shone through the green leaves of the plants in the little sunroom, making a clean look, and the patterned flowers on the chintz-covered couch were naïve and pink in the early light. The girl sat on the sofa with the ragged red square of knitting in her hands and began to cry because the knitting was all wrong. There were holes, and the small blond woman in the silky white uniform who had said that anyone could learn to knit was in the sewing room helping Debby make a black blouse with lavender fish printed on it.

Mrs. Sneider was the only other one in the sunroom where the girl sat on the sofa with the tears crawling like slow insects down her cheeks, falling wet and scalding on her hands. Mrs. Sneider was at the wooden table by the window making a fat woman out of clay. She sat hunched over her clay, glaring angrily at the girl every now and then. Finally the girl got up and went over to Mrs. Sneider to look at the swollen clay woman.

"You make very nice clay things," the girl said.

Mrs. Sneider sneered and began to take the woman apart, tearing off the arms and head and hiding the pieces under the newspaper she was working on.

"You really didn't need to do that, you know," the girl said. "It was a very good woman."

"I know you," Mrs. Sneider hissed, squashing the body of the fat woman back into a shapeless lump of clay. "I know you, always snooping and spying!"

"But I only wanted to look," the girl was trying to explain when the silky white woman came back and sat down on the creaking couch asking, "Let me see your knitting."

"It's all holes," the girl said dully. "I can't remember how you told me. My fingers won't do it."

"Why, it's perfectly fine," the woman countered brightly, getting up to go. "I'd like to see you work on it some more."

The girl took up the red square of knitting and slowly wound the thread over her finger, stabbing at a loop with the slippery blue needle. She had caught the loop but her finger was stiff and far away and would not make the yarn go over the needle. Her hands felt like clay, and she let the knitting fall in her lap and began to cry again. Once she began to cry there was no stopping.

For two months she had neither cried nor slept, and now she still did not sleep, but the crying came more and more, all day long. Through her tears she stared out of the window at the blur the sunlight made on the leaves, which were turning bright red. It was sometime in October; she had long ago lost track of all the days and it really didn't matter because one was like another and there were no nights to separate them because she never slept anymore.

There was nothing to her now but the body, a dull puppet of skin and bone that had to be washed and fed day after day after day. And her body would live on for sixty-odd years or more. After a while they would get tired of waiting and hoping and telling her that there was a God or that someday she would look back on this as if it were a bad dream.

Then she would drag out her nights and days chained to a wall in a dark solitary cell with dirt and spiders. They were safe outside the dream, so they could jargon away. But she was caught in the nightmare of the body, without a mind, without anything, only the soulless flesh that got fatter with the insulin and yellower with the fading tan.

That afternoon as always she went out alone into the walled yard behind the ward, carrying a book of short stories which she did not read because the words were nothing but dead black hieroglyphics that she could not translate to colored pictures anymore.

She brought the warm white woolen blanket which she somehow liked to wrap around her and went to lie on a ledge of rock under the pine trees. Hardly anyone came out here. Only the little black-clad ancient women from the third-floor ward used to walk out in the sun now and then and sit stiff against the flat board fence, facing shut-eyed into the light like dried-up black beetles until the student nurses came to call them in for supper.

While she lay in the grass, black flies hovered around her, buzzing monotonously in the sun, and she stared at them as if by concentrating she could shrink herself into the compass of a fly's body and become an organic part of the natural world. She envied even the green grasshoppers that sprang about in the long grass at her feet and once caught a shiny black cricket, holding it in her hand and hating the small insect because it seemed to have a creative place in the sun while she had none, but lay there like a parasitic gall on the face of the earth.

She hated the sun too, because it was treacherous. Yet it was only the sun that talked to her still, for all the people had tongues of stone. Only the sun consoled her a little, and the apples which she picked in the orchard. She hid the apples under her pillow so that when the nurses came to lock up her closet and drawers during the insulin treatment she could still go into the bathroom with an apple in her pocket and shut the door to eat in large, ravenous bites.

If only the sun would stop at the height of its strength and crucify the world, devour it for once and for all with her lying there on her back. But the sun tilted, weakened, and betrayed her and slid down the sky until she felt again the everlasting rising of the night.

Now that she was on insulin the nurses made her come in early so that they could ask her every fifteen minutes how she felt and lay their cool hands on her forehead. All that was a farce, so she said only each time they wanted to know: "I feel the same. The same." And it was true.

One day she asked a nurse why she couldn't stay out till the sun went down, because she wouldn't move and was just lying there, and the nurse had said it was dangerous because she might have a reaction. Only she never had a reaction. She just sat there and stared or sometimes embroidered on the brown chicken she was making on a yellow apron and refused to talk.

There was no purpose in changing her clothes, because every day she sweated in the sun and got her plaid cotton shirt wet, and every day her long black hair got oilier. Daily she grew more oppressed by the suffocating sense of her body aging in time.

She felt the subtle slow, inevitable corruption of her flesh that yellowed and softened hour by hour. She imagined the waste piling up in her, swelling her full of poisons that showed in the blank darkness of her eyes when she stared into the mirror, hating the dead face that greeted her, the mindless face with the ugly purple scar on the left cheek that marked her like a scarlet letter.

A small scab began to form at each corner of her mouth. She was sure that this was a sign of her coming desiccation and that the scabs would never heal but would spread over her body, that the backwaters of her mind would break out on her body in a slow, consuming leprosy.

Before supper the smiling young student nurse came with a tray of orange juice thick with sugar for the girl to drink to terminate the treatment. Then the dinner bell rang, and she walked wordless into the small dining room with the five round white-linen-covered tables. She sat rigidly opposite a big bony woman who had graduated from Vassar and was always doing double-crostics. The woman tried to get the girl to talk, but she just answered in monosyllables and kept eating.

Debby came into supper late, rosy and breathless from walking, because she had ground privileges. Debby seemed to be sympathetic, but she smiled in a sly way and was in league with all the rest and wouldn't tell the girl: you are a cretin and there is no hope for you.

If someone would once say that, the girl would believe them because she had known for months that this was true. She had gone on circling at the brink of the whirlpool, pretending to be clever and gay, and all the while these poisons were gathering in her body, ready to break out behind the bright, false bubbles of her eyes at any moment crying: Idiot! Impostor!

Then came the crisis, and now she sat trapped for sixty years inside her decaying body, feeling her dead brain folded up like a gray, paralyzed bat in the dark cavern of her living skull.

A new woman in a purple dress was on the ward tonight. She was sallow as a mouse and smiled secretly to herself as she walked precisely down the hall to the dining room, stepping with one foot after the other along a crack between the floorboards. When she came to the doorway she turned sideways, keeping her eyes demurely on the floor, and lifted first her right foot, then her left, over the crack as if stepping over an invisible little stile.

Ellen, the fat, laughing Irish maid, kept bringing dishes out from the kitchen. When Debby asked for fruit for dessert instead of pumpkin pie, Ellen brought her an apple and two oranges and right there at the table Debby began to peel them and cut them up in pieces into a cereal dish. Clara, the girl from Maine with the blond Dutch bob, was arguing with tall, heavy Amanda, who lisped like a little child and complained continually that there was a smell of coal gas in her room.

The others were all together, warm, active, and noisy. Only the girl sat frozen, withdrawn inside herself like a hard, shriveled seed that nothing could awaken. She clutched her milk glass in one hand, asking for another piece of pie so she could postpone for a little longer the beginning of the sleepless night that would speed in the same accelerating way, without stopping, into the next day. The sun ran faster and faster around the world, and she knew that her grandparents would soon die, and that her mother would die, and that there would finally be left no familiar name to invoke against the dark.

During those last nights before her blackout the girl had lain awake listening to the thin thread of her mother's breathing, wanting to get up and twist the life out of the fragile throat, to end at once the process of slow disintegration which grinned at her like a death's head everywhere she turned.

She had crawled into bed with her mother and felt with growing terror the weakness of the sleeping form. There was no more sanctuary in the world. Creeping back to her own bed then, she had lifted up the mattress, wedging herself in the crevice between mattress and bedsprings, longing to be crushed beneath the heavy slab.

She had fought back to darkness and lost. They had jolted her back into the hell of her dead body. They had raised her like Lazarus from the mindless dead, corrupt already with the breath of the grave, sallow-skinned, with purple bruises swelling on her arms and thighs and a raw open scar on her cheek that distorted the left side of her face into a mass of browning scabs and yellow ooze so that she could not open her left eye.

At first they thought she would be blind in that eye. She had lain awake the night of her second birth into the world of flesh, talking to a nurse who was sitting up with her, turning her sightless face toward the gentle voice and saying over and over again, "But I can't see, I can't see."

The nurse, who had also believed that she was blind, tried to comfort her, saying, "There are a lot of other blind people in the world. You'll meet a nice blind man and marry him someday."

And then the full realization of her doom began to come back to the girl from the final dark where she had sought to lose herself. It was no use to worry about her eyes when she could not think or read. It would make no difference if her eyes were blank, blind windows now, because she could neither read nor think.

Nothing in the world could touch her. Even the sun shone far off in a shell of silence. The sky and leaves and people receded, and she had nothing to do with them because she was dead inside, and not all their laughter nor all their love could reach her anymore. As from a distant moon, extinct and cold, she saw their supplicant, sorrowful faces, their hands stretching out to her, frozen in attitudes of love.

There was nowhere to hide. She became more and more aware of dark corners and the promise of secret places. She thought longingly of drawers and closets and the black open gullets of toilets and bathtub drains. On walks with the fat, freckled recreational therapist she yearned toward flat pools of standing water, toward the seductive shadow under wheels of passing cars.

At night she sat up in bed with the blanket wrapped around her, making her eyes go over and over the words of the short stories in the tattered magazines she carried about until the night nurse came in with her flashlight and turned out the reading lamp. Then the girl would lie curled up rigidly under her blanket and wait open-eyed until the morning.

One night she hid the pink cotton scarf from her raincoat in the pillowcase when the nurse came around to lock up her drawers and closet for the night. In the dark she had made a loop and tried to pull it tight around her throat. But always just as the air stopped coming and she felt the rushing grow louder in her ears, her hands would slacken and let go, and she would lie there panting for breath, cursing the dumb instinct in her body that fought to go on living.

Tonight at supper when the rest had gone, the girl took her milk glass down to her room while Ellen was busy stacking dishes in the kitchen. There was no one in the corridor. A slow lust spread through her like the rise of a flood tide.

She went to her bureau and, taking a towel from the bottom drawer, she wrapped up the empty glass and put it on the floor of her closet. Then with a strange heavy passion, as if caught in the compulsion of a dream, she stamped on the towel again and again.

There was no sound, but she could feel the voluptuous sensation of the glass crushing underneath the thicknesses of the towel. Bending down, she unwrapped the broken pieces. Amid the glitter of small fragments lay several long shards. She selected the two sharpest of these and hid them under the inner sole of her sneaker, folding the rest of the bits back in the towel.

In the bathroom she shook the towel out over the toilet bowl and watched the glass strike the water, sinking slowly, turning, catching the light, descending into the dark funneled hole. The lethal twinkle of the falling fragments reflected in the dark of her mind, tracing a curve of sparks that consumed themselves even as they fell.

At seven the nurse came in to give the evening insulin shot. "What side?" she asked, as the girl bent mechanically over the bed and bared her flank.

"It doesn't matter," the girl said. "I can't feel them any more."

The nurse gave an expert jab. "My, you certainly *are* black and blue," she said.

Lying on the bed, wound round with the heavy wool blanket, the girl drifted out on a flood of languor. In the blackness that was stupor, that was sleep, a voice spoke to her, sprouting like a green plant in the dark.

"Mrs. *Pat*terson, Mrs. *Pat*terson, Mrs. *Pat*terson!" the voice said more and more loudly, rising, shouting. Light broke on seas of blindness. Air thinned.

The nurse Mrs. Patterson came running out from behind the girl's eyes. "Fine," she was saying, "fine, let me just take off your watch so you won't bang it on the bed."

"Mrs. Patterson," the girl heard herself say.

"Drink another glass of juice." Mrs. Patterson was holding a white celluloid cup of orange juice to the girl's lips.

"Another?"

"You've already had one."

The girl remembered nothing of the first cup of juice. The dark air had thinned and now it lived. There had been the knocking at the gate, the banging on the bed, and now she was saying to Mrs. Patterson words that could begin a world: "I feel different. I feel quite different."

"We have been waiting for this a long time," Mrs. Patterson said, leaning over the bed to take the cup, and her words were warm and round, like apples in the sun. "Will you have some hot milk? I think you'll sleep tonight."

And in the dark the girl lay listening to the voice of dawn and felt flare through every fiber of her mind and body the everlasting rising of the sun.

Superman and Paula
Brown's New Snowsuit

Story, 1955

The year the war began I was in the fifth grade at the Annie F. Warren Grammar School in Winthrop, and that was the winter I won the prize for drawing the best Civil Defense signs. That was also the winter of Paula Brown's new snowsuit, and even now, thirteen years later, I can recall the changing colors of those days, clear and definite as patterns seen through a kaleidoscope.

I lived on the bay side of town, on Johnson Avenue, opposite the Logan Airport, and before I went to bed each night, I used to kneel by the west window of my room and look over to the lights of Boston that blazed and blinked far off across the darkening water. The sunset flaunted its pink flag above the airport, and the sound of waves was lost in the perpetual droning of the planes. I marveled at the moving beacons on the runway and watched, until it grew completely dark, the flashing red and green lights that rose and set in the sky like shooting stars. The airport was my Mecca, my Jerusalem. All night I dreamed of flying.

Those were the days of my technicolor dreams. Mother believed that I should have an enormous amount of sleep, and so I was never really tired when I went to bed. This was the best time of the day, when I could lie in the vague twilight, drifting off to sleep, making up dreams inside my head the way they should go. My flying dreams were believable as a landscape by Dali, so real that I would awake with a sudden shock, a breathless sense of having tumbled like Icarus from the sky and caught myself on the soft bed just in time.

These nightly adventures in space began when Superman started invading my dreams and teaching me how to fly. He used to come roaring by in his shining blue suit with his cape whistling in the wind, looking remarkably like my Uncle Frank, who was living with Mother and me. In the magic whirring of his cape I could hear the wings of a hundred seagulls, the motors of a thousand planes.

I was not the only worshipper of Superman in our block. David Sterling, a pale, bookish boy who lived down the street, shared my love for the sheer poetry of flight. Before supper every night, we listened to Superman together on the radio, and during the day we made up our own adventures on the way to school.

The Annie F. Warren Grammar School was a red brick building, set back from the main highway on a black tar street, surrounded by barren gravel playgrounds. Out by the parking lot David and I found a perfect alcove for our Superman dramas. The dingy back entrance to the school was deep set in a long passageway which was an excellent place for surprise captures and sudden rescues.

During recess, David and I came into our own. We ignored the boys playing baseball on the gravel court and the girls giggling at dodge-ball in the dell. Our Superman games made us outlaws, yet gave us a sense of windy superiority. We even found a stand-in for a villain in Sheldon Fein, the sallow mamma's boy on our block who was left out of the boys' games because he cried whenever anybody tagged him and always managed to fall down and skin his fat knees.

At first, we had to prompt Sheldon in his part, but after a while he became an expert on inventing tortures and even carried them out in private, beyond the game. He used to pull the wings from flies and the legs off grasshoppers, and keep the broken insects captive in a jar hidden under his bed where he could take them out in secret and watch them struggling. David and I never played with Sheldon except at recess. After school we left him to his mamma, his bonbons, and his helpless insects.

At this time my Uncle Frank was living with us while waiting to be drafted, and I was sure that he bore an extraordinary resemblance to Superman incognito. David couldn't see his likeness as clearly as I did, but he admitted that Uncle Frank was the strongest man he had ever known, and could do lots of tricks like making caramels disappear under napkins and walking on his hands.

That same winter, war was declared, and I remember sitting by the radio with Mother and Uncle Frank and feeling a queer foreboding in the air. Their voices were low and serious, and their talk was of planes and German bombs. Uncle Frank had something about Germans in America being put in prison for the duration, and Mother kept saying over and over again about Daddy: "I'm only glad Otto didn't live to see this; I'm only glad Otto didn't live to see it come to this."

In school we began to draw Civil Defense signs, and that was when I beat Jimmy Lane in our block for the fifth-grade prize. Every now and then we would practice an air raid. The fire bell would ring and we would take up our coats and pencils and file down the creaking stairs to the basement, where we sat in special corners according to our color tags, and put the pencils between our teeth so the bombs wouldn't make us bite our tongues by mistake. Some of the little children in the lower grades would cry because it was dark in the cellar, with only the bare ceiling lights on the cold black stone.

The threat of war was seeping in everywhere. At recess, Sheldon became a Nazi and borrowed a goose step from the movies, but his Uncle Macy was really over in Germany, and Mrs. Fein began to grow thin and pale because she heard that Macy was a prisoner and then nothing more.

The winter dragged on, with a wet east wind coming always from the ocean, and the snow melting before there was enough for coasting. One Friday afternoon, just before Christmas, Paula Brown gave her annual birthday party, and I was invited because it was for all the children on our block. Paula lived across from Jimmy Lane on Somerset Terrace, and nobody on our block really liked her, because she was bossy and stuck up, with pale skin and long red pigtails and watery blue eyes.

She met us at the door of her house in a white organdy dress, her red hair tied up in sausage curls with a satin bow. Before we could sit down at the table for birthday cake and ice cream, she had to show us all her presents. There were a great many because it was both her birthday and Christmas time too.

Paula's favorite present was a new snowsuit, and she tried it on for us. The snowsuit was powder blue and came in a silver box from Sweden, she said. The front of the jacket was all embroidered with pink and white roses and bluebirds, and the leggings had embroidered straps. She even had a little white angora beret and angora mittens to go with it.

After dessert we were all driven to the movies by Jimmy Lane's father to see the late afternoon show as a special treat. Mother had found out that the main feature was *Snow White* before she would let me go, but she hadn't realized that there was a war picture playing with it.

The movie was about prisoners of the Japanese who were being tortured by having no food or water. Our war games and the radio programs were all made up, but this was real, this really happened. I blocked my ears to shut out the groans of the thirsty, starving men, but I could not tear my eyes away from the screen.

Finally, the prisoners pulled down a heavy log from the low rafters and jammed it through the clay wall so they could reach the fountain in the court, but just as the first man got to the water, the Japanese began shooting the prisoners dead, and stamping on them, and laughing. I was sitting on the aisle, and I stood up then in a hurry and ran out to the girls' room, where I knelt over a toilet bowl and vomited up the cake and ice cream.

After I went to bed that night, as soon as I closed my eyes, the prison camp sprang to life in my mind, and again the groaning men broke through the walls, and again they were shot down as they reached the trickling fountain. No matter how hard I thought of Superman before I went to sleep, no crusading blue figure came roaring down in heavenly anger to smash the yellow men who invaded my dreams. When I woke up in the morning, my sheets were damp with sweat.

Saturday was bitterly cold, and the skies were gray and blurred with the threat of snow. I was dallying home from the store that afternoon, curling up my chilled fingers in my mittens, when I saw a couple of kids playing Chinese tag out in front of Paula Brown's house.

Paula stopped in the middle of the game to eye me coldly. "We need someone else," she said. "Want to play?" She tagged me on the ankle then, and I hopped around and finally caught Sheldon Fein as he was bending down to fasten one of his fur-lined overshoes. An early thaw had melted away the snow in the street, and the tarred pavement was gritted with sand left from the snow trucks. In front of Paula's house somebody's car had left a glittering black stain of oil slick.

We went running about in the street, retreating to the hard, brown lawns when the one who was "It" came too close. Jimmy Lane came out of his house and stood watching us for a short while, and then joined in. Every time he was "It," he chased Paula in her powder blue snowsuit, and she screamed shrilly and looked around at him with her wide, watery eyes, and he always managed to catch her.

Only one time she forgot to look where she was going, and as Jimmy reached out to tag her, she slid into the oil slick. We all froze when she went down on her side as if we were playing statues. No one said a word, and for a minute there was only the sound of the planes across the bay. The dull, green light of late afternoon came closing down on us, cold and final as a window blind.

Paula's snowsuit was smeared wet and black with oil along the side. Her angora mittens were dripping like black cat's fur. Slowly, she sat up and looked at us standing around her, as if searching for something. Then, suddenly, her eyes fixed on me.

"You," she said deliberately, pointing at me, "you pushed me."

There was another second of silence, and then Jimmy Lane turned on me. "You did it," he taunted. "You did it."

Sheldon and Paula and Jimmy and the rest of them faced me with a strange joy flickering in the back of their eyes. "You did it, you pushed her," they said.

And even when I shouted "I did not!" they were all moving in on me, chanting in a chorus, "Yes, you did, yes, you did, we saw you." In the well of faces moving toward me I saw no help, and I began to wonder if Jimmy had pushed Paula, or if she had fallen by herself, and I was not sure. I wasn't sure at all.

I started walking past them, walking home, determined not to run, but when I had left them behind me, I felt the sharp thud of a snowball on my left shoulder, and another. I picked up a faster stride and rounded the corner by Kellys'. There was my dark brown shingled house ahead of me, and inside, Mother and Uncle Frank, home on furlough. I began to run in the cold, raw evening toward the bright squares of light in the windows that were home.

Uncle Frank met me at the door. "How's my favorite trooper?" he asked, and he swung me so high in the air that my head grazed the ceiling. There was a big love in his voice that drowned out the shouting which still echoed in my ears.

"I'm fine," I lied, and he taught me some jujitsu in the living room until Mother called us for supper.

Candles were set on the white linen tablecloth, and miniature flames flickered in the silver and the glasses. I could see another room reflected beyond the dark dining-room window where the people laughed and talked in a secure web of light, held together by its indestructible brilliance.

All at once the doorbell rang, and Mother rose to answer it. I could hear David Sterling's high, clear voice in the hall. There was a cold draft from the open doorway, but he and Mother kept on talking, and he did not come in. When Mother came back to the table, her face was sad. "Why didn't you tell me?" she said. "Why didn't you tell me that you pushed Paula in the mud and spoiled her new snowsuit?"

A mouthful of chocolate pudding blocked my throat, thick and bitter. I had to wash it down with milk. Finally I said, "I didn't do it."

But the words came out like hard, dry little seeds, hollow and insincere. I tried again. "I didn't do it. Jimmy Lane did it."

"Of course we'll believe you," Mother said slowly, "but the whole neighborhood is talking about it. Mrs. Sterling heard the story from Mrs. Fein and sent David over to say we should buy Paula a new snowsuit. I can't understand it."

"I didn't do it," I repeated, and the blood beat in my ears like a slack drum. I pushed my chair away from the table, not looking at Uncle Frank or Mother sitting there, solemn and sorrowful in the candlelight.

The staircase to the second floor was dark, but I went down the long hall to my room without turning on the light switch and shut the door. A small unripe moon was shafting squares of greenish light along the floor and the windowpanes were fringed with frost.

I threw myself fiercely down on my bed and lay there, dry-eyed and burning. After a while I heard Uncle Frank coming up the stairs and knocking on my door. When I didn't answer, he walked in and sat down on my bed. I could see his strong shoulders bulk against the moonlight, but in the shadows his face was featureless.

"Tell me, honey," he said very softly, "tell me. You don't have to be afraid. We'll understand. Only tell me what really happened. You have never had to hide anything from me, you know that. Only tell me how it really happened."

"I told you," I said. "I told you what happened, and I can't make it any different. Not even for you I can't make it any different."

He sighed then and got up to go away. "Okay, honey," he said at the door. "Okay, but we'll pay for another snowsuit anyway just to make everybody happy, and ten years from now no one will ever know the difference."

The door shut behind him and I could hear his footsteps growing fainter as he walked off down the hall. I lay there alone in bed, feeling the black shadow creeping up the underside of the world like a flood tide. Nothing held, nothing was left. The silver airplanes and the blue capes all dissolved and vanished, wiped away like the crude drawings of a child in colored chalk from the colossal blackboard of the dark. That was the year the war began, and the real world, and the difference.

In the Mountains

Story, 1954

Rocketing up along the mountain road in the bus, with the day graying into blackness, they came into snow blithering and spitting dry against the windows. Outside, beyond the cold glass panes rose the mountains, and behind them more mountains, higher and higher. Higher than Isobel had ever seen, crowding tall against the low skies.

"I can feel the land folding away," Austin told her confidently as the bus climbed, "and I can feel the way the rivers lie, and how they come down making valleys."

Isobel did not say anything. She kept looking past him out of the window. On all sides the mountains shot up into the evening sky, and their black stone slopes were chalked with snow.

"You know what I mean, don't you," he persisted, looking at her intensely in the new way he had since he had been living at the sanatorium. "You know what I mean, don't you, about the contours of the land?"

Isobel avoided his eyes. "Yes," she replied. "Yes, I think it's wonderful." But she did not care anymore about the contours of the land.

Pleased because of her saying it was wonderful, Austin put his arm about her shoulder. The old man at the far end of the long back seat was looking at them, and his eyes were kind. Isobel smiled at him and he smiled back. He was a nice old man and she did not care any more the way she used to when people saw Austin put his arm around her.

"I've been thinking a long time about how good it would be to have you up and all," he was saying. "For the first time, seeing this place. It's been six months now, hasn't it?"

"Just about. You left medical school the second week in fall."

"I can forget those six months, being with you again this way." He grinned down at her. Still strong, she thought, and sure of himself, and even now, although everything was changed for her, she felt a touch of the old hurting fear, just remembering the way it had been.

His arm lay warm and possessive across her shoulders, and through her wool coat she could feel the hard length of his thigh against hers. But even his fingers, now playing with her hair, twining gently in her hair, did not make her want to go to him.

"It is a long time since the fall," she said. "And it has been a long trip up to the san."

"But you made it," he said proudly. "The subway connections and the crosstown taxi and all. You always hated traveling alone. You always were so sure you would get lost."

She laughed. "I manage. But you. Aren't you tired from the trip down from the san, down and now back, all in one day?"

"Of course I'm not tired," he scoffed. "You know I don't get tired."

He had always scorned weakness. Any kind of weakness, and she remembered how he mocked her being tender at the killing of the guinea pigs.

"I know," she said, "but I thought that now, after being in bed so much . . ."

"You know I don't get tired. Why do you think they let me go down to the city to meet you? I feel fine," he declared.

"You look fine too," she said to pacify him, and fell silent.

In Albany he had been waiting at the bus terminal when her taxi skidded to the curb, and he had looked just the way she remembered him, his blond hair cropped short and close to his tall-boned skull, and his face pink with the cold. No change there.

Living with a bomb in your lung, he had written her from medical school after they told him, is no different from living any other way.

You can't see it. You don't feel it. But you believe it because they tell you and they know.

"Will they let me see you most of the time?" she began then.

"Most. Except after lunch at rest hour. But Doc Lynn is getting me passes while you're here. You're staying at his house, so it's legal."

"What's legal?" She slanted a curious look at him.

"Don't say it like that," he laughed. "My visiting you, that's all. Just so long as I'm back in bed by nine o'clock."

"I can't understand the rules they have. They keep you strictly on drugs and make sure you go to bed at nine o'clock, and yet they let you come down to the city, and they let me come up here. It doesn't follow."

"Well, every place has a different system. Up here they let us have an ice-skating rink, and they're pretty lax about most things. Except walk hours."

"What do they say about walk hours?" she asked.

"Separate walk hours for the separate sexes. Never coincide."

"But why? That's silly."

"They figure the affairs up here are quick enough without that."

"Oh, really?" she laughed.

"But I can't see that sort of thing. No point to it."

"Oh?" Her tone needled him.

"No," he said seriously. "There's no future in that sort of thing up here. Gets too complicated. Just take what happened to Lenny, for instance."

"You mean Lenny the punchy fighter you wrote me about?"

"That's the one. Fell for a Greek girl up here. Well, he married her over the holidays. Back here now with her, she being twenty-seven, he twenty."

"Good lord, why did he marry her?"

"Nobody knows. Says he loves her, that's all. His parents are as upset as hell."

"Affairs are one thing," she said. "But signing your life away because you're lonely, because you're afraid of being lonely, that's something else again."

He gave her a quick look. "That sounds funny coming from you."

"Maybe," she said defensively. "But that's the way I figure it. That's the way I figure it now anyway."

He was looking at her so curiously that she broke the tension with a little laugh, and, lifting her gloved hand, she patted his cheek. Aloof staccato pats, but he did not know the difference, and she saw that her spontaneous gesture had made him happy. His arm tightened about her shoulder in response.

From somewhere in front of the bus there was a cold draft of air coming. It blew back, freezing and cutting. Three seats ahead a man had opened a window.

"God, it's cold," Isobel exclaimed aloud, pulling her green and black plaid scarf closer about her throat.

The old man at the other end of the back seat heard her and smiled, saying, "Yes, it's the open window. I wish they would shut it. I wish someone would ask them to shut it."

"Shut it for him," she whispered to Austin. "Shut it for the old man."

Austin looked down at her keenly. "Do you want it shut?" he asked.

"I don't care really. I like fresh air. But the old man, he wants it shut."

"I will shut it for you, but I won't shut it for him. Do you want it shut?"

"Shh, not so loud," she said, fearing that the old man would hear. It was not like Austin to be so angry. He was angry; his jaw was tight, and his mouth shut firm. He got angry like cold steel.

"All right, I want it shut then," she said, sighing.

He got up and went front three seats and asked the man to please shut the window. Coming back to her, he smiled. "I did that for you. No one else."

"That's silly," she said. "Why are you so mean about the old man? What are you trying to prove?"

"Did you see him? Did you see the way he looked at me? He was perfectly able to get up and shut it himself. And he wanted me to do it."

"I wanted you to do it too."

"That's different. That's altogether different."

She kept quiet then, feeling sorry for the old man and hoping he hadn't heard. The rhythmic jolting of the bus and the warmth was making her drowsy. Her eyelids drooped, lifted, and drooped again. The sleep waves started to come up under her, and she wanted to flatten out and go away on them.

Leaning her head back on Austin's shoulder, she let herself be lulled by the rocking of the bus in the circle of his arms. Intervals of warm blind languor, and then "We're coming to the stop," he was saying gently in her ear. "Mrs. Lynn will be ready for you, and I have an evening pass until nine."

Slowly Isobel opened her eyes and let the lights and the people and the old man come back. She straightened up, yawning hugely. The back of her neck was stiff from leaning her head against the arm Austin still kept around her shoulders.

"But I don't see anything," she said, rubbing a dark clear spot on the steamed window glass and peering out. "I don't see anything at all."

Outside the window the darkness was broken only by the flash of headlights on tall banks of snow that went careening backwards into the blackness of the trees, into the overhanging blackness of the mountains.

"In just a minute," he promised. "You'll see. We're almost there. I'll go and tell the bus driver when it's time to stop."

He stood up then, and began edging his way down the narrow aisle. The passengers turned their heads to look as he went by. Everywhere he went people always turned to look.

She glanced again through the window. Out of the confused dark sprouted sudden rectangles of light. Windows of a house low-eaved in a pine grove.

Austin was beckoning her to come to the door. He had taken her suitcase from the rack already. She rose and went to him, rocking unsteadily down the aisle with the motion of the bus and laughing.

Abruptly the bus swung to a stop, and the door folded back into itself with an accordion wheeze.

Austin leaped down the high step into the snow and reached up his arms to help her. After the warm damp air inside the bus the coldness struck at her dry and sharp as the blade of a knife.

"Oh, all the snow! I've never anywhere seen so much snow!" she exclaimed, stepping down beside him.

The bus driver heard her and laughed, closing the door from inside and starting to drive away. She watched the lighted window squares move by, misted with steam, and the face of the old man looked out at them from the back. Impulsively, she lifted her arm and waved to him. His return wave was like a salute.

"Why did you do that?" Austin asked, curious.

"I don't know," she laughed up at him. "I just felt like it. I just felt like it, that's all." Numb from sitting still so long, she stretched and stamped her feet in the soft powder of snow. He stared carefully at her a moment before he spoke.

"It's just over there," he said, pointing to the blazing windows of the low-eaved house. "Mrs. Lynn's is just over there, up the driveway. And the san is only a little farther along the road, around the bend."

Picking up her suitcase, he took her arm, and they started walking between the tall banks of snow, up the drive to the house, the stars blinking cold and distant overhead. As they tramped up the front walk, the door of the house opened and a shaft of light sliced out across the snow.

"Hello there." With languid blue eyes and blond hair crisping about her smooth-skinned face, Emmy Lynn met them at the doorway. She wore black tapered slacks and a pale blue plaid lumbershirt.

"I've been waiting for you all," she drawled, and her voice had the slow, clear quality of honey. "Here, let me take your things."

"God, she's lovely," Isobel whispered to Austin, while Emmy Lynn was hanging their coats in the hall closet.

"That's a doctor's wife for you," Austin said. And it was only when she saw him looking down at her intently that she realized he was not joking.

Emmy Lynn came back to them, smiling drowsily. "You two go in the living room and take it easy awhile. I'm going upstairs and read in bed a little. If there's anything you want, just call."

"My room . . ." Isobel began.

"At the head of the stairs. I'll take your suitcase up. Just lock the front door after Austin goes, will you?" Emmy Lynn turned and padded cat-like over the rug in her moccasins to the foot of the stairs.

"Oh, I almost forgot . . ." She turned back with a grin. "Coffee's hot on the stove in the kitchen." And she was gone.

Blue-patterned wallpaper in the hall widened into a long living room with a log fire dying in the grate. Crossing to the couch, Isobel sank into the soft depths of the cushions and Austin came to sit beside her.

"Will you have coffee?" Austin asked her. "She said there is some in the kitchen."

"Yes," Isobel said. "Yes, I think I need something hot to drink."

He came back bringing two steaming cups and set them on the coffee table.

"You too?" she said, surprised. "You never used to like coffee."

"I have learned to drink it," he told her, smiling. "Black, the way you do, without cream or sugar."

She bent her head quickly so that he could not see into her eyes. It shocked her to see him acquiesce this way. He who had been so proud. Lifting her coffee cup, she drank slowly the scalding black liquid, saying nothing.

I am reading a book, he had written in one of his latest letters, where the man is a soldier and the girl he has made pregnant dies, and oh, I began thinking that you were the girl, and I was the man, and I could not stop thinking about how terrible it was for days.

She had wondered a long time about that, about him alone in his room reading day after day, worrying about the imaginary man and the dying girl. It was not like him. Before, always, he used to say how silly she was to feel sorry for people in books because they were not real. It was not like him to worry about the girl dying in the book.

Together they finished the coffee, tilting the cups and draining the last warm drops of liquid. In the fireplace one thin blue flame flared, small and clear, and went out. Under the white ash of the gutted log, coals still showed red, fading.

Austin reached for her hand. She let him interlace his fingers with hers, and she knew that her hand was cool and unresponsive.

"I have been thinking," Austin said to her then, slowly, "all this long time I have been away I have been thinking about us. We have been through a lot together, you know."

"Yes," she said guardedly. "Yes, I know."

"Remember," he began, "that Friday night we stayed in town so late we missed the last bus out, and the crazy boys we thumbed a ride back home with?"

"Yes," she said, remembering how it was all so lovely and hurting then. How everything he said had hurt her.

"That crazy guy," he persisted, "in the back seat. Remember him? The one who kept tearing up the dollar bill in little pieces and letting them fly out the open window?"

"I'll never forget that," she said.

"That was the night we saw the baby born," he said. "Your first time at the hospital, and you had your hair all wound up under a white cap, and a white coat on, and your eyes were all dark and excited over the mask."

"I was afraid someone would find out I wasn't a medical student."

"You dug your nails into my hand while they tried to get the kid to breathe," he went on. "You didn't say anything, but your nails left little red crescents in the palm of my hand."

"That was half a year ago. I'd know better now."

"I don't mean that. I liked it, the red marks. It was a good hurt, and I liked it."

"You didn't say so then."

"I didn't say a lot of things then. But I have been thinking up here of all the things I never told you. All the time up here when I am lying in bed, I remember the way it was with us."

"It is because you have been away so long that you remember all the time," she said. "When you get back to med school and the old fast life again you won't think like this. It is not good for you to think so hard."

"That is where you are wrong. I did not want to admit it for a long time, but I think I needed this. Getting away and thinking. I am beginning to learn who I am."

She looked down into her empty coffee cup, stirring aimless dry circles with her spoon.

"Tell me then," she said softly, "who are you?"

"You already know," he said. "You already know better than anyone."

"You sound sure of that. I am not so sure."

"Oh, but you do know. You have seen the rotten streak in me and you have come back, no matter how bad it was. You have always come back."

"What are you trying to tell me?"

"Can't you see?" he said simply. "I mean you have taken me always the way I am, no matter what. Like that time I told you about Doris, and you cried and turned away. I thought for sure that was the end then, with you sitting crying on the other side of the car, looking out at the river and not talking."

"I remember that," she said. "It was going to be the end."

"But then you let me kiss you. After all that, you let me kiss you, still crying, and your mouth tasted wet and salty from the tears. You let me kiss you and it was all right again."

"That was a long time ago. It is different now."

"I know it is different now because I never want to make you cry again. Do you believe that? Do you know what I'm trying to say?"

"I think so but I am not sure. You have never before talked to me like this, you know. You always let me guess at what you meant."

"That is all over now," he said. "And my getting out of here won't make it any different. I will get out of here, and we will begin again. A year is not a very long time. I do not think it will take me more than a year, and then I will come back."

"I have to know something," she said. "I have to ask it of you in words to make sure."

"Do you need words now?" he said.

"I have to know. Tell me, why did you want me to come?"

He looked at her and his eyes reflected her fear. "I needed you very badly," he confessed, quite low. He hesitated, then said quietly, "It is unfortunate that I can't kiss you."

He put his face into the hollow between her neck and shoulder, blinding himself with her hair, and she could feel the sudden wet scalding of his tears.

Stricken, she did not move. The patterned blue wall of the rectangular room fell away, and the warm geometric light fell away, and outside the snow-covered mountains bulked hugely through the irrevocable dark. There was no wind at all and it was hushed and still.

Initiation

Story, July 1952

The basement room was dark and warm, like the inside of a sealed jar, Millicent thought, her eyes getting used to the strange dimness. The silence was soft with cobwebs, and from the small, rectangular window set high in the stone wall there sifted a faint bluish light that must have been coming from the full October moon. She could see now that what she was sitting on was a woodpile next to the furnace.

Millicent brushed back a strand of hair. It was stiff and sticky from the egg that they had broken on her head as she knelt blindfolded at the sorority altar a short while before. There had been a silence, a slight crunching sound, and then she had felt the cold, slimy egg-white flattening and spreading on her head and sliding down her neck. She had heard someone smothering a laugh. It was all part of the ceremony.

Then the girls had led her here, blindfolded still, through the corridors of Betsy Johnson's house and shut her in the cellar. It would be an hour before they came to get her, but then Rat Court would be all over and she would say what she had to say and go home.

For tonight was the grand finale, the trial by fire. There really was no doubt now that she would get in. She could not think of anyone who had ever been invited into the high school sorority and failed to get through initiation time. But even so, her case would be quite different. She would see to that. She could not exactly say what had decided her revolt, but it definitely had something to do with Tracy and something to do with the heather birds.

What girl at Lansing High would not want to be in her place now? Millicent thought, amused. What girl would not want to be one of the elect, no matter if it did mean five days of initiation before and after school, ending in the climax of Rat Court on Friday night when they made the new girls members? Even Tracy had been wistful when she heard that Millicent had been one of the five girls to receive an invitation.

"It won't be any different with us, Tracy," Millicent had told her. "We'll still go around together like we always have, and next year you'll surely get in."

"I know, but even so," Tracy had said quietly, "you'll change, whether you think you will or not. Nothing ever stays the same."

And nothing does, Millicent had thought. How horrible it would be if one never changed . . . if she were condemned to be the plain, shy Millicent of a few years back for the rest of her life. Fortunately there was always the changing, the growing, the going on.

It would come to Tracy, too. She would tell Tracy the silly things the girls had said, and Tracy would change also, entering eventually into the magic circle. She would grow to know the special ritual as Millicent had started to last week.

"First of all," Betsy Johnson, the vivacious blonde secretary of the sorority, had told the five new candidates over sandwiches in the school cafeteria last Monday, "first of all, each of you has a big sister. She's the one who bosses you around, and you just do what she tells you."

"Remember the part about talking back and smiling," Louise Fullerton had put in, laughing. She was another celebrity in high school, pretty and dark and Vice-President of the Student Council. "You can't say anything unless your big sister asks you something or tells you to talk to someone. And you can't smile, no matter how you're dying to." The girls had laughed a little nervously, and then the bell had rung for the beginning of afternoon classes.

It would be rather fun for a change, Millicent mused, getting her books out of her locker in the hall, rather exciting to be part of a closely knit group, the exclusive set at Lansing High. Of course, it wasn't a school organization. In fact, the principal, Mr. Cranton, wanted to do away with initiation week altogether, because he thought it was undemocratic and disturbed the routine of school work. But there wasn't really anything he could do about it. Sure, the girls had to come to school for five days without any lipstick on and without curling their hair, and of course everybody noticed them, but what could the teachers do?

Millicent sat down at her desk in the big study hall. Tomorrow she would come to school, proudly, laughingly, without lipstick, with her brown hair straight and shoulder length, and then everybody would know, even the boys would know, that she was one of the elect. Teachers would smile helplessly, thinking perhaps: So now they've picked Millicent Arnold. I never would have guessed it.

A year or two ago, not many people would have guessed it. Millicent had waited a long time for acceptance, longer than most. It was as if she had been sitting for years in a pavilion outside a dance floor, looking in through the windows at the golden interior, with the lights clear and the air like honey, wistfully watching the gay couples waltzing to the never-ending music, laughing in pairs and groups together, no one alone.

But now at last, amid a week of fanfare and merriment, she would answer her invitation to enter the ballroom through the main entrance marked "Initiation." She would gather up her velvet skirts, her silken train, or whatever the disinherited princesses wore in the story books, and come into her rightful kingdom . . . The bell rang to end study hall.

"Millicent, wait up!" It was Louise Fullerton behind her, Louise who had always before been very nice, very polite, friendlier than the rest, even long ago, before the invitation had come.

"Listen," Louise walked down the hall with her to Latin, their next class, "are you busy right after school today? Because I'd like to talk to you about tomorrow."

"Sure. I've got lots of time."

"Well, meet me in the hall after home room then, and we'll go down to the drugstore or something."

Walking beside Louise on the way to the drugstore, Millicent felt a surge of pride. For all anyone could see, she and Louise were the best of friends.

"You know, I was so glad when they voted you in," Louise said.

Millicent smiled. "I was really thrilled to get the invitation," she said frankly, "but kind of sorry that Tracy didn't get in, too."

Tracy, she thought. If there is such a thing as a best friend, Tracy has been just that this last year.

"Yes, Tracy," Louise was saying, "she's a nice girl, and they put her up on the slate, but . . . well, she had three blackballs against her."

"Blackballs? What are they?"

"Well, we're not supposed to tell anybody outside the club, but seeing as you'll be in at the end of the week I don't suppose it hurts." They were at the drugstore now.

"You see," Louise began explaining in a low voice after they were seated in the privacy of the booth, "once a year the sorority puts up all the likely girls that are suggested for membership . . ."

Millicent sipped her cold, sweet drink slowly, saving the ice cream to spoon up last. She listened carefully to Louise, who was going on, ". . . and then there's a big meeting, and all the girls' names are read off and each girl is discussed."

"Oh?" Millicent asked mechanically, her voice sounding strange.

"Oh, I know what you're thinking," Louise laughed. "But it's really not as bad as all that. They keep it down to a minimum of catting. They just talk over each girl and why or why not they think she'd be good for the club. And then they vote. Three blackballs eliminate a girl."

"Do you mind if I ask you what happened to Tracy?" Millicent said.

Louise laughed a little uneasily. "Well, you know how girls are. They notice little things. I mean, some of them thought Tracy was just a bit *too* different. Maybe you could suggest a few things to her."

"Like what?"

"Oh, like maybe not wearing knee socks to school, or carrying that old bookbag. I know it doesn't sound like much, but well, it's things like that which set someone apart. I mean, you know that no girl at Lansing would be seen dead wearing knee socks, no matter how cold it gets, and it's kiddish and kind of green to carry a bookbag."

"I guess so," Millicent said.

"About tomorrow," Louise went on. "You've drawn Beverly Mitchell for a big sister. I wanted to warn you that she's the toughest, but if you get through all right it'll be all the more credit for you."

"Thanks, Lou," Millicent said gratefully, thinking, this is beginning to sound serious. Worse than a loyalty test, this grilling over the coals. What's it supposed to prove anyway? That I can take orders without flinching? Or does it just make them feel good to see us run around at their beck and call?

"All you have to do really," Louise said, spooning up the last of her sundae, "is be very meek and obedient when you're with Bev and do just what she tells you. Don't laugh or talk back or try to be funny, or she'll just make it harder for you, and believe me, she's a great one for doing that. Be at her house at seven-thirty."

And she was. She rang the bell and sat down on the steps to wait for Bev. After a few minutes the front door opened and Bev was standing there, her face serious.

"Get up, gopher," Bev ordered.

There was something about her tone that annoyed Millicent. It was almost malicious. And there was an unpleasant anonymity about the label "gopher," even if that was what they always called the girls being initiated. It was degrading, like being given a number. It was a denial of individuality.

Rebellion flooded through her.

"I said get up. Are you deaf?"

Millicent got up, standing there.

"Into the house, gopher. There's a bed to be made and a room to be cleaned at the top of the stairs."

Millicent went up the stairs mutely. She found Bev's room and started making the bed. Smiling to herself, she was thinking: How absurdly funny, me taking orders from this girl like a servant.

Bev was suddenly there in the doorway. "Wipe that smile off your face," she commanded.

There seemed something about this relationship that was not all fun. In Bev's eyes, Millicent was sure of it, there was a hard, bright spark of exultation.

On the way to school, Millicent had to walk behind Bev at a distance of ten paces, carrying her books. They came up to the drugstore, where there already was a crowd of boys and girls from Lansing High waiting for the show.

The other girls being initiated were there, so Millicent felt relieved. It would not be so bad now, being part of the group.

"What'll we have them do?" Betsy Johnson asked Bev. That morning Betsy had made her "gopher" carry an old colored parasol through the square and sing "I'm Always Chasing Rainbows."

"I know," Herb Dalton, the good-looking basketball captain, said. A remarkable change came over Bev. She was all at once very soft and coquettish.

"You can't tell them what to do," Bev said sweetly. "Men have nothing to say about this little deal."

"All right, all right," Herb laughed, stepping back and pretending to fend off a blow.

"It's getting late." Louise had come up. "Almost eight-thirty. We'd better get them marching on to school."

The "gophers" had to do a Charleston step all the way to school, and each one had her own song to sing, trying to drown out the other four. During school, of course, you couldn't fool around, but even then, there was a rule that you mustn't talk to boys outside of class or at lunch time . . . or any time at all after school. So the sorority girls would get the most popular boys to go up to the "gophers" and ask them out, or try to start them talking, and sometimes a "gopher" was taken by surprise and began to say something before she could catch herself. And then the boy reported her and she got a black mark.

Herb Dalton approached Millicent as she was getting an ice cream at the lunch counter that noon. She saw him coming before he spoke to her, and looked down quickly, thinking: He is too princely, too dark and smiling. And I am much too vulnerable. Why must he be the one I have to be careful of?

I won't say anything, she thought, I'll just smile very sweetly.

She smiled up at Herb very sweetly and mutely. His return grin was rather miraculous. It was surely more than was called for in the line of duty.

"I know you can't talk to me," he said, very low. "But you're doing fine, the girls say. I even like your hair straight and all."

Bev was coming toward them, then, her red mouth set in a bright, calculating smile. She ignored Millicent and sailed up to Herb.

"Why waste your time with gophers?" she caroled gaily. "Their tongues are tied, but completely."

Herb managed a parting shot. "But that one keeps *such* an attractive silence."

Millicent smiled as she ate her sundae at the counter with Tracy. Generally, the girls who were outsiders now, as Millicent had been, scoffed at the initiation antics as childish and absurd to hide their secret envy. But Tracy was understanding, as ever.

"Tonight's the worst, I guess, Tracy," Millicent told her. "I hear that the girls are taking us on a bus over to Lewiston and going to have us performing in the square."

"Just keep a poker face outside," Tracy advised. "But keep laughing like mad inside."

Millicent and Bev took a bus ahead of the rest of the girls; they had to stand up on the way to Lewiston Square. Bev seemed very cross about something. Finally she said, "You were talking with Herb Dalton at lunch today."

"No," said Millicent honestly.

"Well, I *saw* you smile at him. That's practically as bad as talking. Remember not to do it again."

Millicent kept silent.

"It's fifteen minutes before the bus gets into town," Bev was saying then. "I want you to go up and down the bus asking people what they eat for breakfast. Remember, you can't tell them you're being initiated."

Millicent looked down the aisle of the crowded bus and felt suddenly quite sick. She thought: How will I ever do it, going up to all those stony-faced people who are staring coldly out of the window . . .

"You heard me, gopher."

"Excuse me, madam," Millicent said politely to the lady in the first seat of the bus, "but I'm taking a survey. Could you please tell me what you eat for breakfast?"

"Why . . . er . . . just orange juice, toast and coffee," she said.

"Thank you very much." Millicent went on to the next person, a young businessman. He ate eggs sunny side up, toast and coffee.

By the time Millicent got to the back of the bus, most of the people were smiling at her. They obviously know, she thought, that I'm being initiated into something.

Finally, there was only one man left in the corner of the back seat. He was small and jolly, with a ruddy, wrinkled face that spread into a beaming smile as Millicent approached. In his brown suit with the forest-green tie he looked something like a gnome or a cheerful leprechaun.

"Excuse me, sir," Millicent smiled, "but I'm taking a survey. What do you eat for breakfast?"

"Heather birds' eyebrows on toast," the little man rattled off.

"*What?*" Millicent exclaimed.

"Heather birds' eyebrows," the little man explained. "Heather birds live on the mythological moors and fly about all day long, singing wild and sweet in the sun. They're bright purple and have *very* tasty eyebrows."

Millicent broke out into spontaneous laughter. Why, this was wonderful, the way she felt a sudden comradeship with a stranger.

"Are you mythological, too?"

"Not exactly," he replied, "but I certainly hope to be some day. Being mythological does wonders for one's ego."

The bus was swinging into the station now; Millicent hated to leave the little man. She wanted to ask him more about the birds.

And from that time on, initiations didn't bother Millicent at all. She went gaily about Lewiston Square from store to store asking for broken crackers and mangoes, and she just laughed inside when people stared and then brightened, answering her crazy questions as if she were quite serious and really a person of consequence. So many people were shut up tight inside themselves like boxes, yet they would open up, unfolding quite wonderfully, if only you were interested in them. And really, you didn't have to belong to a club to feel related to other human beings.

One afternoon Millicent had started talking with Liane Morris, another of the girls being initiated, about what it would be like when they were finally in the sorority.

"Oh, I know pretty much what it'll be like," Liane had said. "My sister belonged before she graduated from high school two years ago."

"Well, just what *do* they do as a club?" Millicent wanted to know.

"Why, they have a meeting once a week . . . each girl takes turns entertaining at her house . . ."

"You mean it's just a sort of exclusive social group . . ."

"I guess so . . . though that's a funny way of putting it. But it sure gives a girl prestige value. My sister started going steady with the captain of the football team after she got in. Not bad, I say."

No, it wasn't bad, Millicent had thought, lying in bed on the morning of Rat Court and listening to the sparrows chirping in the gutters.

She thought of Herb. Would he ever have been so friendly if she were without the sorority label? Would he ask her out (if he ever did) just for herself, no strings attached?

Then there was another thing that bothered her. Leaving Tracy on the outskirts. Because that is the way it would be; Millicent had seen it happen before.

Outside, the sparrows were still chirping, and as she lay in bed Millicent visualized them, pale gray-brown birds in a flock, one like the other, all exactly alike.

And then, for some reason, Millicent thought of the heather birds. Swooping carefree over the moors, they would go singing and crying out across the great spaces of air, dipping and darting, strong and proud in their freedom and their sometime loneliness. It was then that she made her decision.

Seated now on the woodpile in Betsy Johnson's cellar, Millicent knew that she had come triumphant through the trial of fire, the searing period of the ego which could end in two kinds of victory for her. The easiest of which would be her coronation as a princess, labeling her conclusively as one of the select flock.

The other victory would be much harder, but she knew that it was what she wanted. It was not that she was being noble or anything. It was just that she had learned there were other ways of getting into the great hall, blazing with lights, of people and of life.

It would be hard to explain to the girls tonight, of course, but she could tell Louise later just how it was. How she had proved something to herself by going through everything, even Rat Court, and then deciding not to join the sorority after all. And how she could still be friends with everybody. Sisters with everybody. Tracy, too.

The door behind her opened and a ray of light sliced across the soft gloom of the basement room.

"Hey, Millicent, come on out now. This is it." There were some of the girls outside.

"I'm coming," she said, getting up and moving out of the soft darkness into the glare of light, thinking: This is it, all right. The worst part, the hardest part, the part of initiation that I figured out myself.

But just then, from somewhere far off, Millicent was sure of it, there came a melodic fluting, quite wild and sweet, and she knew that it must be the song of the heather birds as they went wheeling and gliding against wide blue horizons through vast spaces of air, their wings flashing quick and purple in the bright sun.

Within Millicent another melody soared, strong and exuberant, a triumphant answer to the music of the darting heather birds that sang so clear and lilting over the far lands. And she knew that her own private initiation had just begun.

Sunday at the Mintons'

Story, Spring 1952

If Henry were only, sighed Elizabeth Minton as she straightened a map on the wall of her brother's study, not so fastidious. So supremely fastidious. She leaned dreamily aslant his mahogany desk for a moment, her withered, blue-veined fingers spread whitely against the dark, glossy wood.

The late morning sunlight lay in pale squares along the floor, and the dust motes went drifting, sinking in the luminous air. Through the window she could see the flat sheen of the green September ocean that curved far beyond the blurred horizon line.

On a fine day, if the windows were open, she could hear the waves fall. One would crash and go slipping back, and then another and another. On some nights, when she was lingering half-awake about to be engulfed in sleep, she would hear the waves, and then the wind would begin in the trees until she could not tell one sound from the other, so that, for all she knew, the water might be washing in the leaves, or the leaves falling hushed, drifting into the sea.

"Elizabeth," Henry's voice echoed deep and ominous down the cavernous hallway.

"Yes, Henry?" Elizabeth answered her older brother meekly. Now that they were back together in the old house again, now that she was looking after Henry's wants once more, she could at times fancy herself a little girl, obedient and yielding, as she had been long ago.

"Have you finished tidying the study?" Henry was coming down the hall. His slow, ponderous footstep sounded outside the door. Nervously Elizabeth lifted her slender hand to her throat, fingering, as if for security, her mother's amethyst brooch, which she always wore pinned to the collar of her dress. She glanced about the dim room. Yes, she had thought to dust the lamp shades. Henry could not tolerate the dust.

She peered at Henry, who was now standing in the doorway. In the vague light she could not see his features clearly, and his face loomed round and somber, his substantial shadow blending with the darkness of the hall behind. Squinting at the indistinct form of her brother, Elizabeth felt an odd pleasure in observing him without her glasses. He was invariably so clear, so precise, and now for once he was quite thoroughly obscured.

"Daydreaming again, Elizabeth?" Henry chided sadly, seeing a characteristic far-off look in her eyes. It had always been that way with the two of them, Henry coming out to find her reading in the garden under the rose arbor or building castles in the sand by the sea wall, Henry telling her that Mother needed help in the kitchen or that the silver needed polishing.

"No, Henry," Elizabeth drew herself up to her fragile height. "No, Henry, not at all. I was just about to put the chicken in the oven." She brushed past her brother with the merest suggestion of an indignant flounce.

Henry stared after his sister as her heels tapped lightly down to the kitchen, her lavender skirt balancing and swaying about her shins with an alarming hint of impertinence. She had never been a practical girl, Elizabeth, but she had at least been docile. And now this . . . this almost defiant attitude of hers, recurring so often of late. Ever since she had come to live with him in his retirement, in fact. Henry shook his head.

Out in the pantry Elizabeth was rattling china plates and silverware, setting out the dishes for the Sunday meal, piling the grapes and apples high in the cut-glass dish for the table centerpiece, pouring ice water into the tall, pale green goblets.

In the dimness of the austere dining room she moved, a soft violet figure in the half-light of the drawn portieres. It was thus that her mother had moved years ago . . . when was it? How long? Elizabeth had lost track of the time. But Henry could tell her. Henry would remember the exact day, the very hour of Mother's death. Scrupulously exact Henry was about such things.

Seated at the head of the table at dinner, Henry bowed his head and said grace in his deep voice, letting the words come rolling rich and rhythmic as a Biblical chant. But just as Henry reached the amen, Elizabeth sniffed something burning. Uncomfortably she thought of the potatoes.

"The potatoes, Henry!" She jerked up out of her chair and hurried to the kitchen, where the potatoes were slowly blackening in the oven. Turning off the flame, she lifted them out on the counter, dropping one on the floor first as it scalded her thin, sensitive fingers.

"It's just the skins, Henry. They'll be all right," she called into the dining room. She heard an annoyed snort. Henry did always look forward so to his buttered potato skins.

"You haven't changed in all these years, I see, Elizabeth," Henry moralized as she returned to the dining room bearing a dish containing the burned potatoes. Elizabeth sat down, shutting her ears against Henry's rebuke. She could tell that he was about to begin a long, reproachful oration. His voice oozed sanctimoniousness like plump golden drops of butter.

"I sometimes wonder at you, Elizabeth," Henry went on, cutting laboriously into a particularly stubborn piece of chicken. "I wonder how you managed to fend for yourself all these years you've worked alone in the library in town, what with your daydreaming and such."

Elizabeth bent her head over her plate quietly. It was easier to think of something else while Henry was lecturing. When she was small she always used to block her ears to shut out the sound of his voice as he marshaled her to duty, carrying out Mother's directions with such perseverance. But now she found it quite simple to escape Henry's censure unobtrusively by drifting off into a private world of her own, dreaming, musing on anything that chanced into her thoughts. She remembered now about how the horizon blurred pleasantly into the blue sky so that, for all she knew, the water might be thinning into air or the air thickening, settling, becoming water.

They ate on in silence, Elizabeth moving now and then to clear away some dishes, to refill Henry's glass of water, to bring in the dessert bowls of blackberries and cream from the kitchen. As she went about, her full lavender skirt brushing and rustling against the stiff, polished furniture, she felt oddly that she was merging into someone else, her mother perhaps. Someone who was capable and industrious about household tasks. Strange that she, after all these years of independence, strange that she should again be back with Henry, circumscribed once more by domestic duties.

She gazed then at her brother, who was bent over his dessert, ladling spoonful after spoonful of berries and cream into his cavernous mouth. He blended, she thought, with the dim, translucent gloom of the shaded dining room, and she liked to see him sitting so, in the artificial twilight, when she knew that beyond the drawn blinds the sun shone, exact and brilliant.

Elizabeth lingered over washing the lunch dishes while Henry went to pore over some of the maps in his study. There was nothing he liked better than making charts and calculations, Elizabeth thought, her hands fumbling in the warm soap suds as she stared out of the kitchen window to the blinking flashes of blue water beyond. Always when they were small Henry would be making charts and maps, copying from his geography book, reducing things to scale, while she would dream over the pictures of the mountains and rivers with the queer foreign names.

In the depths of the dishpan the silver collided blindly with the glassware in little tinkling crescendoes of sound. Elizabeth put a few last plates into the pan of soapy water and watched them tilt and sink to the bottom. After she was through she would join Henry in the parlor, where they would read together for a while, or perhaps go for a walk. Henry thought the fresh air was so healthful.

Somewhat resentfully Elizabeth remembered all the long days she had spent in bed when she was small. She had been a sallow, sickly child, and Henry had always come in to see her with his round, ruddy face aglow, beaming with vigor.

There would come a time, Elizabeth thought, as she had thought so many times before, when she would confront Henry and say something to him. She did not know quite what, but it would be something rather shattering and dreadful. Something, she was sure of it, extremely disrespectful and frivolous. And then she would see Henry for once nonplused, Henry faltering, wavering helplessly, without words.

Smiling to herself, her face rapt with inner enjoyment, Elizabeth joined Henry, who was looking at a book of maps in the parlor.

"Come here, Elizabeth," Henry directed, patting the seat on the sofa beside him. "I have found a most interesting map of the New England states I want you to see."

Obediently Elizabeth went to sit beside her brother. The two of them sat on the couch for a while, holding the encyclopedia between them and perusing the shiny pages with the pale pink and blue and yellow maps of states and counties. All at once Elizabeth glimpsed a familiar name in the middle of Massachusetts.

"Wait a minute," she exclaimed. "Let me look at all the places I have been. Here"—she traced a line with her finger up over the surface of the page west from Boston to Springfield—"and up here"—her finger swung to the corner of the state to North Adams—"and then just over the borderline into Vermont when I went to visit Cousin Ruth . . . when was it? Last spring . . ."

"The week of April sixth," Henry prompted.

"Yes, of course. You know, I never thought," she said, "of what direction I was going in on the map . . . up, down or across."

Henry looked at his sister with something like dismay.

"You never have!" he breathed incredulously. "You mean you never figure whether you're going north or south or east or west?"

"No," flashed Elizabeth, "I never do. I never saw the point."

She thought of his study, then, the walls hung with the great maps, carefully diagramed, meticulously annotated. In her mind's eye she could see the black contour lines painstakingly drawn and the faint blue wash of color about the shore of continents. There were symbols, too, she recalled. Stylized clumps of grass to indicate the swamps and green patches for the parks.

She imagined herself wandering, small and diminutive, up the finely drawn contour lines and down again, wading through the shallow blue ovals of lakes and shouldering her way among stiff symmetrical clumps of swamp grass.

Then she pictured herself with a round, white-faced compass in her hand. The compass needle spun, quivered, quieted, pointing always north, no matter where she turned. The relentless exactness of the mechanism irritated her.

Henry was looking at her still with something akin to shock. She noted that his eyes were very cold and very blue, rather like the waters of the Atlantic on the encyclopedia map. Fine black lines rayed out from the pupil. She saw the short black fringe of lashes drawn suddenly distinct and clear. Henry would know where north was, she thought desperately. He would know precisely where north was.

"Really, I don't think direction matters so much. It's the place you're going to that's important," she announced petulantly. "I mean, do you truly think about the direction you're going in all the time?"

The very room seemed to take offense at this open insolence. Elizabeth was sure she saw the rigid andirons stiffen, and the blue tapestry above the mantel had paled perceptibly. The grandfather clock was gaping at her, speechless before the next reproving tick.

"Of course I think where I'm going on the map," Henry declared staunchly, a ruddy color rising to his cheeks. "I always trace out my route beforehand, and then I take a map with me to follow as I travel."

Elizabeth could see him now, standing brightly in the morning on the flat surface of a map, watching expectantly for the sun to come up from the east. (He would know exactly where east was.) Not only that, he would know from which direction the wind was blowing. By some infallible magic he could tell from which slant of the compass the wind veered.

She visualized Henry in the center of the map, which was quartered like an apple pie under the blue dome of a bowl. Feet planted firmly he stood with pencil and paper making calculations, checking to see that the world revolved on schedule. At night he would watch the constellations go ticking by like luminous clocks, and he would call them cheerily by name, as if greeting punctual relatives. She could almost hear him bellowing heartily: "What ho, Orion, old man!" Oh, it was thoroughly unbearable.

"I suppose telling direction is something anyone can learn," Elizabeth murmured at last.

"Of course," Henry told her, beaming at her humility. "I would even lend you a map to use for practice."

Elizabeth sat quite still while Henry turned the pages of the encyclopedia, studying maps that he found of special interest. Elizabeth was cherishing the way she would a dear, slandered friend, the vague, imprecise world in which she lived.

Hers was a twilight world, where the moon floated up over the trees at night like a tremulous balloon of silver light and the bluish rays wavered through the leaves outside her window, quivering in fluid patterns on the wallpaper of her room. The very air was mildly opaque, and forms wavered and blended one with the other. The wind blew in gentle, capricious gusts, now here, now there, coming from the sea or from the rose garden (she could tell by the scent of water or of flowers).

She winced under the benevolent brightness of Henry's patronizing smile. She wanted to say something brave and impudent, then, something that would disturb the awful serenity of his features.

Once, she remembered, she had ventured to say something spontaneous and fanciful . . . what was it? About wanting to lift up the tops of people's heads like teapot lids and peer inside to find out what they were thinking. Henry had stiffened at that, had cleared his throat and said with a sigh, as if speaking to an irresponsible child, something like "And what would you expect to find inside? Not cogs and wheels certainly, nor thoughts stacked about like sheaves of paper, labeled and tied up with ribbon!" And he had smiled at his ponderous wit.

No, of course not, Elizabeth had told him, deflated. She thought now of how it would be in her mind, a dark, warm room, with colored lights swinging and wavering, like so many lanterns reflecting on the water, and pictures coming and going on the misty walls, soft and blurred like Impressionist paintings. The colors would be broken down in small tinted fragments, and the pink of the ladies' flesh would be the pink of the roses, and the lavender of the dresses would mingle with the lilacs. And there would be, from somewhere sweetly coming, the sound of violins and bells.

Henry's mind, she was certain, would be flat and level, laid out with measured instruments in the broad, even sunlight. There would be geometric concrete walks and square, substantial buildings with clocks on them, everywhere perfectly in time, perfectly synchronized. The air would be thick with their accurate ticking.

There was a sudden brightening outside, and the room seemed to expand in the fresh light. "Come, it will be a fine afternoon for a walk," Henry said, rising from the couch, smiling, and holding out a square, substantial hand to her.

Every Sunday afternoon after dinner it was his habit to take her for a stroll along the boulevard by the ocean. The brisk salt air, he said, would be a bracing tonic for her. She was always a bit sallow, a bit pinched about the cheeks.

In the blowing air Elizabeth's gray hair would loosen and flutter about her face in a wispy halo, damp and moist. But in spite of the healthful breeze she knew that Henry disliked to see her hair untidy and was glad to have her smooth it back in the accustomed bun and secure it with a long metal hairpin.

Today the air was clear, yet warm for early September, and Elizabeth stepped out on the front porch with a sudden gaiety, her gray cloth coat open loosely over her lavender dress. In the distance she could see a small pile of dark clouds that might be a storm rising slowly on the far horizon. Like tiny grape clusters the purple clouds were, with the gulls wheeling in cream white flakes against them.

Down against the stone foundations of the boardwalk the waves were breaking powerfully, the great green crests hanging suspended in a curve of cold glass, veined bluish, and then, after a moment of immobility, toppling in a white surge of foam, the layers of water flaring up the beach in thin sheets of mirrored crystal.

Her hand resting securely on Henry's arm, Elizabeth felt tethered, like a balloon, safely in the wind. Breathing in the drafts of fresh air made her feel peculiarly light, almost inflated, as if at a slightly stronger puff of wind she would go lifting, tilting out over the water.

Far, far out on the horizon the grape clusters were swelling, dilating, and the wind was queerly warm and pushing. The September sunlight seemed suddenly diluted, weakened.

"Henry, I think there's going to be a storm."

Henry scoffed at the distant looming clouds. "Nonsense," he said resolutely. "It will blow off. The wind is wrong."

The wind was wrong. Blowing in impulsive, freakish gusts, the wind teased Elizabeth. It flickered at the edge of her petticoat. Playfully it blew a strand of hair in her eye. She felt strangely mischievous and elated, secretly pleased that the wind was wrong.

Henry was stopping by the seawall. He was taking his massive gold watch from his waistcoat pocket. The tide, he said, should be high in fifteen minutes now. At seven minutes past four exactly. They would watch it from the old pier that jutted out over the rocks.

Elizabeth felt a mounting exhilaration as they walked out on the boards of the pier, which creaked and complained beneath them. Between the cracks she could see the deep green water winking up at her. The seething waves seemed to be whispering something mysterious to her, something that was unintelligible, lost in the loudness of the wind.

Giddily she felt the moss-covered piles of the pier sway and squeak beneath them in the strong pull of the tide.

"Out here," said Henry, leaning over the railing at the end of the pier, his conservative blue pin-stripe suit rippling in the skittish wind, which lifted the carefully combed hairs from the crown of his head until they vibrated, upstanding in the air, like the antennae of an insect.

Elizabeth bent over the railing beside her brother, staring down into the waves churning up on the rocks below. Her lavender skirt kept billowing and flapping about her legs, and although she tried to hold it down with her thin, frail fingers it would still blow about rebelliously.

Something was pricking her throat. Absently she lifted one hand only to feel her amethyst brooch loosen, slip through her fingers and fall, raying purple flashes as it spun down to lie on the rocks below, sparkling spitefully.

"Henry," she cried, clinging to him. "Henry—Mother's brooch! Whatever shall I do?" Henry's gaze followed her pointing hand, her angular, trembling index finger, down to where the brooch lay glinting. "Henry," she cried, half-sobbing, "you must get it for me. The waves will take it!"

Henry, handing her his black bowler hat, was suddenly responsible and protecting. He leaned over the railing to see what was the best possible footing. "Never fear," he said bravely, and the words were flung back at him by the derisive wind. "Never fear, there is a ladder of sorts. I will get your brooch for you."

Carefully, expertly, Henry began his descent. He placed his feet, one after the other, precisely in the angles of the wooden crosspieces, letting himself down at last onto the dry, mossy top of the rocks, where he stood in triumph. The waves crashed a little below him, rhythmically rising and falling, making ominous knocking sounds in the caverns and crevices among the great rocks. Steadying himself with one hand on the lowest rung of his improvised ladder, Henry leaned bulkily to pick up the brooch. He bent slowly, majestically, puffing a little from his heavy dinner.

Elizabeth realized that the wave must have been coming for quite some time, but she had not noticed that it was so much taller than the rest. There it was, though, a great bulk of green water moving slowly, majestically inward, rolling inexorably on, governed by some infallible natural law, toward Henry, who was just straightening, about to smile up at her, the brooch in his hand.

"Henry," she whispered in an ecstasy of horror as she leaned forward to watch the wave engulf the rock, spilling an enormous flood of water over the very spot on which Henry stood, surging up around his ankles, circling in two whirlpools about his knees. For a long moment Henry balanced valiantly, a colossus astride the roaring sea, an expression of unusual and pained surprise growing on his white, uplifted face.

Henry's arms revolved in the air like two frantic plane propellers as he felt the moss go sliding, slipping away under his submerged, well-polished shoes, and with a last helpless look, faltering, fumbling, without words, he toppled back into the depth of the next black wave. With a growing peace Elizabeth watched the flailing arms rise, sink and rise again. Finally the dark form quieted, sinking slowly down through level after level of obscurity into the sea. The tide was turning.

Musingly Elizabeth leaned on the railing, her pointed chin cupped in her blue-veined hands. She envisioned a green, aquatic Henry dropping through layers of clouded water like a porpoise. There would be seaweed in his hair and water in his pockets. Weighted by the round gold watch, by the white-faced compass, he would sink down to the ocean floor.

The water would ooze inside his shoes and seep into the workings of his watch until the ticking stopped. Then no amount of irritated shaking and knocking would be able to jar the works into motion again. Even the mysterious and exact cogs of the compass would rust, and Henry could shake and prod them, but the fine quivering needle would stick stubbornly, and north would be everywhere he turned. She pictured him taking his afternoon stroll alone on Sundays, walking briskly in the dilute green light, prodding curiously at the sea anemones with his cane.

And then she thought of his study with all the maps and the sea serpents drawn decoratively in the middle of the Atlantic Ocean; of Neptune sitting regally on a wave with his trident in his hand and the crown on his blown white hair. Even as she meditated, the features of Neptune's kingly visage blurred, puffed, rounded, and there, turned to look at her, was the startled face of a much altered Henry. Shivering without his waistcoat, without his pin-stripe suit, he sat huddled on the crest of the wave, teeth chattering. And as she looked, she heard a minute and pathetic sneeze.

Poor Henry. Her heart went out to him in pity. For who would look after him down there among all those slippery, indolent sea creatures? Who would listen to him talk about the way the moon controlled the tides or about the density of atmospheric pressure? She thought sympathetically of Henry and how he never could digest shellfish.

The wind was rising again, and Elizabeth's skirts lifted in a fresh gust, billowing, belling up, filled with air. She tilted dangerously, letting go of the railing, trying to smooth down her petticoats. Her feet rose from the planking, settled, rose again, until she was bobbing upward, floating like a pale lavender milkweed seed along the wind, over the waves and out to sea.

And that was the last anyone saw of Elizabeth Minton, who was enjoying herself thoroughly, blowing upward, now to this side, now to that, her lavender dress blending with the purple of the distant clouds. Her high-pitched, triumphant, feminine giggle mingled with the deep, gurgling chuckle of Henry, borne along beneath her on the outgoing tide.

The afternoon was shading into twilight. There was a sudden tug at Elizabeth's arm. "Come along home, Elizabeth," Henry said. "It's getting late."

Elizabeth gave a sigh of submission. "I'm coming," she said.

Among the Bumblebees

Story, Early 1950s

In the beginning there was Alice Denway's father, tossing her up in the air until the breath caught in her throat, and catching her and holding her in a huge bear hug. With her ear against his chest, young Alice could hear the thunder of his heart and the pulse of blood in his veins, like the sound of wild horses galloping.

For Alice Denway's father had been a giant of a man. In the blue blaze of his eyes was concentrated the color of the whole overhead dome of sky, and when he laughed, it sounded as if all the waves of the ocean were breaking and roaring up the beach together. Alice worshiped her father because he was so powerful, and everybody did what he commanded because he knew best and never gave mistaken judgment.

Alice Denway was her father's pet. Ever since Alice was very little, people had told her that she favored her father's side of the family and that he was very proud of her. Her baby brother Warren favored their mother's side of the family, and he was blond and gentle and always sickly. Alice liked to tease Warren, because it made her feel strong and superior when he began to fuss and cry. Warren cried a lot, but he never tattled on her.

There had been that spring evening at the supper table when Alice was sitting across from her brother Warren, who was eating his chocolate pudding. Chocolate pudding was Warren's favorite dessert, and he ate it very quietly, scooping it up carefully with his little silver spoon. Alice did not like Warren that night because he had been good as gold all day, and Mother had said so to Father when he came home from town. Warren's hair was gold and soft too, the color of dandelions, and his skin was the color of his glass of milk.

Alice glanced to the head of the table to see if her father was watching her, but he was bent over his pudding, spooning it up, dripping with cream, into his mouth. Alice slid down in her chair a little, staring innocently at her plate, and stretched her leg out under the table. Drawing her leg back, she straightened it in a sharp, swift kick. The toe of her shoe struck one of Warren's frail shins.

Alice watched him carefully from under her lowered lashes, concealing her fascination. The spoonful of pudding halfway to his lips dropped out of his hand, tumbling streakily down his bib to the floor, and a look of surprise sprouted in his eyes. His face crumpled into a mask of woe and he began to whine. He did not say anything, but sat there meekly, tears oozing out of the corners of his shut eyes, and blubbered wetly into his chocolate pudding.

"Good lord, doesn't he do anything but cry?" Alice's father scowled, lifting his head, and making a scornful mouth. Alice glared at Warren in safe contempt.

"He is tired," her mother said, with a hurt, reproving look at Alice. Bending over the table, she stroked Warren's yellow hair. "He hasn't been well, poor baby. You know that."

Her mother's face was tender and soft like the Madonna pictures in Sunday school, and she got up and gathered Warren into the circle of her arms, where he lay curled, warm and secure, sniffling, his face turned away from Alice and the father. The light made a luminous halo of his soft hair. Mother murmured little crooning noises to quiet him and said, "There, there, angel, it is all right now. It is all right."

Alice felt the lump of pudding stop in the back of her throat as she was about to swallow, and she almost gagged. Working hard with her mouth, she finally got it down. Then she felt the steady encouraging level of her father's gaze upon her, and she brightened. Looking up into his keen blue eyes, she gave a clear triumphant laugh.

"Who's my girl?" he asked her fondly, tweaking at a pigtail.

"Alice is!" she cried out, bouncing in her chair.

Mother was taking Warren upstairs to bed. Alice was aware of the retreating back, of the measured clicking of her mother's heels going away up the stairs, sounding faintly on the floor above. There came the sound of water running. Warren was going to have a bath, and Mother would tell him a made-to-order story. Mother told Warren a story every night before she tucked him in bed because he was good as gold all day.

"Can I watch you correct tonight?" Alice asked her father.

"*May,*" said her father. "Yes, you may, if you are very quiet." He wiped his lips on his napkin, folded it, and tossed it on the table, pushing back his chair.

Alice followed her father into the den and went to sit in one of the big, slippery leather chairs near his desk. She liked to watch him correcting the papers he brought home from town in his briefcase, fixing up all the mistakes that people had made during the day. He would go reading along, and then all at once stop, pick up his colored pencil and make little red gashes here and there where the words were wrong.

"Do you know," her father had said once, looking up suddenly from his work, "what will happen tomorrow when I hand these papers back in class?"

"No," said Alice, shivering a little. "What?"

"There will be," her father intoned in mock severity, with a black frown, "a weeping and wailing and a gnashing of teeth."

Alice had thought, then, of the great hall at the college where her father stood, high upon a platform. She had been there once with Mother, and there had been hundreds of people who came to listen to her father talk and tell them wonderful strange things about how the world was made.

She had pictured him standing up there, handing down papers to the people, calling them by name, each one. He would look the way he did when he scolded Mother sometimes, strong and proud, and his voice would be hard, with a sharp edge to it. From up there, like a king, high on a throne, he would call out the names in his thundering voice, and the people would come, trembling and frightened, to take their papers. And then, rising mournfully, there would be the sound of weeping, of wailing, and gnashing of teeth. Alice hoped that she would be there some day when the people were gnashing their teeth; she was sure that it would make a terrible and awe-inspiring noise.

Tonight, she sat and watched her father correct papers until it was time for her to go to bed. The light of the study lamp circled his head with a crown of brightness, and the vicious little red marks he made on the papers were the color of the blood that oozed out in a thin line the day she cut her finger with the bread knife.

Every day, that year, when her father came home just before supper, he would bring her surprises from town in his briefcase. He would come in the front door, take off his hat and his heavy rough coat with the cold silk lining, and set the briefcase down on a chair. First he would unbuckle the straps, and then he would take out the newspaper that came all folded and smelling of ink. Then there would be the sheaves of papers he had to correct for the next day. And at the very bottom there would be something especially for her, Alice.

It might be apples, yellow and red, or walnuts wrapped in colored cellophane. Sometimes there would be tangerines, and he would peel off the pock-marked orange skin for her and the spongy white threads that laced over the fruit. She would eat the sections one by one, the juice spurting sweet and sharp into her mouth.

In the summertime, when it was very nice out, her father did not go to town at all. He would take her to the beach when Mother had to stay at home with Warren, who always coughed and fretted because he had asthma and couldn't breathe without the steam kettle beside his bed.

First Father would go for a swim himself, leaving her on the shore, with the small waves collapsing at her feet and the wet sand sliding up cool between her toes. Alice would stand ankle-deep, watching him admiringly from the edge of the breakers, shielding her eyes against the blinding glare of summer sun that struck silent and brilliant on the surface of the water.

After a while she would call to him, and he would turn and begin swimming shoreward, carving a line of foam behind him with his legs and cleaving the water ahead with the powerful propellers of his arms. He would come to her and lift her onto his back, where she clung, her arms locked about his neck, and go swimming out again. In an ecstasy of terror, she would hold on to him, her soft cheek prickling where she laid her face against the back of his neck, her legs and slender body trailing out behind her, floating, moving effortlessly along in her father's energetic wake.

And gradually, there on her father's back, Alice's fear would leave her, and the water, black and deep beneath her, would seem calm and friendly, obeying the skillful mastery of her father's rhythmic stroke and supporting both of them upon the level waves. The sunshine, too, fell warm and cordial upon her thin arms, where the skin was stippled with gooseflesh. The summer sun did not burn her skin raw and red, the way it did Warren's, but turned her a lovely brown shade, the color of cinnamon toast.

After swimming, her father would take her for a brisk run up and down the beach to make her dry again, and as she raced him along the flat, hard-packed sand at the water's edge, laughing into the teeth of the wind, she would try to match her steps to the easy piston-powered pace of his swift stride. Then it seemed to Alice, as she felt the growing strength and sureness of her young limbs, that some day she, too, would be able to ride the waves in safe dominion, and that the sunlight would always bend deferentially to her, docile and generous with its creative warmth.

Alice's father feared nothing. Power was good because it was power, and when the summer storms came, with the crackling blue sheet lightning and the ear-splitting thunderclaps, like the sound of a city toppling block by block, Alice's father would roar with laughter as Warren scurried to hide in the broom closet, his fingers in his ears and his pale face grave with terror. Alice learned to sing the thunder song with her father: "Thor is angry. Thor is angry. Boom, boom, boom! Boom, boom, boom! We don't care. We don't care. Boom, boom, boom!" And above the resonant resounding baritone of her father's voice, the thunder rumbled harmless as a tame lion.

Sitting on her father's lap in the den, watching the waves at the end of the street whipped to a ragged froth of foam and blown spray against the seawall, Alice learned to laugh at the destructive grandeur of the elements. The swollen purple and black clouds broke open with blinding flashes of light, and the thunderclaps made the house shudder to the root of its foundations. But with her father's strong arms around her and the steady reassuring beat of his heart in her ears, Alice believed that he was somehow connected with the miracle of fury beyond the windows, and that through him, she could face the doomsday of the world in perfect safety.

When it was the right time of year, her father took her into the garden and showed her how he could catch bumblebees. That was something no one else's father could do. Her father caught a special kind of bumblebee that he recognized by its shape and held it in his closed fist, putting his hand to her ear. Alice liked to hear the angry, stifled buzzing of the bee, captured in the dark trap of her father's hand, but not stinging, not daring to sting. Then, with a laugh, her father would spread his fingers wide, and the bee would fly out, free, up into the air and away.

One summer, then, Alice's father did not take her out to catch bees. He lay inside the house on the couch and Mother brought him trays with orange juice in tall glasses, and grapes, and plums to eat. He drank a lot of water, for he was very thirsty all the time. Alice would go often into the kitchen for him and get a pitcher of water with ice cubes to make it cold, and she would bring him a glass, frosted with water drops.

It went on like that for a long while, and Father would not talk much to anyone who came into the house. At night, after Alice was in bed, she could hear Mother speaking to Father in the next room, and her voice would go along very soft and low for a while, until Father would get cross and raise his voice like thunder, and sometimes he would even wake up Warren, who began to cry.

One day, after a night like this, the doctor came to see Father. He brought a black briefcase and silver tools, and after he had left, Father began to stay in bed. It was the doctor's orders. There was whispering, always now, upstairs instead of talking, and the doctor wanted the blinds in Father's room kept down because the sunlight was too bright and hurt Father's eyes.

Alice could only go to see Father once in a while now because they kept the door shut most of the time. Once when she was sitting on a chair by the bed, talking to him softly about how the violet seeds were ready to collect in their dry brown pods in the garden, the doctor came. Alice could hear the front door open downstairs and Mother asking him in. Mother and the doctor stood together for a while in the downstairs hall, the low murmur of their voices sounding solemn and indistinct.

Then the doctor came upstairs with Mother, bringing his black bag and smiling a foolish bright smile. He pulled playfully at Alice's pigtail, but she switched it away from him with a pout and a toss of her head. Father winked at her, but Mother shook her head.

"Be nice, Alice," she begged. "The doctor's here to help Father."

That was not true. Father did not need any help. The doctor was making him stay in bed; he shut out the sun and that was making Father unhappy. Father could tell the plump silly doctor to go out of the house, if he wanted to. Father could slam the door after him and order him never to come back again. But instead, Father let the doctor take a big silver needle out of the black bag and swab a sterile place on Father's arm and stab the needle in.

"You should not look," Mother told Alice gently.

But Alice was determined to look. Father did not wince at all. He let the needle go in and looked at her with his strong blue eyes, silently telling her that really he did not care, really he was only humoring Mother and the absurd fat little doctor, two harmless conspirators. Alice felt her eyes fill up with tears of pride. But she blinked back the tears and did not cry. Father did not like anyone to cry.

The next day Alice went to visit her father again. From the hall she glimpsed him lying in bed in the shaded room, his head on the pillow, and the light, pale and dusty orange, filtering through the drawn blinds.

She tiptoed into the room, which smelled sweet and strange with alcohol. Father was asleep, lying motionless on the bed except for the rhythmic rising and falling of the blankets over his chest and the sound of his breathing. In the muted light, his face was the sallow color of candle wax, and the flesh was lean and taut about his mouth.

Alice stood looking down at her father's gaunt face, clenching and unclenching her thin hands by her side and listening to the slow thread of his breathing. Then she leaned over the bed and put her head down on the bedclothes above his chest. From somewhere, very faint and far off, she could hear the weak pulsing of his heart, like the fading throb of a distant drum.

"Father," she said in a small pleading voice. "Father." But he did not hear, withdrawn as he was into the core of himself, insulated against the sound of her supplicant voice. Lost and betrayed, she slowly turned away and left the room.

That was the last time that Alice Denway saw her father. She did not know then that in all the rest of her life there would be no one to walk with her, like him, proud and arrogant among the bumblebees.

Grateful acknowledgment is made for permission to reprint:

"The Day Mr. Prescott Died" and "The Wishing Box," which first appeared in *Granta* (1956 and 1957).

"The Fifteen-Dollar Eagle," which first appeared in the *Sewanee Review* in 1960.

"The Daughters of Blossom Street" and "The Fifty-Ninth Bear," which first appeared in the *London Magazine* (1960 and 1961).

"Johnny Panic and the Bible of Dreams," which first appeared in *Atlantic Monthly* in September 1968.

"Mothers," which first appeared in the October 1972 issue of *McCall's*, under the title "The Mother's Union."

"Context," which first appeared in the *London Magazine* (1962).

"A Comparison," which was written for a BBC Home Service program, "The World of Books," in July 1962.

"Ocean 1212-W," which was broadcast on the BBC in 1962 and published in *The Listener* in 1963.

"America! America!" which first appeared in *Punch* in April 1963.

"Initiation," which first appeared in *Seventeen* in January 1953.

"Sunday at the Mintons," which first appeared in *Mademoiselle* in August 1952.

"Superman and Paula Brown's New Snowsuit," which first appeared in *Smith Review* in Spring 1955.

"In the Mountains," which first appeared in *Smith Review* in Fall 1954.

"All the Dead Dears," which first appeared in *Gemini* in Summer 1957. (Thanks are due to Richard Steuble for finding this story.)

"Day of Success," which first appeared in *Bananas* in 1975.

"Cambridge Notes," which first appeared in *The American Poetry Review* in May/June 1978.